ISBN 978-1-397-31489-5
PIBN 11375078

This book is a reproduction of an important historical work. Forgotten Books uses
state-of-the-art technology to digitally reconstruct the work, preserving the original format
whilst repairing imperfections present in the aged copy. In rare cases, an imperfection in
the original, such as a blemish or missing page, may be replicated in our edition. We do,
however, repair the vast majority of imperfections successfully; any imperfections that
remain are intentionally left to preserve the state of such historical works.

For support please visit www.forgottenbooks.com

ANNOUNCEMENT

OF THE

College of Physicians and Surgeons

of Ontario

1921 - - 1922

Report of Proceedings of Ontario Medical Council

JUNE, 1921

REGISTRATION OFFICE

COLLEGE OF PHYSICIANS AND SURGEONS
OF ONTARIO

170 University Avenue, Toronto

JULY—1921

ANNOUNCEMENT

———OF THE———

College of Physicians and Surgeons

OF ONTARIO

FOR 1921—1922

REGISTRATION OFFICE

COLLEGE OF PHYSICIANS AND SURGEONS OF ONTARIO

170 University Avenue, Toronto

JULY—1921

THE ARMAC PRESS, Limited
TORONTO

The Red Ink Appeal

THE Workmen's Compensation Board and the Board of License Commissoners for Ontario decline to recognize the claims or honour the prescriptions respectively of members, with whose addresses they are not acquainted.

If each member, when first locating, or later when changing his address, would notify the Registrar of the same, occasion for irritation or annoyance, due to the action of these Boards in this regard, would be at once removed.

It is of moment to the Members of the College, to bear in mind, that, under statutory enactment, the College is bound in each calendar year to supply certain Government Boards with a list of those of its members who are in good standing, and practicing in the Province of Ontario. A member is not in good standing who does not pay his fees, and until the Annual Certificate is taken out, representing payment of annual assessment dues, the College cannot assure these Boards in any given enquiry, that the certificate for the calendar year has been taken out, and that, therefore, the member concerned is in good standing in the College for the calendar year in question.

The Annual Assessment Fee of two dollars for each calendar year is due on and from the first day of January of said year.

Members will be drawn upon through the Bank for Assessment Dues in those cases only, in which such members indicate by letter to the College a desire to have drafts made upon them. In cases where drafts are not duly honoured, the practice of sending them will be discontinued.

CONTENTS

CONTENTS—*Continued*

COUNCIL OF
The College of Physicians and Surgeons
OF ONTARIO

Territorial Representatives

G. R. Cruickshank, M.D., Windsor, Ont. ....Division No. 1
G. M. Brodie, M.D., Woodstock, Ont. ....   "   2
A. S. Thompson, M.D., Strathroy, Ont. ....   "   3
A. T. Emmerson, M.D., Goderich, Ont.   4
J. J. Walters, M.D., Kitchener, Ont.   5
S. McCallum, M.D., Thornbury, Ont.   6
Election to be held in   7
E. T. Kellam, M.D., Niagara Falls, Ont.   8
R. H. Arthur, M.D., Sudbury, Ont.   9
A. D. Stewart, M.D., Fort William, Ont.   10
E. E.King, M.D., Toronto, Ont......................   11
R. T. Noble, M.D., Toronto   12
F. A. Dales, M.D., Stouffville, Ont.   13
T. W. H. Young, M.D., Peterboro, Ont.   14
T. S. Farncomb, M.D., Trenton, Ont.   15
W. Spankie, M.D., Wolfe Island, Ont.   16
R. N. Horton, M.D., Brockville, Ont.   17
J. F. Argue, M.D., Ottawa, Ont.   18

University Representatives

University of Ottawa .... J. L. Chabot, M.A., M.D.C.M., Ottawa
University of Toronto ....J. M. MacCallum, B.A., M.D., Toronto
University of Trinity College .... W. H. Pepler, M.D., Toronto
Queen's University .... J. C. Connell, M.A., M.D., Kingston
Victoria University .... W. L. T. Addison, B.A., M.D., Toronto
Western University .... R. Ferguson, B.A., M.D., London

Homeopathic Representatives

H. Becker, M.D. .... Toronto, Ontario.
W. S. Cody, M.D. .... Hamilton, Ontario.
E. A. P. Hardy, M.D. .... Toronto, Ontario.
C. E. Jarvis, M.D. .... London, Ontario
G. A. Routledge, M.D. .... Lambeth, Ontario

OFFICERS OF
The College of Physicians and Surgeons
OF ONTARIO

President
J. FENTON ARGUE, M.D., Ottawa, Ont.

Vice-President
A. D. STEWART, M.D., Fort William, Ont.

Registrar-Treasurer
H. WILBERFORCE AIKINS, M.D., Toronto, Ont.

Prosecutor
JOHN FYFE, Toronto. Ont.

College Counsel
H. S. OSLER, K.C.

BOARD OF EXAMINERS FOR NOVEMBER EXAMINATIONS
1921

Surgery
> DR. T. H. MIDDLEBRO, Owen Sound, Ont.
> DR. BRUCE ROBERTSON, Toronto, Ont.

Medicine, and Preventive Medicine
> DR. W. T. CONNELL, Kingston, Ont.
> DR. J. P. VROOMAN, Napanee, Ont.

Obstetrics and Gynaecology
> DR. F.R. CLEGG, London, Ont.
> DR. DONALD McKAY, Collingwood, Ont.

Homeopathic Examiners
> DR. E. K. RICHARDSON, Toronto, Ont.
> DR. HUGH PORTER, Hamilton, Ont.

Alternate Homeopathic Examiner
> DR. K. A. McLAREN, Toronto. Ont.

BOARD OF EXAMINERS FOR JUNE EXAMINATIONS, 1922

The Oral and Clinical Examiners

Surgery
> DR. T. H. MIDDLEBRO, Owen Sound, Ont.
> DR. R. R. GRAHAM, Toronto, Ont.

Medicine, and Preventive Medicine
> DR. W. T. CONNELL, Kingston, Ont.
> DR. J. P. VROOMAN, Napanee, Ont.

Obstetrics and Gynaecology
> DR. F. R. CLEGG, London, Ont.
> DR. DONALD McKAY, Collingwood, Ont.

Homeopathic Examiners
> DR. E. K. RICHARDSON, Toronto, Ont.
> DR. HUGH PORTER, Hamilton, Ont.

Alternate Homeopathic Examiner
> DR. K. A. McLAREN, Toronto, Ont.

The Examiners for the Written Examinations

Surgery
> DR. E. R. SECORD, Brantford, Ont.
> DR. BRUCE ROBERTSON, Toronto, Ont.

Medicine, and Preventive Medicine
> DR. W. J. TILLMAN, London, Ont.
> DR. J. T. FOTHERINGHAM, Toronto, Ont.

Obstetrics and Gynaecology
> G. R. MYLKS, Kingston, Ont.
> J. GOW, Windsor, Ont .

Homeopathic Examiners
> DR. E. K. RICHARDSON, Toronto, Ont.
> DR. HUGH PORTER, Hamilton, Ont.

Alternate Homeopathic Examiner
> DR. K. A. McLAREN, Toronto, Ont.

STANDING AND OTHER COMMITTEES
OF THE COUNCIL
FOR 1921—1922

Complaints Committee

Drs. Young, Farncomb, Cody, Kellam and Thompson.

Discipline Committee

Drs. Arthur, Becker, Kellam, Walters and Noble.

Education Committee

Drs. J. M. MacCallum, S. McCallum, Jarvis, Spankie, Cruickshank, Ferguson, Connell, Addison and King.

Executive Committee

Drs. J. M. MacCallum, Stewart, Routledge, Young and Argue.

Finance Committee

Drs. Becker, Dales, Horton, Emmerson and Cruickshank.

Legislative Committee

Drs. King, Hardy, Kellam, Brodie, Emmerson, Farncomb, Dales, Noble, Arthur, Argue, Stewart, Routledge, J. M. MacCallum and Young.

Printing and Property Committee

Drs. Addison, Horton and Thompson.

Registration Committee

Drs. Connell, Hardy, Walters and Ferguson.

Rules and Regulations Committee

Drs. Emmerson, Jarvis, S. McCallum, Brodie, Cruickshank and Horton.

OFFICERS OF
The College of Physicians and Surgeons
OF ONTARIO

FROM 1866 TO 1921—1922

	Presidents	Vice-Presidents
1866—1867	John R. Dickson	Wm. H. Brouse ...
1867—1868	John Turquand	Wm. H. Brouse ...
1868—1869	James A. Grant	Wm. H. Brouse ..,
1869—1870	William Clark	Wm. H. Brouse ...
1870—1871	William H. Brouse	Chas. W. Covernton
1871	Chas. W. Covernton	

*(June to December)

1871—1872	William Clark	James Hamilton ..

†(December, 1871 to June, 1872)

1872—1873	J. F. Dewar	D. Campbell .....
1873—1874	William Clark	John Muir ......
1874—1875	M. Lavell	E. G. Edwards ..
1875—1876	E. G. Edwards	E. M. Hodder ...
1876—1877	Daniel Clark	D. Campbell ....
1877—1878	Daniel Clark	D. Campbell ....
1878—1879	D. Campbell	A. Allison ......
1879—1880	J. D. Macdonald	G. Logan ......
1880—1881	W. Allison	D. Bergin ....
1881—1882	D. Bergin	J. L. Bray ......
1882—1883	J. L. Bray	W. B. Geikie ....
1883—1884	G. Logan	H. W. Day ......
1884—1885	H. W. Day	E. W. Spragge ..
1885—1886	D. Bergin	R. Douglas ......
1886—1887	H. H. Wright	G. Henderson ...
1887—1888	G. Henderson	J. H. Burns ....
1888—1889	J. H. Burns	J. G. Cranston ..
1889—1890	J. G. Cranston	V. H. Moore ....
1890—1891	V. H. Moore	J. A. Williams ..
1891—1892	J. A. Williams	F. Fowler ......
1892—1893	F. Fowler	C. T. Campbell ..
1893—1894	C. T. Campbell	D. L. Philip .....
1894—1895	D. L. Philip	W. T. Harris ....
1895—1896	W. T. Harris	A. F. Rogers ....
1896—1897	A. F. Rogers	J. Thorburn ....
1897—1898	J. Thorburn	J. Henry ....
1898—1899	L. Luton	W. F. Roome ...
1899—1900	W. F. Roome	W. Britton ......
1900—1901	W. Britton	W. W. Dickson ..
1901—1902	L. Brock	W. J. H. Emory .
1902—1903	W. J. H. Emory	J. A. Robertson ..

*The President, Vice-President and Registrar-Treasurer of the College are elected at the Annual Meeting of the Council, and hold office until their successors are elected.

†Dr. William Clark was elected December 19, 1871, at a special meeting of the Council in consequence of the resignation of Dr. C. W. Covernton.

1903—1904......J. A. Robertson ....M. Sullivau .....
1904—1905......M. Sullivau ....A. A. Macdonald .
1905—1906......A. A. Macdonald ....W. H. Moorehouse
1906—1907......W. H. Moorehouse ....W. Spankie .....
1907—1908......W. Spankie ....P. Stuart ....
1908—1909......H. S. Glasgow ....E. A. P. Hardy .
1909—1910......E. A. P. Hardy ....J. Lane ....
1910—1911......J. Lane ....R. J. Gibson ...
1911—1912......R. J. Gibson ....E. Ryan ....
1912—1913......Edward Ryan ....M. O. Klotz .....
1913—1914......M. O. Klotz ....Jas MacArthur ..
1914—1915......James MacArthur ....H. S. Griffin ..
1915—1916......H. S. Griffin ....E. E. King .....
1916—1917......Edmund E. King ....W. E. Crain ....
1917—1918......William E. Crain ....R. Ferguson ....
1918—1919......Robert Ferguson ....A. T. Emmerson .
1919—1920......A. T. Emmerson ....G. A. Routledge .
1920—1921......G. A. Routledge ....J. M. MacCallum .
1921—1922...... J. Fenton Argue ....A. D. Stewart ...

TREASURERS

W. T. Aikins ....1866—1897
H. Wiberforce Aikins ....1897—1915

REGISTRARS AND SECRETARIES

Henry Strange ....May 3, 1866—Sept. 2, 1872
Thomas Pyne ....Sept. 2, 1872—July 15, 1880
Robt. A. Pyne ....July 15, 1880—July 2, 1907
John L. Bray ....July 2, 1907—June 29, 1915

REGISTRAR-TREASURER

H. Wilberforce Aikins 1915

The College of Physicians and Surgeons
OF ONTARIO

Announcement for the Academic Year
1921-1922

"The College of Physicians and Surgeons of Ontario" is the name adopted by the Medical Profession of the Province of Ontario in its corporate capacity. Every legally qualified medical practitioner in the Province is a member of this College. It is not an institution for the teaching of medicine.

The Medical Profession of Ontario was first incorporated under this name by an Act of Parliament of Canada passed in 1866. This Act was subsequently repealed by the Legislature of Ontario in 1869, and now the affairs of the Profession in this Province are regulated by an Act passed in 1874 (37 Vic., Cap. 30), commonly known as the "Ontario Medical Act", and further amended in 1887, 1891, 1893, 1895, 1902, 1905, 1914-1915, and 1918-1919.

By this Act, the "Council of the College of Physicians and Surgeons of Ontario" is empowered and directed to enact bylaws for the regulation of all matters connected with medical education; for the admission and enrolment of students of medicine; for determining from time to time the curriculum of the studies to be pursued by them, and to appoint a Board of Examiners, before whom all candidates must pass a satisfactory examination before they can be enrolled as members of the College, and thus be legally qualified to practise their profession in the Province of Ontario.

The Council, moreover, has power and authority conferred upon it by this Act to fix the terms upon which practitioners of medicine, duly qualified in other countries, may be admitted as members of the College of Physicians and Surgeons of Ontario, this being the only mode in which they can become legally entitled to practise their profession in this Province.

For the information and guidance of students of medicine, the Profession, and the public generally, the Council, in conformity with the Ontario Medical Act, hereby promulgates for the year 1921-1922 the Regulations which herein follow, repealing all others heretofore in force.

Regulations for 1921-1922

Every one who desires to obtain licentiate standing in the Province of Ontario, to enable him to practise medicine therein, must comply with the following requirements:—

SECTION I.

Matriculation,

As preliminary to entrance upon medical studies in any Medical College or University recognized by this College, it is necessary for any one who so enters upon such studies, and who proposes to obtain later the license of this College (except as hereinafter provided), to satisfy the matriculation requirements of the same.

For purposes of registration of matriculation standing, any one of the following credentials will be accepted:

1. A certificate of having graduated in Arts or Science in any university of His Majesty's Dominions, or any other university approved of by this Council.

2. A certificate from the Registrar of any chartered Canadian University conducting a full Arts Course, that the holder thereof has passed the examination conducted at the end of the first year in Arts by such university.

3. A certificate of having passed the Senior Arts matriculation conducted by any chartered university of Canada.

4. A certificate of having passed the joint university senior matriculation examination in Arts as conducted by the Matriculation Board of Ontario.

5. A certificate of having passed the joint university examination for junior matriculation in Arts conducted by the Matriculation Board of Ontario.

6. A certificate of having passed the Junior matriculation in Arts, conducted by any Canadian University engaged in teaching medicine.

The qualifying certificate may be presented personally at the Office of the College, or may be sent by mail. If, upon inspection in the office, it is found satisfactory, it will be returned to the applicant, with an identification declaration form, which, when duly executed, will need to be sent back to the office, together with the associated fee of twenty-five dollars, when the applicant's standing will be registered.

SECTION II.

Curriculum

1. Every student who enters upon the study of medicine after Sept. 1, 1920, must spend a period of six years in actual professional studies, except as hereinafter provided; and the prescribed period of studies shall include six sessions of thirty teaching weeks in each session.

The Registrar of this College shall be required to exact from each candidate a certificate of graduation in Medicine from his College Registrar, and evidence that he has attended lectures for a full term of thirty weeks in each session, and further that such certificates must show that the candidate has attended not less than eighty per cent of such lectures, including hospital and laboratory work.

2. Graduates in Arts or Science of any college or university recognized by the Council shall be permitted to present themselves for their examination in five years, provided that during such course two years have been spent in the course of physics, chemistry, biology, and physiology, and examinations passed in these subjects while taking said university course.

3. Every student must attend the undermentioned courses in a University, College or School of Medicine approved of by the Council.

A course of thirty teaching weeks shall consist of at least sixty hours.

A course of fifteen teaching weeks shall consist of at least thirty hours.

Biology—One course of thirty teaching weeks.

Physiological Anatomy—One course of thirty teaching weeks.

Anatomy—Two courses of thirty teaching weeks each in descriptive and practical anatomy.

Each student will be required to prove that he has carefully dissected the entire human body.

Medical and Surgical Anatomy—One course of thirty teaching weeks.

Physiology—Two courses of thirty teaching weeks each.

Histology—One course of thirty teaching weeks.

Embryology—One course of fifteen teaching weeks.

Chemistry—Two courses of thirty teaching weeks each.

Medical Physics—One course of thirty teaching weeks.

Materia Medica, Pharmacy and Pharmacology—One course of thirty teaching weeks.

Medicine—Three courses of thirty teaching weeks each.

Clinical Medicine—Three courses of thirty teaching weeks each.

Surgery—Three courses of thirty teaching weeks each.

Clinical Surgery—Three courses of thirty teaching weeks each.

Midwifery—Two courses of thirty teaching weeks, and one course in Clinical Obstetrics, which shall consist of attendance upon not less than ten cases of labour.

Gynæcology—Two courses of thirty teaching weeks each.

Pathology and Bacteriology—Three courses of thirty teaching weeks each.

Diseases of Children—One course of thirty teaching weeks.

Therapeutics, Physio-Therapy (including Hydro-Therapy, Electro-Therapy, Massage and Manipulative treatment, X-Ray and Radio-Therapy)—One course of thirty teaching weeks.

Diseases of the Eye, Ear, Nose and Throat—Two courses of thirty teaching weeks each.

Hygiene and Preventive Medicine—Two courses of thirty teaching weeks.

Psychology—One course of fifteen teaching weeks.

Psychiatry—One course of fifteen teaching weeks.

Every student must serve as interne in a recognized hospital for at least six months.

4. Courses prescribed for Homeopathic students:

Candidates wishing to be registered as Homeopathists must conform with the requirements regarding matriculation as found in Section 1.

Such candidates must also have complied with the full curriculum of studies prescribed from time to time by the Council for all medical students, but the full time of attendance upon lectures and hospitals required by the curriculum of the Council may be spent in such Homeopathic Medical Colleges in the United States or Europe as may be recognized by a majority of the Homeopathic members of the Council, and when such teaching body has been established in Ontario, it shall be optional for such candidates to pursue in part or in full the required curriculum in Ontario.

5. Graduates in medicine from "recognized" colleges outside the Dominion of Canada who desire to qualify themselves for registration must complete fully the practical and clinical curriculum required by the Council, and shall pass before the examiners appointed by the Council all the examinations hereinafter prescribed.

6. Graduates from other than "recognized" Colleges outside the Dominion of Canada who desire to qualify for registration by examination shall submit to the Executive of the Council their

credentials and the Executive shall have power to decide the eligibility of the candidate.

7. The following Schools in the United States are "recognized" as "Accredited Colleges":

University of California Medical School, Berkeley-San Francisco, California.

Leland Stanford Junior University School, San Francisco, California.

Yale University School of Medicine, New Haven, Conn.

North Western University School, Chicago, Ill.

Rush Medical College, Chicago, Ill.

Indiana University School of Medicine, Indianapolis, Indiana.

Johns Hopkins University, Baltimore, Maryland.

Harvard University Medical School, Boston, Mass.

University of Michigan Medical School, Ann Arbor, Mich.

Washington University Medical School, St. Louis, Missouri.

University of Minnesota Medical School, Minneapolis, Minn.

University of Nebraska College of Medicine, Omaha, Nebraska. (Seat of University, Lincoln, Nebraska.)

Columbia University College of Physicians and Surgeons, New York, N.Y.

Cornell University Medical College, New York, N.Y.

Syracuse University College of Medicine, Syracuse, N. Y.

Ohio State University College of Medicine, Columbus, Ohio.

Western Reserve University School of Medicine, Cleveland, Ohio.

Jefferson Medical College, Philadelphia, Pa.

University of Pennsylvania, Philadelphia, Pa.

University of Pittsburgh School of Medicine, Pittsburgh, Pa.

HOMEOPATHIC COLLEGES

Hahnemann Medical College of Philadelphia.

Hahnemann Medical College and Hospital of Chicago.

University of Michigan Homeopathic Medical School.

College of Homeopathic Medicine of the Ohio State University.

New York Homeopathic College and Flower Hospital.

8. Reciprocal relations in issuing certificates have been entered into with the State Board of Pennsylvania.

SECTION III.

Examinations—Date and Place, and requirements of

1. There shall be one Examination held by the Medical Council, and that at the end of the sixth year of medical study.

2. Every applicant for this examination must be a graduate of an approved Medical College, and must present certificates of attendance covering a period of six years, except as provided in paragraph 2, Section II.

3. The following shall be the subjects for said examination:

(1) Medicine and Preventive Medicine.

(2) Surgery.

(3) Obstetrics and Gynæcology.

4. The examination shall consist of two examinations on each subject: (1) "written" and (2) "oral" and "clinical."

5. Sixty per cent. of the marks will be required to pass in each subject. A candidate must take all three subjects at one examination, but he will only be required to pass subsequently on any subject or subjects upon which he has failed.

6. The Annual Examination in the Spring of each year shall be held in Toronto, Kingston and London, at such date as shall be fixed by Annual By-law. There shall also be a Supplemental Examination in the Fall of each year held only in the City of Toronto for candidates who failed in one or more subjects at the Annual Examination.

7. Candidates who intend to be examined by the Homeopathic Examiners shall signify their intention to the Registrar at least two weeks previous to the commencement of the examinations, due notice of which must be given to examiner by Registrar. Homeopathic students are to be examined by examiners approved by a majority of the Homeopathic members of the Council.

8. The Fall Examination for 1921 begins at nine o'clock on the morning of Tuesday, November 8th.

9. The Spring Examination for 1922 begins on Tuesday, June 6th.

SECTION IV.

Examinations—Duties of Registrar and Board of Examiners

Rules for the guidance of the Registrar and the Board of Examiners:

1. The Registrar or a deputy Registrar must be present at every examination, and each student must produce evidence satisfactory to the Registrar or Deputy Registrar of his identity.

2. At the end of each written examination upon any subject, the answers to the questions are to be handed by the candidates to the Registrar, who will open the envelopes, in which they are hereinafter directed to be enclosed, and to each set of papers affix a number by which the author will be known to the Board of Examiners during the examination. The Registrar will then deliver the papers to those members of the Board of Examiners appointed by the Council to examine upon the subject, upon which these candidates have just been writing.

3. The papers when delivered to the members of the Board of Examiners appointed by the Council to examine on the subject, are to be by them examined, and the relative value of answers marked by means of numbers on a blank form which will be furnished to them by the Registrar.

4. The percentage in all subjects of the Professional Examinations shall range from 0 to 100, of which sixty per cent. will be required to pass in each subject.

5. The value awarded by the Examiners to the answers of candidates and confirmed by the Board of Examiners is final; and is not subject to revision.

6. In the event of any alterations or erasures in the marks of a paper, or of any question in a paper, the same shall be initialed by both Examiners.

7. The Examiners shall, on completion of their work, conjointly certify to the schedule of marks and books. Their report, including schedule of marks and books, completed and duly certified, shall be final, and shall forthwith be filed with the Registrar.

8. The Examiner shall return the schedule to the Registrar, with values inserted, within fifteen days of the close of examinations on his subject. From these values a general schedule shall be prepared by a chartered accountant associated with the Registrar, which schedule shall be inspected and signed by the President before the results are announced.

9. The Registrar, in notifying the members of the Board of Examiners, will direct attention to the following instructions, a copy of which he shall enclose.

(a) In preparation of questions Examiners will confine themselves to the principles common to the standard text-books.

(b) In referring to diseases or operations of any kind, the name of such disease or operation most commonly in use must be employed, and the Examiners shall refrain as far as possible from the use of proper names and ambiguous questions.

(c) In the preparation of the paper, opposite each question shall be placed the value of a full and correct answer thereof—the whole of such numbers to amount to 100.

(d) In the reading of papers the Examiners shall mark in colored pencil what they regard as the numerical value of the answers given for each question opposite the same.

(e) The oral and clinical examinations are to be made as practical, demonstrative or clinical as possible, and shall occupy at least thirty minutes.

(f) Candidates shall be known to the Examiners by numbers only.

(g) There shall be a dual Board of Examiners, namely one set of two examiners in each subject who shall conjointly set and examine each paper in the Written Examination and another set of two examiners in each subject who shall conjointly examine each student in the Oral and Clinical Examination.

(h) In the event of any alteration or erasures in the marks of a paper, or of any question in a paper, the same shall be initialed by both examiners.

(i) The Examiners shall meet at the close of the examination for consultation and consideration of reports before these are forwarded to the Registrar. The Examiners shall, on the completion of their work, conjointly certify to the schedules of marks and books. Their report, including schedules of marks and books completed and duly certified, shall be final, and shall forthwith be filed with the Registrar.

10. Candidates for oral examinations will be divided into classes alphabetically, and notified of the time at which they shall present themselves for examination. Such students shall wait in an adjoining room, and appear before the Examiners when summoned.

11. The Examiners in each subject shall meet at a convenient point to prepare the examination papers, and shall send each paper to the Registrar by registered mail at least two weeks before the date of examination. (The Examiners shall approve of the proofs before printing.)

12. As no appeal is now permitted from the findings of the Board, the President, with the Vice-President as his alternate, shall attend the usual meeting held by the Board of Examiners preparatory to handing in the Schedule of Examination Marks to the Registrar for consultation and consideration of said Schedule with the Examiners.

SECTION V.

Examinations—Rules for Candidates in the Examination Hall

1. Each candidate shall receive from the Registrar a programme containing a list of subjects upon which the candidate is to be examined, and it will admit him to the examination hall during the progress of the examination upon such subjects, but at no other time.

2. Candidates must write the answers to the question given by the Examiners legibly and neatly upon one side of each page of a book, which will be furnished to each candidate, and the number of each question, as it appears in the examination paper, is to be put at the head of the answer to it, in such a manner as to have the first page facing outward to the view; the papers then to be folded once and enclosed in an envelope, on the outside of which each candidate is to write his name. The packet is then to be handed to the Registrar or his Deputy. No signature, number or sign, by which the writer could be recognized by the Examiner, is to be written or marked on any portion of the book to be enclosed in the envelope.

3. The questions of the Examiners in the Homeopathic subjects will be handed, at the beginning of the general examination on the same subject, by the Registrar or Deputy, to such candidates as shall have given him notice in accordance with Section III., subsec. 7.

They shall write the answers to these questions in the same hall with the other candidates, and hand their papers, when finished, to the Registrar in the same manner as provided for other candidates, to be by him given for examination to the Homeopathic members of the Board of Examiners appointed to examine on that subject.

4. No candidate will be allowed to leave the hall after the questions are given out, until his answers have been handed in.

5. No one shall be allowed in the hall during the hours of examination, except those who are actually undergoing examination, or members of the Council or officials connected therewith.

6. Any candidate who may have brought any book or reference paper into the hall must deposit it with the Registrar before the examination begins.

7. Candidates must not communicate with each other while examinations are going on by writing, signs, words, or in any manner whatever.

8. Candidates must at all times bear themselves toward the Registrar or Deputy and Examiners with the utmost deference and

respect; and they will not be permitted in any manner to manifest approbation or disapprobation of any member of the Board of Examiners during the progress of the examination.

9.　Candidates must not only conduct themselves with decorum while an examination is going on, but they will be held strictly responsible for any impropriety of conduct during the whole progress both of the written and the oral examinations.

10.　Any infraction of the above rules will lead to the exclusion of the candidate who is guilty of it for the remainder of the examination; and he will not receive credit for any examination papers which may have been handed to the Registrar or Deputy previous to his being detected in such misconduct.

11.　And he may be debarred from further privileges at the discretion of the Council.

SECTION VI.

Registration of British Medical Practitioners

Registration in the Register of The College of Physicians and Surgeons of Ontario confers the right to practise medicine, surgery and midwifery in the Province of Ontario under the provisions of The Ontario Medical Act.

It is necessary according to the provisions of The Ontario Medical Act and Regulations of the Council of The College of Physicians and Surgeons of Ontario, passed in accordance therewith, that any person applying to be registered as a British Medical Practitioner should produce to the Registrar documents or certificates as follows:

1.　A certificate that the applicant is duly registered in the Medical Register of the United Kingdom of Great Britain and Ireland. (This certificate is obtained from the Registrar of the British Medical Council.)

2.　Satisfactory evidence of identity.

3.　Satisfactory evidence of good character.

4.　Satisfactory evidence that diploma or diplomas in respect of which the applicant was registered in the Medical Register of the United Kingdom was or were granted to him at a time when he was not domiciled in the Province of Ontario or in the course of a period of not less than five years, during the whole of which he resided out of the Province of Ontario.

5. The documents and the prescribed fee (one hundred dollars) should, together with the enclosed forms duly filled in, be transmitted to the address set forth hereunder:

The Registrar of The College of Physicians
and Surgeons of Ontario,
170 University Avenue,
Toronto.

SECTION VII.

MEDICAL COUNCIL OF CANADA
Registration of Licentiates of the Medical Council of Canada

Licentiates of the Medical Council of Canada can register their standing as such in the various Provinces of Canada, and acquire by virtue of such registration the right to engage in the practice of medicine in any Province in which they may choose to register, subject only to local Medical Council requirements.

The requirements of the College of Physicians and Surgeons of Ontario, to permit of such registration, call for production of official certificate from the Medical Council of Canada of licentiate standing therein, evidence of good character, and payment of fee of seventy-five dollars.

☞ Medical students, proposing to ultimately acquire the license of the Medical Council of Canada by examination, are advised to bear in mind, that, with a view to being permitted to become candidates for such examination, they must furnish to the Registrar of the Medical Council of Canada an official certificate issued by one of the Provincial Medical Councils, that they have fully satisfied the requirements of the Medical Council of the Province in question, as to matriculation standing, and as to possession of a degree in medicine from a University or Medical College approved by the Medical Council in question.

They are further advised to remember, if they propose to obtain such a certificate (technically known as an "enabling certificate") in the Province of Ontario, that they must register their matriculation standing (of whatever nature and wherever obtained) with the College of Physicians and Surgeons of Ontario, before they enter upon their medical studies in any University or Medical College. (The matriculation requirements of the College of Physicians and Surgeons of Ontario will be found set out in detail on page 12 of the Annual Announcement.)

The fee associated with registration of matriculation in Ontario is twenty-five dollars. This fee is never, under any circumstances, refunded.

The fee associated with the issuing of an enabling certificate is also twenty-five dollars. A refund of twenty dollars of this amount is made in those cases, in which students who have paid the twenty-five dollar fee for the enabling certificate, and who have later obtained licentiate standing in the Medical Council of Canada, register the same at some later date in Ontario, with the College of Physicians and Surgeons of Ontario.

(Full information as to requirements of the Medical Council of Canada can be had, by making application to Dr. R. W. Powell, Registrar, Medical Council of Canada, 180 Cooper Street, Ottawa, from whom also must be obtained the blank enabling certificate forms, to be filled in by the Registrar of a Provincial Council.)

SECTION VIII.

Fees

1. The following scale of fees has been established by the Council of the College of Physicians and Surgeons of Ontario:

    (a) Registration of Matriculation standing..............$25.00

    (b) Fee for Final examination (this includes registration of licentiate standing, when so obtained, and issuance of diploma)...................$75.00

    (c) Annual Assessment Dues...................................$2.00

        (This fee is due and payable on and from the first day of January of each calendar year, and covers the calendar year in question. The payment of this fee, which is imposed annually upon every member of the College, under By-law of the Council, is a sine qua non of good standing in the College. No member can claim recognition as such before the Courts of Law of the Province of Ontario, to whom the Annual Certificate, representing the payment of this fee, has not been issued.)

    (d) Fee payable by licentiates of the Medical Council of Great Britain, who ask to be registered as licentiates of the College of Physicians and Surgeons of Ontario...$100 00

    (e) Fee payable by licentiates of the Canada Medical Council, who ask to be registered as licentiates of the College of Physicians and Surgeons of Ontario $75 00

(f) Fee payable by licentiates of the College, for Official Certificate, indicating the date of their registration with the College, and of their being in good standing in the College at the time of the issuing of the Certificate, for presentation to the Canada Medical Council. (This applies equally to those licentiates who propose offering themselves for examination before the Canada Medical Council, and those licentiates of not less than ten years' standing, who seek registration with the Canada Medical Council, without examination.) $5   00

(g) Fee payable by matriculants of the College, who ask for official enabling certificate to permit them to appear before the Medical Council of Canada for examination $25   00

(A refund of twenty dollars is made to those matriculants of the College, who have paid the twenty-five dollar fee for such enabling certificate, and who later become licentiates of the College, either by passing its examinations, or by registration with it of Canada Medical Council licentiate standing.)

(h) Fee payable by matriculants or licentiates of the College, for certificate of standing in the College, for presentation to State Medical Registration Boards in the United States $25   00

2. All fees must be paid in lawful money of Canada, to the Treasurer of the College. The Office of the College is at 170 University Avenue, Toronto. Payments may be made in person or by mail.

3. Examination fees to accompany application form of candidates for examination, and to be in the hands of the Registrar not less than two weeks before the date set for the beginning of the examinations.

4. No candidate will be admitted to any examination until the fee for such examination is paid in full.

5. Candidates who have failed in any professional examination in one or more subjects will be allowed to take the next ensuing Spring examination, without payment of further fee, but any Supplemental Examination taking place in the Fall calls for the payment of a fee of twenty-five dollars ($25.00).

6. If a membership diploma is accidentally destroyed, it may be replaced, with the consent of the Council or Executive Committee, upon presentation of statutory declaration as to manner of its destruction, and payment of cost of replacement.

Examination Questions, 1920

FINAL EXAMINATIONS, NOVEMBER, 1920.

MEDICINE

N.B.—Questions of equal value.   Answer five questions only.

1. Diphtheritic laryngitis or membranous croup. Discuss onset, course, symptoms, differential diagnosis, and treatment. Outline precautions to be taken with patient and family to prevent extension of the infection.

2. Discuss etiology and describe onset, course, symptoms and diagnosis of multiple or disseminate sclerosis.

3. (a) Give usual appearances, diagnosis and treatment of Lupus vulgaris.

(b) Describe the commoner skin rashes which may follow the injection of curative sera, with course and treatment.

4. Discuss the symptoms, course, prognosis and the treatment of diabetes mellitus.

5. Discuss etiology of lesions leading to stenosis of mitral valve, together with common course, symptoms and treatment of this condition.

6. Duodenal ulcer. Describe the onset, course, symptoms and differential diagnosis of this condition and outline treatment.

W. T. Connell, M.D.

J. P. Vrooman, M.D.

SURGERY

All questions of equal value.

I.—Describe the treatment of a recent compound fracture of the middle third of the bones of the leg.

II.—A baby of six months of age is suddenly seized with abdominal pain and vomiting and soon displays the usual symptoms of shock. Discuss the diagnosis.

III.—Describe the symptoms, pathology and treatment of psoas abscess.

IV.—Name the different forms of swellings occurring within the scrotum. Discuss the differential diagnosis.

V.—Describe the anatomy and technique of an amputation in the lower portion of the thigh.

T. H. Middlebro, M.B., F.R.C.S., Eng.,

W. E. Gallie, M.B., F.R.C.S., Eng.

OBSTETRICS AND GYNAECOLOGY

All questions of equal value.

1. Give the symptoms, diagnosis and treatment of extrauterine pregnancy.
2. Give the etiology, clinical course and treatment of phlegmasia alba dolens.
3. Discuss the etiology and treatment of abortion.
4. Give pathology, diagnosis and treatment of Salpingitis due to gonococcus.
5. Discuss the etiology and diagnosis of uterine bleeding in a woman of forty-five years of age.

ERNEST WILLIAMS, } *Examiners.*
DONALD McKAY,

EXAMINATIONS, JUNE, 1921

MEDICINE AND PREVENTIVE MEDICINE

N.B.—Answer *five* questions only. Questions of equal value.

1. Discuss the modes of onset, symptoms, course and differential diagnosis of epidemic encephalitis (encephalitis lethargica).

Outline the preventive measures you would consider necessary in connection with a case.

2. Describe the usual lesions, diagnosis and treatment of
   (a) Ringworm of the scalp.
   (b) Psoriasis.
   (c) Impetigo Contagiosa.

3. Discuss the symptoms, diagnosis and general prognosis of diabetes mellitus.

Outline your management of a case in a stout male of 45 years showing symptoms of moderate severity.

4. Describe the onset, symptoms, differential diagnosis and treatment of tuberculous peritonitis.

4. Discuss the onset, symptoms, differential diagnosis and treatment of diphtheria.

Outline the methods of spread, and the means of protection of exposed individuals.

6. A linotype operator aged 46, rather intemperate, presents himself complaining of loss of power of both hands noticed for past four or five days, with wrist drop. Discuss further examinations you would make, with differential diagnosis.

W. T. Connell, M.D.
J. P. Vrooman, M.D.

SURGERY

Examiners: Dr. T. H. Middlebro
Dr. Roscoe R. Graham

Time—2½ hours.   All questions of equal value.

(1) Fracture of the Humerus at or near the Lower End.
  (a) Give the surgical anatomy of the factors concerned in displacement.
  (b) Diagnosis.
  (c) Treatment.
(2) Discuss the diagnosis of the commoner causes of Obstruction of the Bowels.
(3) Discuss Chronic Cholecystitis with regard to
  (a) Etiology.
  (b) Differential Diagnosis
  (c) Treatment
  (d) Prognosis
(4) A woman 45 years of age presents herself with a chronic lump in her Breast.
  (a) Give a differential diagnosis, with differentiating clinical signs and symptoms.
  (b) Detail the advice you would give, provided malignancy could not be excluded by clinical examination.
(5) Describe the symptoms of the secondary stage of Syphilis.

OBSTETRICS AND GYNAECOLOGY.

All questions of equal value.

  I. Give fully the treatment of Eclampsia.
 II. Chronic Salpingitis, give
      a. Etiology.
      b. Symptoms.
III. Breech Presentation, give
      a. Diagnosis.
      b. Management.
 IV. Uterine Fibroids, give
      a. Varieties.
      b. Symptoms.
      c. Treatment.
  V. Give your treatment of the following Complications of Pregnancy:
      a. Concealed Accidental Haemorrhage.
      b. Pruritus Vulvae.
      c. Vomiting.

ERNEST WILLIAMS,
DONALD McKAY,
Examiners.

By-Laws of the Council

OF

The College of Physicians and Surgeons

OF ONTARIO

BY-LAWS

BY-LAW No. 1.

In the following by-laws, unless there be something in the subject or context inconsistent therewith, the words:

1. "The Council" shall mean "the Medical Council of the College of Physicians and Surgeons of Ontario."

2. "Member" shall mean "Member of the College of Physicians and Surgeons of Ontario."

3. "The College" shall mean "the College of Physicians and Surgeons of Ontario."

BY-LAW No. 2.

Elections

1. (a) In the event that an election shall require to be held for the election of a new Council or to fill a vacancy caused by the death, resignation or disqualification of any member elected from a territorial division to the Council, the Registrar shall send to all members entitled to vote at such election (except those registered as Homeopathic members) a circular letter stating that an election will be held for the purpose of electing a new Council or to fill such vacancy (as the case may be), that nominations will be received within thirty days after the date on which such circular letter shall be mailed, and that nomination by twenty members entitled to vote is necessary to render a candidate eligible for election.

(b) In the case of an election of a new Council the Registrar shall advertise in the medical journals published in Toronto (for a period of thirty days after the date on which the said circular letter shall be mailed) the fact that elections for the Council are to be held, stating the last date on which nominations will be received, and the approximate time of holding the elections.

2. In the event of only one candidate being nominated in any territorial division, the Registrar shall notify him that he has been duly elected a member of the Council, but if more than one candidate eligible for election is nominated, the Council, or the Executive Committee, or (in the absence of an appointment so made) the Registrar on the recommendation of such Executive Committee shall appoint a member of the College, resident in such division, to act as returning officer, and shall mail to all registered members entitled to vote (except those registered as Homeopathic members) a voting paper and circular letter of instructions, which shall be similar to the forms set out in Schedules "A" and "B" respectively appended to this by-law. Such voting paper duly filled out must reach the returning officer on or before the first juridical day after the expiration of fifteen days following the mailing thereof by the Registrar.

3. The returning officer shall, on the day and time stated in the circular letter of instructions and not prior thereto, open the envelopes, carefully count and examine the voting papers, make a record of the entire number of votes cast, and of the name and address of the person receiving the greatest number of votes, who shall be declared elected as the representative of the division, and in case two or more candidates receive an equality of votes the returning officer shall give the casting vote for one of such candidates which shall decide the election.

4. The returning officer shall permit all or any of the candidates in the division or their agents duly appointed and authorized in writing to act on their behalf to be present when the envelopes are opened and the votes counted, and to examine all voting papers to satisfy themselves as to the voting papers being properly filled up, and that the persons signing the voting papers are duly registered members of the College and entitled to vote at the election.

5. (a) The returning officer shall seal up and return all voting papers connected with the election to the Registrar within six days from the time appointed for holding the election.

(b) The returning officer shall return all envelopes containing voting papers, received after the date and hour mentioned in circular letter of instructions to the Registrar, unopened and marked "too late." Such envelopes shall bear his stamp as returning officer of the division.

6. The Registrar, on receiving declaration from the returning officer, declaring a candidate has received the largest number of votes in the division, shall forthwith inform the candidate declared elected that he has been chosen to represent said division in the Medical Council of the College of Physicians and Surgeons of Ontario, and the Registrar shall inform each member so elected of

the time and place of the first meeting of the Council after the said election shall have taken place.

7. At the said meeting of the Council the Registrar shall submit all the papers and documents sent to him by the returning officer or officers (as the case may be).

8. The fee for the returning officer for each election shall be twenty-five dollars.

SCHEDULE "A"

College of Physicians and Surgeons of Ontario

VOTING PAPER

Medical Registration Office, University Ave., Toronto.	Election of Territorial Representative to the Medical Council.
The name of the Candidate for whom your vote is cast .... Residence of Candidate	I .... residing at .... in the County of .... do solemnly affirm that I am registered under the Ontario Medical Act; That the signature affixed hereto is my proper handwriting; That I have signed no other voting paper at this election; That I have not voted in any other division at this election; That I am a resident of this division in which I now vote; That this Voting Paper was executed on the day of the date hereof by me. Witness my hand this .... day of .... Signed ....

SCHEDULE "B"

College of Physicians and Surgeons of Ontario.

Election of Territorial Representatives to the Medical Council.

The voting paper herewith enclosed is to be filled up carefully, using ink, and placed in the enclosed envelope, which is directed to the returning officer and mailed in time to reach him not later than 2 o'clock p.m. on....................................,the............day of.................... 192................

Sign your name to voting paper, using ink.

(Signed) ....

Registrar, Toronto, Ontario.

By-Law No. 3

Election of Homeopathic Members

1. This by-law shall apply only to the election of the Homeopathic Members of the Medical Council.

2. In the event that an election shall require to be held for the election of a new Council the Registrar shall send to every registered Homeopathic member of the College a circular letter stating that an election will be held for the purpose of electing a new Council, and that nominations will be received within thirty days after the date on which such circular letter shall be mailed. In the event of the death or resignation of any member of the Council representing the Practitioners of the Homeopathic System of Medicine, the remaining representatives of the Homeopathic System in the Council may fill such vacancy by selecting from amongst the duly registered Practitioners in Homeopathy a person to fill the said vacancy.

3. In the event of only five candidates being nominated for the new Council (or in the case of a vacancy, one candidate) the Registrar shall notify them that they have been duly elected members of the Council, but if more than five candidates eligible for election are nominated (or in the case of a vacancy, one candidate) the Registrar shall act as returning officer, and shall mail to every registered Homeopathic member of the College a voting paper and circular letter of instructions which shall be similar in form to those set out in Schedules "A" and "B" respectively appended to this by-law.

4. Such voting paper duly filled out must reach the Registrar on or before the first juridical day after the expiration of fifteen days from the mailing thereof by the Registrar.

5. The Registrar shall on the day and time stated in the circular letter of instructions, and not prior thereto, open the envelopes, carefully count and examine the voting papers, count the votes, make a record of the votes cast, and inform by letter the five candidates (or in the case of an election to a vacancy, one candidate) having the largest number of votes, that they are elected as the Homeopathic representatives on the Council. The Registrar shall, after carefully counting the votes contained in the envelopes, seal up the voting papers and all other documents, etc., sent to him connected with such election, and present them to the Council at its next meeting.

6. No voting paper shall be counted that is not properly filled out in accordance with the instructions contained in the circular letter accompanying the voting paper despatched to the voter.

7. The Registrar shall permit any candidate, or his agent duly appointed and authorized in writing, to act on his behalf, to be present at the counting of the votes and to satisfy himself as to the voting papers being properly filled up, and that the persons signing the voting papers are duly registered members of the College and entitled to vote at the election.

SCHEDULE "A"

Coll. Phys. and Surgs., Ont......Office of Medical Registrar
University Avenue, Toronto

HOMEOPATHIC ELECTIONS, 19......

The Medical Council.

VOTING PAPER

The name of the Candidate or Candidates for whom you cast vote:	Name of Voter .... Residence of Voter ....
1 .... 2 .... 3 .... 4 .... 5	I .... of the .... of.............. do solemnly affirm that I am registered under the Ontario Medical Act; That I have not voted before at this election; That the signature to this is in my own hand-writing, as witness my hand this ....day of .... Signed ....

Note: In the case of an election to a vacancy a vote is to be cast for only one candidate.

SCHEDULE "B"

Election for Homeopathic Representatives to the Medical Council.

The voting paper herewith enclosed is to be filled up carefully and put into the enclosed envelope, which is directed to the Registrar, and mailed in time to reach him not later than two o'clock p.m. on ....

Sign your name to voting paper, using ink.

Signed..
Registrar.

By-Law No. 4.

Meetings

1. The Council shall hold one session annually in the City of Toronto, commencing on the first Tuesday in July of each year at the hour of two o'clock p.m.

2. The Executive Committee may at any time convene a special session.

3. It shall be the duty of the President to convene a special session upon the written requisition of at least one-half of the members of the Council.

4. Any such requisition, and the notice calling any special session, shall specify the object of the meeting. The requisition shall be signed by the members making the same, and shall be deposited at the office of the Registrar. It may consist of several documents in like form, each signed by one or more of the requisitionists. The session must be convened for the purpose specified in the requisition and in the notice calling the meeting, and only such business as is mentioned in the notice calling such special session shall be transacted thereat.

5. In case the President, for fourteen days after the deposit of such requisition, fails to give notice of the special session, the requisitionists may themselves give notice of the meeting which shall be held within six weeks after the deposit of the requisition therefor.

6. Special sessions shall be held at such time and place as shall be mentioned in the notice calling the same.

By-Law No. 5

Officers

1. The Officers of the Council shall be a President, Vice-President, Registrar, Treasurer, Public Prosecutor, Auditor, and Solicitor, and such others as the Council may deem necessary.

2. Except as provided in Article 4 the President shall preside at all sessions. In his absence the Vice-President shall take the chair, and in the absence of both these officers, the members of the Council then present shall choose some one of their number as Chairman.

3. The President and Vice-President shall be ex-officio members of all committees, standing and special, except the Committee on Discipline and the Executive Committee.

4. The Registrar shall furnish upon request information on any subject within his jurisdiction to the Council, or any of the Committees. He shall make report to the Council of the conduct of his office, and shall perform all duties imposed upon him by the Ontario Medical Act and the By-laws of the Council, and shall be subject to the direction of the Council.

5. The Treasurer shall collect all dues, receive and account for all moneys due to the College, pay out moneys only upon cheques signed by the President or Vice-President, or Chairman of the Finance Committee, and countersigned by the Treasurer.

6. The Treasurer shall give to the College a bond in amount and form satisfactory to the Council, and the premium thereon shall be paid by the College.

7. The Registrar, Treasurer and Public Prosecutor may retire from their offices by giving one month's notice in writing of their intention so to do, and such resignation, if accepted, shall take effect upon expiration of such notice.

The Council when requiring to dispense with their services shall give to these three officers one month's notice in writing of their intention so to do, or one month's salary in lieu of notice.

BY-LAW No. 6—PROCEEDING AT MEETINGS

ORGANIZATION

1. At the first meeting of the new Council the Registrar shall call the Council to order, read over the names of members, and request it to elect a Committee on Credentials, and upon the reception and adoption of the Committee's Report the Registrar shall call upon the Council to elect a President.

2. The Officers shall be elected after nomination by open vote, the vote being taken on the nominees in the order in which they were nominated. In the case of an equality of votes, the presiding officer, as on all other questions, shall give the casting vote, provided an equality of votes for the office of President shall be decided by the member present, representing the greatest number of registered practitioners. When only one candidate is nominated it shall be the duty of the presiding officer to declare him duly elected.

3. The first business of the annual session, after the organization of the Council, shall be the election of officers and the appointment of a Committee to nominate the standing committees.

Orders of the Day

4. The general order of business for the day shall be as follows:

(a) Calling names of members and marking them as present or absent.

(b) Reading of the Minutes.

(c) Reading of communications, petitions, etc.

(d) Reception of reports of committees.

(e) Notices of motion.

(f) Motions of which notice has been given at a previous meeting.

(g) Inquiries.

(h) Consideration of Reports.

(i) Unfinished business from previous meeting.

(j) Miscellaneous business.

All resolutions and reports must be taken up as they appear in the Order of the Day, and no variation of the foregoing order of business shall be permitted, except by consent of the Council.

Rules of Order

5. When any member is about to speak in debate he shall rise in his place and address the presiding officer, confining himself to the question under debate.

6. When two or more members rise at the same time the presiding officer shall name the member who is first to speak.

7. No member, while speaking, shall be interrupted by another, except upon a point of order, or for the purpose of explanation. The member so rising shall confine himself strictly to the point of order, or the explanation.

8. If any member, in speaking or otherwise, transgress the rules, the presiding officer shall, or any member may, call him to order, in which case the member so called shall immediately sit down, unless permitted to explain.

9. No member shall speak more than once upon any motion. except the proposer thereof, who shall be permitted to reply, nor shall any member speak longer than a quarter of an hour on the same question without the permission of the Council, except in explanation, and he must then not introduce new matter.

10. Any member of the Council may require the question under discussion to be read at any time of the debate, but not so as to interrupt the speaker.

11. When the matter under consideration contains distinct propositions, under the request of any member the vote upon each proposition shall be taken separately.

12. No member shall speak to any question after the same has been put by the presiding officer.

13. Notices shall be given of all motions for introducing new matters other than matters of privilege and petitions at a previous meeting to that at which it comes up for discussion, unless dispensed with by a two-thirds vote of the members present. Any matter when once decided by the Council shall not be reintroduced during that session, unless by a two-thirds vote of the Council then present.

14. A motion must be put in writing and seconded before it is stated by the presiding officer, and then shall be disposed of only by a vote of the Council, unless the mover, by permission of the Council, withdraws it. Every member present shall vote unless excused by the Council.

15. At the close of the annual session the minutes of the last meeting shall be read, approved and signed by the presiding officer.

16. In all cases not provided for by these rules, resort shall be had to the procedure of Parliament.

17. The Registrar shall make a list of all motions and reports on the table in the order in which they were received, which shall be considered under the heading "General Orders of the Day."

18. The presiding officer shall preserve order and decorum during each session of the Council, and protect the members in the enjoyment of their rights and privileges. He shall decide all questions of order, giving his reasons for such decision, and citing the rule applicable to the case, subject, however, to an appeal to the Council, and in case of an appeal it shall be put by the presiding officer in the following words: "Shall the chair be sustained?"

19. All questions of order upon which an appeal has been made from the decision of the presiding officer shall be decided by a direct vote of the Council without debate.

20. The presiding officer shall declare all votes, but, if any members demand it, such presiding officer, without further debate on the question, shall require the members voting in the affirmative and negative, respectively, to stand until they are counted, and he shall then declare the result. At the request of any two members the yeas and nays shall be taken and recorded.

21. The presiding officer shall not give any other than a casting vote, but may express his opinion on any subject under debate.

22. The presiding officer shall consider a motion to adjourn as always in order; but no second motion to the same effect shall be made until after some intermediate business has been transacted. This motion must be put without debate.

23. No motion except to adjourn shall be introduced unless it be written in ink and contains the names of the mover and seconder.

24. Every motion shall be read by the mover, standing in his place; it shall then be handed to the presiding officer, who shall read and submit it to the Council.

25. When a question is under debate, no other motion shall be entertained except a motion to amend, to commit, to postpone, or to lay on the table, or a motion for the previous question, or for adjournment, which last shall always be in order except when the Council is in Committee of the Whole.

26. Amendments, whether in Committee or in Council, shall be submitted to the vote before the original motion, in the reverse order in which they are moved.

27. A motion for commitment, until it is decided, shall preclude all amendments to the main question.

28. A motion to postpone shall include a day to be named for the further consideration of the question.

29. A motion to lay on the table shall be taken without debate; when it prevails the subject matter shall not be revived during the session except by a two-thirds vote of the Council.

30. The "previous question" until it is decided shall preclude all amendments to the main question, and shall be put, without debate, in the following words: "Shall the main question be now put?" If this motion be resolved in the affirmative, the original question is to be put forthwith, without amendments or debate.

31. Whenever the presiding officer shall consider that a motion before the Council is contrary to the By-laws or inconsistent with the report or other matter to which it was intended to refer, it shall be his duty to rule it out of order.

By-Law No. 7

Committees

1. The Standing Committees shall be the following:
(a) Registration, consisting of five members.
(b) Education, consisting of nine members.
(c) Finance, consisting of five members.

(d)   Rules and Regulations, consisting of six members.

(e)   On Complaints, consisting of five members.

(f)   On Printing and Property, consisting of three members.

And the following Statutory Committees:

(g)   Executive, consisting of five members.

(h)   On Discipline, consisting of not less than five members.

2.   A majority of the members of any committee shall constitute a quorum, provided the said quorum be not less than three members.

3.   When a committee presents its Report it shall be received without motion or debate. On reaching the order of business, "The Consideration of Reports," the reports previously received shall be taken up in order of their reception, and may be acted on directly by the Council, or referred to the Committee of the Whole.

4.   On motion of any member the Council may resolve itself into a Committee of the Whole for the consideration of a By-Law, report, or other matter, when the presiding officer shall leave the Chair, naming a member to act as Chairman of the Committee, who shall have the same authority in Committee as the President in the Chair of the Council.

5.   When any report of the Committee of the Whole is submitted to the Council, as provided in the preceding section, it shall be either adopted or rejected, or referred back to committee with instructions to amend or postpone to a time to be fixed for asking the concurrence of the Council.

6.   The By-Laws of the Council, except as provided by Article 4, Sections 8 and 19, shall be observed in Committee of the Whole; and the motion for the previous question or for an adjournment can be received; but a member may at any time move that the Committee now rise, or that it shall rise and report progress.

7.   On motion in committee to rise, or to rise and report progress, the question shall be decided without debate.

8.   Committees appointed to report on any subject referred to them by the Council shall report a statement of facts and also their opinion thereon in writing, and it shall be the duty of the Chairman to sign and present the report.

9.   All petitions and communications on any subject within the cognizance of the standing committee shall, on presentation, be referred by the presiding officer to the proper committee without any motion; but it shall be competent for the Council by a two-thirds vote to enter upon the immediate consideration thereof.

10. Every member who shall introduce a petition or motion upon any subject which is referred to a select committee appointed to consider such motion or petition, shall, during the sittings of the Council, be one of the Committee, without being named by the Council, and shall be the convener of the said Committee.

11. Any member of the Council may be placed upon a Committee notwithstanding the absence of such member at the time of his being appointed to such committee.

By-Law No. 8

Duties of the Committees

1. *Education Committee.*—The Education Committee shall have supervision of the curriculum and all matter pertaining thereto, and to the examination of those who seek registration.

2. *Finance Committee.*—The Finance Committee shall have the supervision of the fiscal concerns of the Council, and report the condition of the various funds. It shall prepare and report a detailed statement of the estimates required by the Council. It shall also consider and report on all matter referred to the committeee by the Council.

3. *Registration Committee.*—The Registration Committee shall examine and report upon all applications for registration as matriculants or as practitioners. It shall also examine the registers pertaining to the same, and all matters generally concerning registration.

4. *Committee on Complaints.*—The Committee on Complaints shall deal with all complaints against the Council or its officers.

5. *Printing and Property Committee.*—The Printing and Property Committee shall supervise all matters pertaining to the College Building and its requirements, and shall have supervision over all stenographic work and printing required by the Council.

6. *Rules and Regulations Committee.*—The Rules and Regulations Committee shall consider all matters pertaining to the rules and regulations of the Council.

7. *Discipline Committee.*—The Discipline Committee shall consider all complaints against members of the College of Physicians and Surgeons of Ontario that may be referred to it by the Council or the Executive Committee and shall be governed in its procedure by the Ontario Medical Act.

The Discipline Committee appointed shall consist of five members, three of whom shall form a quorum for the transaction of business.

The said Committee shall hold office for one year, provided that any member of such Committee appointed in any year shall continue to be a member thereof, until all business brought before it during the year of office has been reported upon to the Council.

8. *Executive Committee.*—The Executive Committee shall take cognizance of, and action upon, all such matters as may require immediate interference or attention between the adjournment of the Council and its next meeting, and all such acts shall be valid only until the next ensuing meeting of the Council; but the Committee shall have no power to alter, repeal or suspend any by-law of the Council.

By-Law No. 9

By-Laws

1. Every By-Law shall be introduced upon motion specifying the title thereof, and shall come up for consideration at the next session of the Council. Every By-Law, however, shall be first referred to the Committee of the Whole.

2. No By-Law shall be introduced either in blank or imperfect form.

3. Each clause, the title and the preamble, shall be considered and passed upon in Committee of the Whole, and the By-Law, after being adopted by the Council, shall be signed by the President or Vice-President and the Registrar, and sealed with the corporate seal of the College.

By-Law No. 10

The Seal

1. The seal of the College shall be in the custody of the Registrar, and shall not be affixed to any instrument except by the authority of a resolution of the Council and in the presence of the President or Vice-President, and the Registrar. The President or Vice-President and the Registrar shall sign every instrument to which the seal of the College is so affixed.

2. The seal of the College shall bear the device of a
and have legibly engraved upon it the registered name of the College.

By-Law No. 11

Authentication of Deeds and Documents

1. All Deeds executed on behalf of the College shall be in such form, and contain such powers, provisos, conditions, covenants, clauses and agreements as the Executive Committee shall think fit, and in addition to being sealed with the seal of the College, shall be signed by the President or Vice-President and countersigned by the Registrar.

2. All cheques or orders for payment shall be signed by the President or Vice-President, or Chairman of the Finance Committee, and countersigned by the Treasurer. Bills of exchange lodged with bankers for collection may be drawn on behalf of the College by the Treasurer.

3. Cheques or other negotiable instruments deposited with bankers for collection, and requiring the endorsement of the College, may be endorsed on its behalf by the Treasurer.

4. All moneys belonging to the College shall be deposited with such bankers as the Finance Committee shall from time to time think fit; and every receipt for money paid to the College shall be signed by the Treasurer, such receipt being an effectual discharge for the money therein stated to be received.

By-Law No. 12

Borrowing Powers

The College may, from time to time, at its discretion, raise or borrow, by way of loan or overdraft, any sum of money for the purposes of the College.

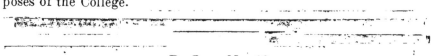

By-Law No. 13

Audit

1. Once at least in every year the accounts of the College shall be examined, and the correctness of the statement of receipts and disbursements, and balance sheet, ascertained by a qualified accountant or a firm of qualified accountants who shall act as auditor or auditors.

2. The auditor or auditors shall be appointed at the annual session, and their remuneration fixed by the Council.

3. The auditor or auditors shall hold office until the next annual session, and shall be eligible for re-election. Any casual vacancy in such office may be filled by the Finance Committee.

4. The auditor or auditors shall be supplied with copies of the statement of receipts and disbursements, and balance sheet intended to be laid before the Council at the annual session, before such session, and it shall be his or their duty to examine the same with the accounts and vouchers relating thereto, and to report thereon.

5. The auditor or auditors shall at all reasonable times have access to the books and accounts of the College.

By-Law No. 14

FEES AND TRAVELING EXPENSES

1. The Sessional Indemnity for members at every Session shall be one hundred and twenty-five dollars, together with twelve and a half dollars for every half-day occupied in traveling from their place of residence to the place of meeting and return, in addition to mileage at the rate of five cents a mile to and from the place of residence, the usual deduction at the rate of twelve and a half dollars per half day being made for absence from meeting.

2. Members of committees, when meeting during the recess of the Council, shall be paid twelve and a half dollars per half day, and mileage as is paid members of the Council at its meetings.

3. Each Examiner shall receive the sum of twenty-five dollars as a retaining fee, and twenty-five dollars per diem for each day's attendance at oral and written examinations and meetings, with the usual allowance of five cents per mile for the distance travelled to and from the examinations to place of residence, and an allowance of twelve and a half dollars for each half day occupied in travelling from his place of residence and return, or from one Examination Centre to another.

By-Law No. 15

EXAMINATIONS

Spring examinations shall be conducted in Toronto, Kingston and London, and also a Fall Examination in Toronto at such times and in such manner as the Council may direct.

By-Law No. 16

Annual Fees

1. Each member of the College shall pay to the Registrar toward the general expenses of the College for each calendar year an annual fee of Two Dollars ($2.00), pursuant to the provisions of the Ontario Medical Act, Revised Statutes of Ontario, 1914, Chap. 161, Section 21, Sub-Sec. 1.

The fee for the calendar year of 1921 is now due and payable.

The annual fees are to be applied toward the general expenses of the College, and shall be due on and from the first day of January of each year, and shall be based upon the levy imposing same made at the Annual Meeting of the Council first preceding the year in question; and such fee shall be deemed to be a debt due by each member to the College, and shall be recoverable with costs of suit in the name of the College of Physicians and Surgeons of Ontario, in the Division Court of the division in which the member resides.

2. The annual fee shall not be due and payable by any members of the College, who by reason of absence from the Province, or otherwise, shall in no way practice Medicine, Surgery or Midwifery in the Province of Ontario during the entire currency of the calendar year for which such annual fee may be imposed, but such member of the College shall notify the Registrar that he is leaving the Province, and inform him when he returns. Upon due notification it shall be the duty of the Registrar to exempt him from the fee imposed for such period of time.

The member so claiming shall prove to the satisfaction of the Registrar that he has not practiced his profession in the Province of Ontario during the year or years for which such fee has been imposed, but shall, if the Registrar require it, make a statutory declaration to that effect, and furnish such other evidence as may be required.

The decision of the Registrar upon such application as to the liability of the applicant for the fee in question shall be final and conclusive, subject to appeal to next meeting of Council.

By-Law No. 17

Annual Certificates

1. Every member shall obtain from the Registrar annually before the last day of January in each year a certificate under the seal of the College that he is a duly registered medical practitioner.

2. Upon payment of all fees and dues payable by such member of the College the Registrar shall write his name on the margin of the certificate and the date thereof, and the certificate shall be deemed to be issued only from such date.

3. No certificate shall be issued to any practitioner who is indebted to the College for any sums payable to the College, nor until the annual fee for such certificate is paid.

4. If a member omits to take out such annual certificate he shall not be entitled thereto until he pays to the College the certificate fee as aforesaid, together with any other fees or dues which he owes to the College.

5. After twelve months' default in taking out such certificate, and if two months' notice of such default be given by registered letter addressed to the registered address of such defaulter, the Registrar shall, if payment has not been made by the defaulter, erase his name from the Register, and the provisions of the Ontario Medical Act as to unregistered medical practitioners shall forthwith apply to such medical practitioner.

6. Such medical practitioner may, unless otherwise disqualified under the Ontario Medical Act, at any time after his name is so erased by the Registrar, obtain re-registration by applying to the Registrar and paying all arrears of fees and dues owing to the College, under this Act, and taking out his certificate as herein provided, and he shall be thereupon reinstated to the full privileges enjoyed by other registered medical practitioners under the Ontario Medical Act.

7. Any fees properly charged by such medical practitioner during the time in which he was in default in payment of any fees or dues to the College shall be legally recoverable upon production of the certificate of registration at the time of suit.

By-Law No. 18

Certificates of Institutions in Great Britain and Ireland

Every medical practitioner registered in the Medical Register of the United Kingdom of Great Britain and Ireland, upon proof to the satisfaction of the Registrar that he is so registered, and that he is of good character, and is by law entitled to practice medicine, surgery and midwifery in the United Kingdom, shall, on application to the said Registrar, and on payment of such fee not exceeding one hundred dollars, which, by Regulation of the Council, shall be from time to time charged for registration, of all persons entitled to be registered in the Province of Ontario, be entitled without examination in the Province of Ontario to be registered under the provisions of the Ontario Medical Act.

Provided that he proves to the satisfaction of the Registrar the following circumstance:

That the diploma or diplomas, in respect of which he was registered in the said Medical Register of the United Kingdom, was or were granted to him at a time when he was not domiciled in the Province of Ontario, or in the course of a period of not less than five years, during the whole of which he resided out of the Province of Ontario.

By-Law No. 19

Executive Committee

The Executive Committee for the ensuing year shall consist of Drs. J. M. MacCallum, Stewart, Routledge, Young and Argue.

By-Law No. 20

Legislative Committee

Drs. King, Hardy, Kellam, Brodie, Emmerson, Farncomb, Dales, Noble and Arthur, together with the Executive Committee, shall be and are, hereby appointed the Legislative Committee for the ensuing year.

By-Law No. 21

Committee on Discipline

1. The Committee appointed under the provisions, and for the purpose of the said sub-section, shall consist of not less than five members, three of whom shall form a quorum for the transaction of business.

2. The said Committee shall hold office for one year, and

member of such Committee, notwithstanding anything to the contrary therein, until all business brought before them during the year of office has been reported upon to the Council.

3. The Committee under said Section shall be known as the "Committee on Discipline."

4. Drs. Arthur, Becker, Kellam, Walters and Noble are hereby appointed the Committee for the purpose of said Sections.

H. WILBERFORCE AIKINS,   J. FENTON ARGUE,
Registrar.   President.

Minutes of the Meeting

OF THE

MEDICAL COUNCIL OF ONTARIO

JUNE, 1921

FIFTY-SIXTH ANNUAL SESSION

FIRST DAY

The Annual Meeting of the Council of the College, first follow-ing the Quadrennial Elections of last Fall, began at two o'clock this afternoon, Tuesday, June 28th, 1921, in the College Chambers.

CALLED TO ORDER

The Registrar called the Council to order, read over the names of members, and requested it to elect a Committee on Credentials.

COMMITTEE ON CREDENTIALS

On motion of Drs. Kellam and Argue, a Committee on Creden-tials, consisting of Drs. King, Kellam, Argue, Brodie and Ferguson, was appointed to examine the election returns of the newly elected Council.

COMPOSITION OF COUNCIL

The Committee retired, examined the returns, and reported as duly and properly elected, the following gentlemen:

TERRITORIAL REPRESENTATIVES

Division No. 1—Dr. G. R. Cruickshank.
    "   " 2—Dr. G. M. Brodie.
    "   " 3—Dr. A. S. Thompson.
    "   " 4—Dr. A. T. Emmerson.
    "   " 5—Dr. J. J. Walters.
    "   " 6—Dr. S. McCallum.
    "   " 7—Dr. H. S. Griffin.
    "   " 8—Dr. E. T. Kellam.
    "   " 9—Dr. R. H. Arthur.
    "   " 10—Dr. A. D. Stewart.
    "   " 11—Dr. E. E. King.
    "   " 12—Dr. R. T. Noble.

Division No. 13—Dr. F. A, Dales.
    "   " 14—Dr. T. W. H. Young.
    "   " 15—Dr. T. S. Farncomb.
    "   " 16—Dr. W. Spankie.
    "   " 17—Dr. R. N. Horton.
    "   " 18—Dr. J. F. Argue.

University Representatives

University of Toronto	-	Dr. J. M. MacCallum.
Queen's University	-	Dr. J. C. Connell.
Trinity University	-	Dr. A. J. Johnson.
Victoria University	-	Dr. W. L. T. Addison.
Western University	-	Dr. R. Ferguson.
University of Ottawa	-	Dr. J. L. Chabot.

Homeopathic Representatives

Dr. H. Becker.
Dr. G. A. Routledge.
Dr. W. S. Cody.
Dr. E. A. P. Hardy.
Dr. C. E. Jarvis.

Roll Call

The roll was responded to as follows: Drs. Addison, Argue, Arthur, Becker, Brodie, Cody, Connell, Cruickshank, Dales, Emmerson, Farncomb, Ferguson, Hardy, Horton, Jarvis, Kellam, King, J. M. MacCallum, S. McCallum, Noble, Routledge, Spankie, Stewart, Thompson, Walters and Young.

President's Address

Dr. Routledge, the retiring President, then addressed the Council as follows:

Gentlemen:—Although the conscientious performance of the labors connected with a responsible office does not entitle the individual who has filled it to any special compliment, inasmuch as he has simply done his duty, yet it is a great satisfaction to me to receive, in vacating the Chair as President, an expression of cordial friendship and goodwill from men who have so materially assisted me in conducting the affairs of the Council during the past year. You know the fable of the bundle of sticks. Separated from each other, even the toughest of them were easily broken, but combined they withstood the strongest pressure. In like manner, my efforts to render assistance to the Council proceedings would have been futile, if they had not been practically sustained by able and energetic assistance. If together we have achieved success, the merit belongs to us in common, for the head is nothing without the arms.

In order to keep up the standing of the College of Physicians and Surgeons of Ontario and protect the general public, we must enlist the sympathy and active support of the Medical Profession and with it co-operation on the part of the government of our country. If we can successfully direct their energies along our line, we will enhance our outlook materially.

It is not my intention to even attempt to criticise the Ontario Medical Council. It has had a useful record of over half a century, and has endeavoured to protect the profession and general public against fads and quacks in medicine and keep up the standard.

Drs. Emmerson and Ferguson, the two past Presidents, in their retiring addresses, were very thorough and painstaking in commenting and making recommendations on the routine work of their Presidential years, and I shall now briefly direct your attention to a few matters concerning the College, which call for notice.

The year through which we have been passing has been one largely of readjustment, in which the interests of the community as a whole, and of those of its integral parts, have been alike concerned.

There cannot be said to have been great general progress in what has been actually accomplished, and yet much has been done in the way of preliminary survey work, which we trust will eventuate in great good for the public and the profession.

Permit me for a brief moment to revert to some of the proceedings of our last Annual Meeting.

A number of matters were discussed, and resolutions passed, having relation to the same, to which I draw your attention once more.

Dr. Brodie's repeated efforts to have Government Analysis of Pharmaceutical preparations and drugs prescribed by members of the Medical Profession for use by their patients seems within reasonable distance of realization. The Council referred this question to its Legislative Committee, to have the latter take it up with the proper authorities. This Committee was primarily charged with the duty of interviewing the Government with regard to legislation sought by the College, to accurately define the meaning of the term "the practice of medicine," and, based upon the same, to determine the extent to which men, inadequately trained, or having no training at all, should be free to exploit the public. The Committee was not called together, in view of the fact, that the Premier very clearly intimated to representatives of the various "cults" interested in perpetuating a situation enuring to their profit, as well as to the Chairman of our Legislative Committee, that changes in the Medical Act would not be made at the then current sitting of the House. Because of this announcement, no meeting of the Committee was held, and consideration of the question of Government Analysis of Pharmaceutical Preparations had to be taken up through correspondence. The Chairman of the Legislative Committee, Dr. Edmund E. King, and I pay him the compliment of saying that he has been indefatigable in his efforts to promote the interests of the College, acting on behalf of the Committee, made extensive enquiries in this connection, and I quote a passage from a letter addressed to him by Dr. J. W. S. McCullough, Chief Officer of Health for Ontario :—

"With reference to the two resolutions of the College of Physicians and Surgeons, I beg to say that the one in reference to a laboratory in connection with the Federal Department of Health was brought forward at the meeting of the Dominion Council on the 18th instant. The Deputy Minister assured me that he expected to have such a laboratory established and when it was established it was proposed to carry on therein the examination of the various drugs and other products used in the treatment of disease."

It looks at length, as if the persistent effort of our representative from Woodstock, to have this service duly instituted, will meet with appropriate reward.

The resolution of Dr. Brodie, with relation to having Coroners notified of deaths occurring in cases, where irregular practitioners have been treating the same within ten days of their death, is at present engaging the attention of the Attorney-General.

You will remember that Dr. Stewart proposed the establishment of a Pension Fund, to meet the requirements of aged or infirm members of the College, who did not have available means to enable them to pass their declining years free from apprehension as to what a dark future might have in store for them. The question of the right of the College to use any portion of its funds for this purpose was submitted to our Solicitor for his opinion. He expressed it as his view, that not only could the Council not, without special legislation permitting it to do so, divert any of its funds in this direction, but that the members of the Council might render themselves personally liable for monies so expended.

Dr. Walters' motion, providing for a special marker for doctors' motor-cars, to be paid for out of the funds of the College, would, in the judgment of our Solicitor, also call for special legislation to become effective.

The Executive Committee, in its meetings held throughout the year, has kept closely in touch with all matters affecting the interests of the College.

The most outstanding one of these is the question of Medical Legislation. This has always been a vexed one, and the prospect of the College obtaining from the Legislature such legislation as it deems essential to best protect the interests of the public is not in any way heightened by reason of its failure to harmonize the views and viewpoints of its own members. Working agreements, based upon mutual concessions, are almost always attainable, and propositions made to the Legislature, representing practical unanimity of view on the part of the profession, could hardly fail to meet with sympathetic response. The community not unreasonably asks of the profession that it live up to its best traditions, and regard as its logical mission the exercise of unremitting care over the welfare of the people. Once convinced of its earnest desire to serve the public faithfully and without limitation, the Legislature will not be found to stand in the way of granting all reasonable requests.

The Medical Council, so long as it enjoys and exercises its present functions must regard its work as largely legislative in character, and as primarily and preeminently concerned with the task of caring for the welfare of the public, while the Ontario Medical Association, more elastic in its constitution and less tied down by statutory limitations, is freer to consociate the interests of the public and those of the profession, and to seek to promote the welfare of the profession as well as that of the public. Credit must be freely given to it for its laudable enterprise in this connection. At its instance, a proposal to form a joint advisory Committee of three of its members, associated with a like number of members of our Council, was formally assented to by our Executive Committee to endeavour to link up the interests of the two bodies.

This Committee, made up of Drs. King, Brodie and Argue, members of our Council, and Drs. Cameron, Burt and Routley, members of the Ontario Medical Association, was called together, and a copy of the report of the proceedings of the Committee will be found on the desk of each member. That ultimate good will come from association of these two representative bodies cannot be doubted. Whether or not, joint effort upon their part will result in present legislation remains to be seen.

With your permission, I should like to devote a few moments to consideration of matters of College concern. Before doing so, I wish to give expression to a feeling of regret, that it falls to my lot to have to remind you of the fact that, since we last met, two members of the College, one, Dr. M. O. Klotz, of Ottawa, a past President of the College, and the other, Dr. A. J. Johnson, of Toronto, at the time of his death a member of the Council, have passed away.

Dr. Klotz, in the course of a comparatively short career, had attained distinction of no mean order, of late years especially as a brilliant surgeon.

Dr. Johnson, while a phyisician, having, and deservedly enjoying, a very large practice, in this city, was better known probably than any practitioner in Ontario, as an expert in cases involving knowledge of medical jurisprudence. For many years preceding his death, his knowledge and skill were in constant requisition, and his services were availed of in almost all important cases of a medico-legal character occurring in the City of Toronto, or in the Province of Ontario. Our Executive Committee has already forwarded a resolution of condolence to the members of the family of the late Dr. Klotz, and I ask you to offer similar expression of the Council's profound sorrow in the loss sustained by the family of the late Dr. Johnson.

There is missing from our midst today the face of Dr. Griffin, one of our members and one of the oldest members in point of service. Dr. Griffin, I regret to say, is at present confined to his house by illness, and cannot therefore be present at this meeting. I would ask that our sympathy and best wishes be conveyed to him.

The Quadrennial Elections of the College were held last October. In the territorial divisions, there were contests in five five divisions only. In each of these, the former sitting member was re-elected. In twelve of the remaining thirteen divisions, the former members were re-elected by acclamation, while in the Middlesex division, Dr. Thompson, of Strathroy, succeeds Dr. F. R. Eccles, of London, retired.

Of the five Homeopathic members of the Council, four of them were again returned, while Dr. W. S. Cody, of Hamilton, was elected to succeed Dr. A. E. Wickins, retired.

The University representatives, as they appeared at the last meeting of the Council, were re-appointed by their respective Universities.

You will join with me, in extending a cordial welcome to Drs. Thompson and Cody, our two new members.

My attention has been drawn by the Registrar to the fact that it is now fourteen years since the date of publication of our last Register.

There are now in print and in the office of the College less copies of the Register, than sufficient to supply each member of the Council with one. Constant demands are being made for copies of the same, which cannot be satisfied, and the office has been obliged to apologize to Medical Councils of sister Provinces,

The Ontario Medical Act is bound in the same volume with the Register. There are many more requests for a copy of the names and of foreign States, for its inability to supply them with copies.

and addresses of our licentiates than for copies of the Ontario Medical Act. Copies of the Medical Act can be had by the public, where required, in the Ontario Statutes, but copies of our Register of names and addresses can be obtained only in this office. It is impossible to know when changes in the Act will be made, following which the Act and a list of licentiates could be published in the one volume, and the cost of the printing of such a combined volume, with the possibility of early changes in the Act, necessitating a correspondingly early printing of another such volume, would not be justified. It comes as a suggestion from the Registrar, that, at a comparatively small cost, the names and addresses of members of the College, known to be resident in Ontario, could be added to the list of those licentiates, who have become such since the publication of our last Announcement, as they will appear in this year's Announcement, and while the Announcement type is still set up, a few hundred extra copies of the lists only could be struck off, sufficient to meet the needs of the College for two or three years to come.

With a view to affording assistance to students, ex-soldiers of the recent war, in recognition of services rendered by them in behalf of the Empire, the Executive Committee gave its formal approval to the practice already adopted by the University of making advances to cover examination fees, such advances being secured by approved notes, running for various periods of time up to two years, without interest. The University has already advanced forty thousand dollars in this way to its students. Advances have been asked for and granted under authority of our Executive Committee to three students, or in all the sum of two hundred and twenty-five dollars ($225.00).

A complicated situation has arisen, in connection with the regulations between the British Medical Council and our own, having to do with registration in Great Britain of our licentiates, who obtained registration in our College, not following our own examinations, but by direct transfer of their standing in the Medical Council of Canada to our College. The General Medical Council of Great Britain feels that it is not free to enter in its Register the names of Ontario licentiates, obtaining their standing in our College in this way, and not following the passing by them of our own College Examinations.

The point raised is one of great importance, and I suggest, that the question be referred to the Education Committee for consideration and report.

The Registrar has supplied me with some facts, to which serious consideration must be given. The number of candidates offering themselves for our examinations is rapidly increasing. At this time last year, there were one hundred and twenty-eight candidates, while this year the number was one hundred and eighty-four. Heretofore, the Examiners have been able to hold their final meeting, shortly preceding the Council Meeting, and to have their report in the hands of the Registrar, so as to enable presentation of the same to be made to the Council at its opening session. This year the report is not yet ready for presentation, and if the number of candidates continues increasing in the future, there will not be a long enough interval between the date of the commencement of the examinations, and that of the holding of the Council Annual Meeting, to allow the Examiners' report to be presented to the Council before the latter adjourns.

Some adjustment or rearrangement of this situation will need to be had, and I recommend that the matter be referred to the Education Committee for consideration and report.

In this connection, I desire to draw your attention to some interesting facts, with relation to the number of licenses being issued by the College. The College has during the past eight years been accepting for registration licentiates of the British Medical Council and the Canada Medical Council. The total number of registration entries from all quarters during the period of time in question has been 1,356. This would make a yearly average of 169, while the number registering this year has been 186, an increase this year alone of over ten per cent.

The number of British registrations has been 64, or an average of 8 a year, while this year such registrations have amounted to 24.

The total number of registrations of licentiates of the Canada Medical Council in the years in question has been 124, the number so registering this year being 22.

The total number of Matriculants and Licentiates of our College, asking for certificates to enable them to approach the Canada Medical Council, has been 270, of which 67, or almost exactly twenty-five per cent. of the whole number of applicants for these eight years have obtained their enabling certificates this year.

Matriculation registrations during the eight years have been 1266 in number, an annual average of 158, and of this number the registrations this year have been 252, an increase above the average of about sixty per cent.

While these figures may be wholly gratifying, it necessarily implies an increase in the operation of all the different services of the College, which in the eight years in question has more than doubled.

It cannot have escaped your attention, that the balance on deposit in the Bank is much in excess of the free balance required to conduct the operations of the College, and I ask you to consider whether some of it might not be profitably invested in high class Dominion or Provincial Securities, which at the present time yield an exceedingly attractive return, with as nearly as possible absolute security. The balance as it appears, in the Annual Statement, will be less in amount by about six or seven thousand dollars, after payments in connection with the holding of the examinations and of the Council Meeting have been met.

In conclusion—I am glad to leave with my able successor, Dr. J. Fenton Argue, a corps of practical and trustworthy men, especially our Registrar, Dr. Aikins, to whom we all heartily wish success, well knowing he will deserve it.

Special Committee on President's Address

Dr. Ferguson and Dr. Argue moved and seconded respectively a resolution that the President's address be referred for consideration to a Special Committee consisting of the following members: Drs. Arthur, Connell, Cruickshank, Hardy and Emmerson.. (Carried.)

ELECTION OF OFFICERS

President

Dr. King nominated for the office of President Dr. J. M. MacCallum.

Dr. MacCallum, addressing the Council, explained graciously why he could not accept the nomination, and asked that his name be withdrawn.

Dr. Addison then moved that Dr. Argue be President. (Carried.)

Dr. Argue then took the Chair.

Vice-President

Dr. Kellam moved that Dr. Stewart be elected as Vice-President.   (Carried.)

Registrar-Treasurer

Dr. Stewart moved that Dr. Aikins be re-appointed as Registrar-Treasurer of the College for the ensuing year.   (Carried.)

Solicitor

Dr. Jarvis moved that Mr. H. S. Osler, K.C., be Solicitor for this year.   (Carried.)

Auditor

Dr. Connell moved that Mr. Henry J. Welch be appointed Auditor for the ensuing year, at the same salary as this year. (Carried.)

Official Stenographer

Dr. Hardy moved that Mr. George Angus be re-appointed as Official Stenographer for the College for the ensuing year. (Carried.)

Official Prosecutor

Dr. Emmerson moved that Mr. John Fyfe be re-appointed as Official Prosecutor for the ensuing year.   (Carried.)

Striking Committee, to Nominate Standing Committees

Dr. Becker moved, seconded by Dr. Arthur, that the following members constitute the Striking Committee to nominate the Standing Committees:—Drs. King, Brodie, Spankie, Dales, Kellam, Farncomb, S. MacCallum, Walters, Cruickshank, Jarvis, Noble, Young, and the Mover and Seconder.

Dr. Cruickshank moved, in amendment, seconded by Dr. Emmerson, that the words "and other Committees" be inserted after the word "Standing" in the original motion. Amendment adopted. Original motion, as amended, was then adopted.

Striking Committee's Report

The Striking Committee then retired, and later reported the following as their selection for the different Committees, in accordance with the terms of their report, which is as follows:

June 28, 1921, 3 P.M.

Your Striking Committee begs to report as follows:
The following names were nominated:

Complaints Committee
Drs. Young, Farncomb, Cody, Kellam, and Thompson.

Discipline Committee
Drs. Arthur, Becker, Kellam, Walters and Noble.

Education Committee
Drs. J M. MacCallum, S. McCallum, Jarvis, Spankie. Cruickshank, Ferguson, Connell, Addison and King.

Executive Committee
Drs. J. M. MacCallum, Stewart, Routledge, Young and Argue.

Finance Committee
Drs. Becker, Dales, Horton, Emmerson and Cruickshank.

Legislative Committee
Drs. King, Hardy, Kellam, Brodie, Emmerson, Farncomb, Dales, Noble, Arthur, Argue, Stewart, Routledge, J. M. MacCallum and Young.

Printing and Property Committee
Drs. Addison, Horton and Thompson.

Registration Committee
Drs. Connell, Hardy, Griffin, Walters and Ferguson.

Rules and Regulations Committee
Drs. Emmerson, Jarvis, S. McCallum, Brodie, Cruickshank and Horton.

Dr. Cruickshank moved the adoption of the report, seconded by Dr. Becker. Motion carried.

Communications

Communications were presented and referred to- Committees, or otherwise, as follows:

Those of Drs. C. Battaglia, W. J. Bussey, M. Fagin, P. N. Gardner, D. M. Hackwell, A. J. Ireland, G. Sewell and A. Ruppert were sent on to the Registration Committee.

That of H. S. Foley, and communications referring to matters affecting jointly the British Medical Council, the Canada Medical Council, and the Ontario Medical Council were referred to the Education Committee.

Those of Dr. G. R. Cruickshank and the Ontario Medical Association were postponed for further consideration.

In the communications relating to Dr. Hett and Dr. S. O. Rogers no action was taken.

Reception of Reports

Dr. King presented the report of the Joint. Advisory Committee.

Dr. Emmerson presented the report of the Representatives of this Council to the Canada Medical Council, concerning the Annual Meeting of the latter.

Notices of Motion

Dr. Brodie—Re Excise Duty on Alcohol used by Physicians for Medicinal Purposes.

Dr. Cruickshank—Re allowance re Federal Income Tax.

Dr. Brodie—Re Provincial Board of Health having Jurisdiction over Prosecution of Irregulars.

Canada Medical Council Report

Dr. Walters moved, seconded by Dr. Horton, that the minutes of the Annual Report of the Canada Medical Council, as they appear appended to the report of our Canada Medical Council Representatives, be received and fyled.   (Carried.)

Dr. Emmerson moved, seconded by Dr. Farncomb, the adoption of the report of the Canada Medical Council Representatives. After discussion, the question of adoption was deferred for further consideration.

Discipline Committee Report

Dr. Stewart moved, seconded by Dr. Horton, that the report of the Discipline Committtee be taken up for consideration at three o'clock tomorrow afternoon.   (Carried.)

Notices of Motion

On motion, the Council reverted to the order of "Notices of Motion."

Dr. King gave notice of motion of his intention to introduce a resolution requiring a course of instruction to be given in the subject of Physical Therapy, etc.

ADJOURNMENT

On motion of Dr. Brodie, the Council then adjourned to meet at ten o'clock tomorrow morning.

Minutes confirmed, June 29th, 1921.

(Sgd.) J. FENTON ARGUE, President.

SECOND DAY OF MEETING

The Council met at ten o'clock in the morning of Wednesday, June 29th, 1921.

Roll Call

The following members responded to the Roll Call: Drs. Addison, Argue, Arthur, Becker, Brodie, Cody, Connell, Cruick-shank, Dales, Emmerson, Farncomb, Ferguson, Hardy, Horton, Jarvis, Kellam, King, J. M. MacCallum, S. McCallum, Noble, Routledge, Stewart, Thompson, Walters and Young.

Griffin, H. S., Late Dr.

Touching reference was made by Drs. Argue and Ferguson to the death yesterday evening of Dr. H. S. Griffin, one of the members of the Council.

Dr. Ferguson moved, seconded by Dr. Dales, that Drs. King, and Kellam be delegated to attend the funeral of the late Dr. Griffin.   (Carried.)

Minutes Read

The minutes of the Council yesterday were read and confirmed.

COMMUNICATIONS

Communication from Nova Scotia Medical Board was referred to the Education Committee.

RECEPTION OF REPORTS

Dr. Connell presented the report of the Registration Committee.

Dr. Becker presented the report of the Finance Committee.

NOTICES OF MOTION

Dr. King gave notice of motion re Post-Graduate Education, to be conducted by the College of Physicians and Surgeons of Ontario.

Motions of which Notice Has Been Given

Dr. Brodie moved, seconded by Dr. Emmerson, that "Resolved that the Executive Committee co-operate with the Ontario Medical Association respecting the Excise Duty on Alcohol, used by Physicians for Medicinal Purposes." (Carried.)

Dr. Cruickshank moved, seconded by Dr. Stewart, that "Whereas, it is neccessary that every Physician should study after graduation in order to serve the public well, and that one who does not do so deteriorates rapidly, and,

Whereas, the reading of medical and scientific journals, the attendance at meetings of medical societies and short-term clinics are among the best means of maintaining a practitioner's usefulness, and,

Whereas, the cost of journeys by employees in the interests of their employers, in every business are allowed as expenses in computing income for taxation purposes,

Therefore, that this Council, composed of elected representatives of the Medical Profession of this Province, places on record, in the interests of justice and the public welfare, that these costs be allowed as legitimate expenses, in computing physicians' income taxes for Federal purposes, and that a copy of these resolutions be sent to the proper authorities." (Carried.)

Dr. Brodie moved, seconded by Dr. Cruickshank, "Resolved that the Executive Committee of this Council take proceedings to secure a change in the Medical Act, whereby the prosecution of those practicing medicine without a license shall be under the jurisdiction of the Provincial Board of Health." (Lost.)

Dr. King moved, seconded by Dr. Kellam, "That the question of adopting a course in Physical Therapy be recommended, and that the Examiners of this Council be instructed that they may examine on this subject, and that the matter be referred to the Education Committee." (Carried.)

Consideration of Reports

Joint Advisory Committee

Dr. King presented the report of the Joint Advisory Committee of the College of Physicians and Surgeons of Ontario, and the Ontario Medical Association.

After discussion of the same, Dr. King moved, seconded by Dr. Brodie, that the report be adopted. '(Carried.)

The Executive Committee of the College of Physicians and Surgeons of Ontario in its meeting as of April 7th last, agreed to and did appoint three of its members, Drs. King, Argue and Brodie, to form, with three members of the Executive of the Ontario Medical Association, an Advisory Committee, to consider questions relating to Medical Legislation.

A meeting of the Advisory Committee was held, and, later, following an interview with the Honourable the Premier, and the Minister of Education, the Joint Committee drew up and issued the following report :—

Toronto, May 26, 1921.

After the first meeting of the Advisory Committee the Chairman was instructed to prepare a statement for the Press, which statement was forwarded to each member of the Committee.

An endeavour was made by letter to the Premier for an appointment with the Premier and the Minister of Education for the purpose of ascertaining whether medical legislation would be introduced at the next Session or not. This letter was written on April 15. No reply was received for two weeks, then a telephone communication revealing the fact that the Session was taking up so much time that it would be impossible to grant an appointment until the House closed. When the Session was over the Minister of Education was unable to grant an appointment for over two weeks. He notified us, however, that the first moment that he could give with the Premier would be given, and on Wednesday, the 18th, we received a message in the afternoon that he and the Premier would receive the Committee on Friday the 20th, at two o'clock in the afternoon.

It was impossible to call the Committee together by mail notice, but each of the members was communicated with by telephone. All approved of the meeting and the object. Dr. Cameron, Dr. Burt and Dr. Argue were not able to be present The President of the Ontario Medical Association was communicated with and he approved of the meeting and hoped that something would be accomplished thereby. Several names as substitutes were suggested by the members of the Committee, some of whom did not see their way clear to act. However, on Friday the Committee met the Premier and the Minister of Education in the Parliament Buildings. There were present Dr. E. E. King, Chairman, Drs. F. C. Clarkson, Brodie and T. C. Routley.

The Chairman in presenting the matter to the Premier said that, ''We are the Advisory Committee appointed by the Executive Committee of the College of Physicians and Surgeons of Ontario, and the Ontario Medical Association. We are desirous of ascertaining the possibility or probability of the Government introducing medical legislation at the next session of the House.

This Committee has to report to the Ontario Medical Association which meets at Niagara on the 31st inst. and 1st, 2nd, and 3rd of June, and to the Medical Council which meets in the latter part of June. Neither body meets again for a year.''

He drew the attention of the Premier to the decision of the Court of Appeal in 1906 in which the definition of the practice of medicine as defined in Medical Act of 1879 was interpreted to mean the administration of drugs.

That since that time the bars had practically been down and Ontario had been overrun by irregular practitioners, that the Public had suffered therefrom, and the Medical Act, through its administrators, the College of Physicians and Surgeons, did not have the power to stop them. Also that the Medical Council for many years had endeavoured to have this matter corrected, the ~~Medical Act amended with the~~ definition of the practice of Medicine brought up to date to cover the situation, and how that the Council had been refused permission to prosecute irregulars under the Act; of the definite promise made by the late Sir James Whitney that the Medical Act would be amended, and that he would appoint a Commission and investigate the whole matter. The Chairman also pointed out that such Commission had been appointed and had presented its report, that the Commissioner's report had been approved by both the College of Physicians and Surgeons and the Ontario Medical Association, and also that neither the Whitney Government, the Hearst Government nor the present Government had ever sustained the Hodgins Report nor accepted its findings.

The Chairman drew the attention of the Premier to the fact that if a definition of the practice of medicine could be now established that it would be possible to protect the Public from the irregulars, and that the definition as given in the Commissioner's Report (page 66 Statutory Changes) was agreeable to the College of Physicians and Surgeons and the Ontario Medical Association.

And furthermore he drew the attention of the Premier to a letter published by the Advisory Committee, (Globe May 3) in which the stand taken by the Profession in regard to the practice of Medicine was clearly put forward. He also said that the Profession insisted upon standing by preliminary education and professional education and the necessity of passing an examination. A license should then be granted, but that no one should be allowed to practice on the Public who did not receive a license to do so. Also that there was no objection to any Cult providing that those practicing had proper educational ground work on which to base their diagnostic ability.

He further asked the Premier if this Committee could assure their bodies that legislation would be introduced next year to cover these facts.

Matters referring to the above were discussed informally by all the Members of the Committee with the Premier. The Premier and the Minister of Education were exceedingly agreeable, received the Committee in a gracious manner and assured the Committee that they recognized the very unsatisfactory condition of affairs, they desired to clarify the atmosphere and hoped that something would be done at the next Session. There could be no definite promise but they would look favourably upon any suggestion that could be made through the Ontario Medical Association or the College of Physicians and Surgeons dealing with the question. That they would take the matter up at once with the Cabinet and see how the matter could be introduced and carried through the House.

He drew the Committee's attention to the fact that in public matters of this kind the opinions of the Members of the House varied considerably, and that in none of the several groups of the House was there an unanimity of opinion. He felt, however, that the situation as it exists was unsatisfactory and that he would do anything in his power in clearing that situation. He drew the attention of the Committee to the large volume of correspondence that had reached him on this matter, and how some of it was from very prominent people.

The Committee was exceedingly well pleased with the reception given and felt that a considerable advance has been made toward getting medical legislation at the next Session.

Canada Medical Council

Dr. Arthur moved, seconded by Dr. Walters, that the report of the Canada Medical Council representatives be adopted. (Carried.)

The report follows:

Toronto, Ontario, June 28th, 1921.

To the President and members of the Council of the College of Physicians and Surgeons of Ontario.

Gentlemen:—Your representatives on the Medical Council of Canada beg to report that:—

1. The Ninth Annual Session of the Medical Council of Canada was held in the City of Ottawa on May 31st and June 1st, 1921.

2. The work was largely routine. Appended is a full copy of the minutes of the Council.

3. The examination centres will be the same as last year, examinations will be held in Montreal and Halifax in October, and in Toronto, Winnipeg and Vancouver, next June.

4. In 1920 there were 102 candidates for examination of whom 67 passed, 22 were referred and 13 were rejected. From May 1920 to June 1921, 55 registered under the ten year clause.

5. One clause in the Executive Committee's report reads,— "The Executive Committee desires to report to Council, that the

agreement with the College of Physicians and Surgeons of British Columbia, to conduct the only qualifying examinations held in the Province, has been carried out in a mutually satisfactory manner and would recommend to other Provincial Councils the advisability of entering upon a similar relationship." Your representatives do not think such an agreement would at the present be a wise undertaking for the Ontario Medical Council, yet we are persuaded this Council should aid in advising those graduating in Ontario the wisdom of taking the examinations of the Medical Council of Canada.

6. It is a matter of regret to the Medical Council of Canada that so few of its examiners have registered with the Council. Some endeavour is being made to have such appointments from those whose names are on the Council's Register.

Respectfully submitted,

(Sgd.) A. T. Emmerson,
Tom S. Farncomb.

Permission was granted by the Council to revert to the order "Notices of Motion," whereupon,

NOTICES OF MOTION

Dr. Ferguson introduced notion of motion relating to continuation of Joint Advisory Committee; and

Dr. Kellam introduced notice of motion re treatment of Amblyopia in children of six years of age and under.

MOTION OF CONDOLENCE

Dr. A. J. Johnson and Dr. H. S. Griffin

Dr. Jarvis moved, seconded by Dr. Noble, that letters of condolence be sent to the families of the late Drs. A. J. Johnson, and H. S. Griffin, and that formal letters conveying the same be committed to the care of a special committee composed of Drs. Addison, Noble and Farncomb.   (Carried.)

ADJOURNMENT

Dr. Stewart moved the adjournment of the Council, to sit again at two o'clock.   (Carried.)

Minutes confirmed, June 29th, 1921.

(Sgd.) J. FENTON ARGUE, President.

The Council met at two o'clock, Wednesday afternoon, June 29th, 1921, in the Council Chambers.

Roll Call

The following members responded to the Roll Call: Drs. Addison, Argue, Arthur, Becker, Brodie, Cody, Connell, Cruickshank, Dales, Emmerson, Farncomb, Ferguson, Hardy, Horton, Jarvis, Kellam, King, J. M. MacCallum, S. McCallum, Noble, Routledge, Stewart, Thompson, Walters and Young.

Minutes Read

The Minutes of this morning's session were read and confirmed.

RECEPTION OF REPORTS

Dr. Hardy presented the report of the Prosecutions Committee.

Dr. Arthur presented the report of the Discipline Committee in the cases of Drs. T. Coleman, H. Mason and W. C. Doyle.

MOTIONS OF WHICH NOTICE HAD BEEN GIVEN

Dr. King moved, seconded by Dr. Young, "That it is in the interest of public welfare, that post-graduate education should be encouraged, that it is the duty of the Council of the College of Physicians and Surgeons of Ontario to see that this matter is promulgated. We therefore feel that the establishment of lectures on the subject or subjects of most vital interest to public welfare should be organized, and also one lecture in the series devoted to the History of Medicine, and that as far as possible these lectures be delivered in Toronto at the same time as the University Post-Graduate Course."

After discussion, the motion was declared as lost.

Two of the members called for the yeas and nays. The vote, as so taken, is herewith recorded:

Yeas: Drs. Cody, Cruickshank, Dales, Emmerson, Hardy, Kellam, King, J. M. MacCallum, Noble, Walters, Young.—11.

Nays: Drs. Addison, Arthur, Becker, Brodie, Connell, Farncomb, Ferguson, Horton, Jarvis, S. McCallum, Routledge, Stewart, Thompson.—13.

Dr. Ferguson moved, seconded by Dr. Cruickshank, "That the recent action of the Executive Committee in appointing a committee to act jointly with a similar Committee from the Ontario Medical Association, as a Special Advisory Committee, for the purposes of medical legislation, be approved, and that the Committee be continued under the Legislative Committee." (Carried.)

Dr. Kellam moved, seconded by Dr. Brodie, "That the attached minute of the Section of Eye and Ear of the Ontario Medical

Association be adopted by the College of Physicians and Surgeons of Ontario"—

Minute of a Meeting of the Section of Eye and Ear Specialists of the Ontario Medical Association.

Niagara Falls, Ontario, June 2nd, 1921.

WHEREAS:

1. Defective vision or near blindness in one eye (Amblyopia) is very common, numbering thousands in the Province, as medical inspection of our school children has shown.

II. This Amblyopia always sets in before five years of age, and unless remedied before six years of age, the loss of vision is permanent.

III It is recognized by authorities in all countries that the eyes of young children cannot be correctly tested for glasses without the use of drugs which a licensed medical practitioner alone may use.

IV. An individual with a defective eye is

    (a)   A loss to the State.

    (b)   A potential total disability instead of a partial disability under the Workmen's Compensation Act.

It has been unanimously resolved by the oculists in session at the Ontario Medical Association that the Ontario Medical Association urge on the Government of Ontario that none but qualified medical practitioners be permitted to test for glasses, or otherwise treat the eyes of children under six years of age.

This was carried, subject to the proviso that it be referred to our solicitor for advice, and later sent to the Joint Advisory Committee.

CONSIDERATION OF REPORTS—REGISTRATION COMMITTEE

Dr. Connell submitted the report of the Registration Committee. The report was read and, upon motion of Dr. Connell, seconded by Dr. Walters, was adopted. The report follows:

THE COLLEGE OF PHYSICIANS AND SURGEONS OF ONTARIO

Registration Committee

Dr. A. Battaglia—Asks for license. Request not granted. Must conform to regulations.

Dr. W. J. Bussey— Must attend one year in a Medical College in Ontario and then pass the examinations.

Dr. M. Fagin—Russian Graduate in Medicine. Will be allowed to take the examinations as soon as he can qualify in the English Language for purposes of the College of Physicians and Surgeons.

Dr. P. N. Gardner—After paying the usual fees and costs will be reinstated.

Dr. D. M. Hackwell—Must take a year's course in an Ontario Medical College and then must pass examinations.

Dr. A. J. Ireland—Served in Royal Army Medical Corps since 1916. Asks for License to Practice. Request granted.

Dr. G. Sewell—Asks for License: Must conform to regulations and pass final examinations.

Dr. A. Ruppert—Asks for reinstatement. Request not granted.

(Sgd.) J. C. CONNELL.

FINANCE COMMITTEE REPORT

The report of the Finance Committee was read, and, upon motion of Dr. Becker, seconded by Dr. Dales, was adopted. The report follows:

FINANCE COMMITTEE

Chairman, H. Becker,

Secretary, F. A. Dales.

To the President and Members of the College of Physicians and Surgeons of Ontario:

Gentlemen:—Your Committee begs to report that it has examined the Treasurer's report, properly audited, and finds a balance in the bank of $45,366.57 as of June 21st, 1921.

The Committee recommends that the Sessional Allowance be $125 and that the travel time allowance be $25 per diem, and mileage as heretofore.

The Committee recommends that the following annual salaries be paid: Registrar-Treasurer, $3,600; Prosecutor, $1,500; Stenographer (Miss Roberts), $1,500, and an honorarium of $300 for past services.

The Committee recommends that the Examiners be paid $25 per diem in addition to the retaining fee of $25 and mileage and travelling allowance.

(Sgd.) H. BECKER, Chairman,
F. A. DALES, Sec'y.

Prosecutor's report

The report of the Prosecutions Committee was presented, and, upon motion of Dr. Hardy, seconded by Dr. Emmerson, the report was taken as read.

Toronto, June 1, 1921.

To the Chairman and Members of the Prosecutions Committee of the Ontario Medical Council.

Dear Sirs:—

I beg leave to submit the annual report re Prosecutions and Investigations.

M. H. Thuna .... Toronto .... Fined $50 and costs or 30 days in Jail. Defendant appealed to County Judge. Appeal dismissed. Fine paid.

M. D. Yaros .... Toronto .... Fined $50 and costs or 30 days in Jail. Fine paid.

C. E. Amsden .... Toronto .... Fined $100 and costs or 30 days in Jail. Fine paid.

E. T. Bellman .... Collingwood .... Fined $25 and costs or 30 days in Jail. Fine paid.

E. T. Bellman .... Collingwood .... Fined $25 and costs or 30 days in Jail. Fine paid.

C. E. Miner .... St. Catharines ....Fined $50 and costs or 30 days in Jail. Fine paid.

Wm. Locke .... Toronto ....Left before he could be served with summons.

M. F. Jarden .... Dunnville .... Charge dismissed.

M. F. Jarden .... Dunnville .... Charge dismissed.

G. A. Keith .... Ottawa .... Fined $25 and costs or 30 days in Jail. Fine paid.

G. A. Keith .... Ottawa ....Fined $25 and costs or 30 days in Jail. Fine paid.

P. E. Marier ....Alfred ....Fined $25 and costs or 30 days in Jail. Fine paid.

E. J. Brackin ....Gananoque ....Fined $25 without costs or 30 days in Jail. Fine paid.

Joseph Richard ....Tilbury ....Fined $25 and costs or 30 days in Jail. Fine paid.

C. E. Amsden ....Toronto ....Fined $100 and costs or 30 days in Jail. Fine paid.

E. L. M. Mack ....Sebright ....Fined $100 and costs or 30 days in Jail. Fine paid.

G. A. Williams ....Toronto ....Fined $25 and costs or 10 days in Jail. Fine paid.

Charlie Joe ....Toronto ....Case dismissed.

Avit Seguin ....Warren ....Fined $25 and costs or 30 days in Jail. Fine not yet paid over by Magistrate.

Avit Seguin ....Warren ....Fined $25 and costs or 30 days in Jail. Fine not yet paid over by Magistrate.

H. E. Barnell ....Espanola ....Fined $50.00 and costs, or 30 days in jail. Fine paid.

H. E. Barnell ....Espanola ....Fined $50 and costs or 30 days in Jail. Fine paid.

H. E. Barnell ....Espanola ....Charge not pressed as he had to refund $40, paid by a patient in first case.

M. J. Levitt ....London ....Fined $100 and costs or 30 days in Jail. Fine not yet received.

M. H. Thuna ....Toronto ....Charge withdrawn on advice of Asst. Crown Att. McFadden as Magistrate ruled that evidence of treatment prior to a previous conviction would not be accepted.

Elzear Montpetit ....St. Eugene ....Fined $25 without costs. Fine paid.

Lucien Tremblay ....Hawkesbury .....Fined $25 without costs or 10 days in Jail. Fine paid.

RECEIPTS—1920-1921

DATE	NAME		
1920			
Sept. 27	M. D. Yaros	Toronto	$50 00
Sept. 29	E. T. Bellman	Collingwood	25 00
Sept. 29	E. T. Bellman	Collingwood	25 00
Oct. 12	C. E. Miner	St Catharines	50 00
Oct. 22	C. E. Amsden	Toronto	100 00
Nov. 16...	M. H. Thuna	Toronto	50 00
Nov. 22	H. R. Brownlee	Kenora	50 00
Dec. 6	P. E. Marier	Alfred	25 00
Dec. 15	E. J. Brækin	Gananoque	25 00
1921			
Jan. 7	Joseph Richard	Tilbury	25 00
Jan. 13	George A. Keith	Ottawa	25 00
Jan. 13	George A. Keith	Ottawa	25 00
Jan. 17	C. E. Amsden	Toronto	100 00
Feb. 23	E. L. M. Mack	Sebright	100 00
Mar. 12	George A. Williams	Toronto	25 00
May 14	Lucien Tremblay	Hawkesbury	25 00
May 18	Elzéar Montpetit	St. Eugene	25 00
May 25	H. E. Barnell	Espanola	50 00
May 25	H. E. Barnell	Espanola	50 00

Total Receipts $850 00
Expenses re Prosecutions 392 14
Expenses re Discipline Committee 42 83

NOTICE OF MOTION

With permission of the Council, Dr. Kellam introduced notice of motion referring to periodical bulletin of information to be sent to the members of the College.

DISCIPLINE COMMITTEE REPORT

At three o'clock P. M., Mr. H. S. Osler being present, consideration of the reports of the Discipline Committee was had.

McKenzie, Dr. D C.

The case of Dr. D. C. McKenzie was put over until to-morrow morning.

Mason, Dr. H.

The case of Dr. Homer Mason was taken up. The Doctor did not appear personally, nor was he represented by counsel. The report of the Discipline Committee in his case is hereto attached:

The report of the Discipline Committee in the case of Dr. Homer Mason was taken up.

After full discussion of the case it was moved by Dr. Walters, seconded by Dr. E. T. Kellam,

AND RESOLVED:

"That the report of the Discipline Committee be adopted and that upon the facts ascertained and appearing in the said report and the evidence therein referred to, the said Dr. Mason be found guilty of infamous and disgraceful conduct in a professional respect and that the said Dr. Mason be suspended for a period of one month.

The Council orders that the said Dr. Mason pay the costs of and incidental to the enquiry." (Carried.)

The yeas and nays were recorded, and appear as under:

Yeas: Drs. Addison, Argue, Arthur, Becker, Brodie, Cody, Connell, Cruickshank, Dales, Emmerson, Farncomb, Ferguson, Hardy, Horton, Jarvis, Kellam, King, J. M. MacCallum, S. McCallum, Noble, Routledge, Stewart, Thompson, Walters, Young—25.

Nays: None.

Doyle, Dr. W. C.

The report of the Discipline Committee in the case of Dr. W. C. Doyle is herewith submitted:

"The report of the Discipline Committee in the case of Dr. Doyle was taken up.

After full discussion of the case it was moved by Dr. Arthur, seconded by Dr. E. T. Kellam,

AND RESOLVED:

That the report of the Discipline Committee be adopted and that upon the facts ascertained and appearing in the said report and the evidence therein referred to the said Dr. Doyle be found not guilty of infamous and disgraceful conduct in a professional respect, but that in view of the convictions against Dr. Doyle the enquiry was justified and that the Council therefore orders that Dr. Doyle be required to pay the costs of and incidental to the enquiry." (Carried.)

Coleman, Dr. T.

The report of the Discipline Committee in the case of Dr. Theobald Coleman was then considered. The report follows:

The report of the Discipline Committee in the case of Dr. Coleman was taken up. The Doctor did not appear personally or by counsel.

After full discussion of the case it was moved by Dr. Walters, seconded by Dr. Becker,

AND RESOLVED:

That the report of the Discipline Committee be adopted and that upon the facts ascertained and appearing therein and the evidence therein referred to the said Dr. Coleman be found guilty of infamous and disgraceful conduct in a professional respect and that the said Dr. Coleman be suspended for a period of six months.

The Council orders that the said Dr. Coleman pay the costs of and incidental to the enquiry.   (Carried.)

The yeas and nays were taken and appear in the attached record:

Yeas: Drs. Addison, Argue, Arthur, Becker, Brodie, Cody, Connell, Cruickshank, Dales, Emmerson, Farncomb, Ferguson, Hardy, Horton, Jarvis, Kellam, King, J. M. MacCallum, S. McCallum, Noble, Routledge, Stewart, Thompson, Walters, Young—25.

Nays: None.

Special Committee

The report of the Special Committee appointed to draw up resolutions of condolence to be sent to Mrs. Dr. A. J. Johnson, and to Mrs. Dr. H. S. Griffin, was presented and taken as read.

ADJOURNMENT

On motion of Dr. King, the Council adjourned to meet at ten o'clock tomorrow morning.

Minutes confirmed, June 30th, 1921.

(Sgd.) J. FENTON ARGUE, President.

THIRD DAY OF COUNCIL MEETING

The Council met at ten o'clock this morning, June 30th, 1921, in the Council Chambers.

Roll Call

The following members were present: Drs. Addison, Argue, Arthur, Becker, Brodie, Cody, Connell, Cruickshank, Dales, Emmerson, Farncomb, Ferguson, Hardy, Horton, Jarvis, Kellam, King, J. M. MacCallum, S. McCallum, Noble, Routledge, Stewart, Thompson, Walters and Young.

Minutes Read

The minutes of yesterday's afternoon meeting were read and confirmed.

Reception of Reports

Dr. Jarvis presented the report of the Rules and Regulations Committee.

Dr. Routledge presented the report of the Board of Examiners, Dr. J. M. MacCallum presented the report of the Education Committee.

Dr. Arthur presented the report of the Discipline Committee in the case of Dr. D. C. McKenzie.

Dr. Addison presented the report of the Printing and Property Committee.

Dr. Arthur presented the report of the Special Committee on· the President's address.

Dr. Connell presented supplementary report of the Registration Committee.

Dr. Becker presented supplementary report of the Finance Committee.

Discipline Committee's Report Considered
re Dr. D. C. McKenzie

With permisssion of the Council, the Discipline Committee's report re Dr. McKenzie was then considered. Mr. H. H. Dewart, K.C., appeared on behalf of Dr. McKenzie and addressed the Council.

Mr. H. W. Shapley appeared on behalf of the College and addressed the Council.

After full discussion of the case, it was moved by Dr. E. T. Kellam, seconded by Dr. Walters,

AND RESOLVED:

"That the report of the Discipline Committee be adopted and that upon the facts ascertained and appearing in the said report and the evidence therein referred to, the said Dr. McKenzie be found guilty of infamous and disgraceful conduct in a professional respect and that the said Dr. McKenzie be suspended for a period of one year.

The Council orders that the said Dr. McKenzie pay the costs of and incidental to the enquiry." (Carried.)

A record of the yeas and nays, as taken in connection with this case, is herewith appended:

Yeas: Drs. Addison, Argue, Arthur, Becker, Brodie, Cody, Connell, Cruickshank, Dales, Emmerson, Farncomb, Ferguson, Hardy, Horton, Jarvis, Kellam, King, J. M. MacCallum, S. McCallum, Noble, Routledge, Thompson, Walters, Young—24.

Nays: None.

MOTIONS OF WHICH NOTICE HAD BEEN GIVEN

Information Bureau and Bulletin

It was moved by Dr. E. T. Kellam, seconded by Dr. J. J. Walters:

"That whereas it would be advantageous to the members of the Council of the College of Physicians and Surgeons, as well as to the members of the Profession at large, to have a bulletin issued at intervals or annually by the Council as to the disposal of recommendations of the Council and as to matters of general welfare to the medical profession, be it resolved, That the Executive Committee be instructed to consider the matter and be given power to act." (Lost.)

CONSIDERATION OF REPORTS—EDUCATION COMMITTEE

After reading same, Dr. J. M. MacCallum moved, seconded by Dr. Ferguson, that the report of the Education Committee be adopted.

Subject to an amendment, moved by Dr. Ferguson and seconded by Dr. Brodie, that in the third paragraph of the report the word "Registrar" be substituted for the word "Solicitor," the motion was declared to be carried.

The report follows:

THE COLLEGE OF PHYSICIANS AND SURGEONS OF ONTARIO

REPORT OF EDUCATION COMMITTEE FOR THE
YEAR ENDING, JUNE, 1921

To the Ontario Medical Council,

Gentlemen:—Your Committee begs to report as follows:

The Registrar of the Nova Scotia Medical Council writes suggesting a uniform date for the Council Examinations in all the

Provinces of the Dominion. Your Committee reports that this would be impracticable in the case of Ontario.

The application of H. S. Foley, Detroit, Mich., was considered. He requests matriculation registration with a view to admission to our license examination. Refused admission to license examination on the ground that his University course is inadequate.

Re Dr. L. E. Sauriol, Kingston, Ontario;—He writes complaining that Registrar King of the British Medical Council declines to register him in Great Britain, because his Ontario Certificate was obtained through the Canada Medical Council examination. We recommend that the opinion of our solicitor be asked as to whether Dr. Sauriol is eligible for registration in Great Britain, under Clause 1, page 33 of the Reciprocity Act with Great Britain and, if not eligible, we further recommend that negotiations through our Registrar be entered into with the Medical Council of Great Britain to remove this anomaly.

In view of the impossibility of a single board of examiners being able to conduct the 1922 Midsummer Examinations in time to meet the purposes of the Council it is recommended by your Committee that a Dual Board of Examiners be appointed, one for the purpose of the Oral and Clinical Examination and the other Board for the purpose of the Written Examination the results thereby being reported as expeditiously as possible. It is therefore recommended that Section 4, Paragraph 9, Clause "G" shall be amended to read as follows:—

"There shall be a dual board of examiners, namely, one set of two examiners in each subject who shall conjointly set and examine each paper in the written examination and another set of two examiners in each subject who shall conjointly examine each student in the Oral and Clinical Examination."

The following examiners are recommended for the Fall Examination of 1921:—

Surgery

Dr. T. H. Middlebro, Owen Sound, Ont.
Dr. R. R. Graham, Toronto, Ont.

Medicine and Preventive Medicine

Dr. W. T. Connell, Kingston, Ont.
Dr. J. P. Vrooman, Napanee, Ont.

Obstetrics and Gynaecology

Dr. F. R. Clegg, London, Ont.
Dr. Donald McKay, Collingwood, Ont.

Homeopathic Examiners
Dr. E. K. Richardson, Toronto, Ont.
Dr. Hugh Porter, Hamilton, Ont.

Alternative Homeopathic Examiner
Dr. K. A. McLaren, Toronto, Ont.

BOARD OF EXAMINERS FOR JUNE EXAMINATIONS, 1922.
THE ORAL AND CLINICAL EXAMINERS

Surgery
Dr. T. H. Middlebro, Owen Sound, Ont.
Dr. R. R. Graham, Toronto, Ont.

Medicine and Preventive Medicine
Dr. W. T. Connell, Kingston, Ont.
Dr. J. P. Vrooman, Napanee, Ont.

Obstetrics and Gynaecology
Dr. F. R. Clegg, London, Ont.
Dr. Donald McKay, Collingwood, Ont.

Homeopathic Examiners
Dr. E. K. Richardson, Toronto, Ont.
Dr. Hugh Porter, Hamilton, Ont.

Alternative Homeopathic Examiner
Dr. K. A. McLaren, Toronto, Ont.

THE EXAMINERS FOR THE WRITTEN EXAMINATIONS, 1922

Surgery
Dr. E. R. Secord, Brantford, Ont.
Dr. Bruce Robertson, Toronto, Ont.

Medicine and Preventive Medicine
Dr. W. J. Tillman, London, Ont.
Dr. J. T. Fotheringham, Toronto, Ont.

Obstetrics and Gynaecology
Dr. G. R. Mylks, Kingston, Ont.
Dr. J. Gow, Windsor, Ont.

Homeopathic Examiners
Dr. E. K. Richardson, Toronto, Ont.
Dr. Hugh Porter, Hamilton, Ont.

Alternative Homeopathic Examiner
Dr. K. A. McLaren, Toronto, Ont.

The Committee recommend that the Announcement, Section No. 2 Curriculum, Paragraph No. 3, shall read after the word "Therapeutics": Physio-Therapy (including Hydro-Therapy, Electro-Therapy, Massage and Manipulative treatment, X-ray and Radio-Therapy.)

The following Colleges were recommended to be added to the accredited list, namely:—

Columbus Homeopathic College, Ohio.

New York Homeopathic College and Flower Hospital

To be struck off the present list:—

Boston Homeopathic Collége.

Add to Therapeutics section:—

Section 3, Paragraph 3, (1) "Medicine" shall read "Medicine and Preventive Medicine."

The dates recommended for the Examinations are as follows:—

The Fall Examination, the 2nd Tuesday in November, 1921.

The Midsummer Examination, Tuesday, June 6th, 1922.

Respectfully submitted,

(Sgd.) J. M. MacCallum, Chairman.

R. Ferguson, Secretary.

EXAMINATIONS

Dr. Routledge, Chairman of the Board of Examiners, submitted the annual report of the results of the examinations, held in the Fall of 1920, and in the Spring of 1921.

Following the reading of the Report, Dr. Routledge moved, seconded by Dr. Kellam, its adoption. Motion declared carried.

The report follows:—

EXAMINATION RETURNS

FALL 1920

Applications   46

Failed to appear   1

Tried 45

Passed 34

Failed 11

2   Failed on all Subjects.
2   Failed on Medicine.
4   Failed on Surgery.
1   Failed on Obstetrics.
1   Failed on Surgery and Obstetrics.
1   Failed on Medicine and Surgery.

SPRING 1921

Applications   184
Failed to appear   5
—
Tried 179
Passed 140
Failed 39

7 Failed on all subjects.
7 Failed on Medicine.
9 Failed on Surgery.
4 Failed on Obstetrics.
2 Failed on Surgery and Obstetrics.
6 Failed on Medicine and Surgery.
4 Failed on Medicine and Obstetrics.
—
39

(Sgd.)   G. A. ROUTLEDGE,
Chairman, Board of Examiners.

PRINTING AND PROPERTY COMMITTEE REPORT

After the report of the Printing and Property Committee had been read, its adoption was moved by Dr. Addison, seconded by Dr. Thompson, and it was carried.

The report is as follows:

Your Printing and Property Committee would report that they have inspected the building of the College from cellar to roof, and would report that the building is old and that the inner walls and floors are settling.   The lower floor is shored under the safe, and is reported by architects to be in safe condition for the present. The building is kept in an excellent condition of cleanliness.   There are some minor repairs necessary to the fences and furnace, and we would request authority to deal with these repairs, as found necessary.

The Committee would report that the printing of the Announcement was let last year to the lowest tenderer, the Armac Press, and would recommend that the procedure of last year be followed this year.

They would recommend that, pending probable legislation re the Medical Act, the publication of the complete Register be postponed, and that additions to the Register continue to be published in the Announcement, and special copies of the above-mentioned part be printed, to be used as a supplement to the existing published Register.

Special Committee on President's Address

The Special Committee appointed to review the President's address presented its report. After reading of the same, Dr. Arthur moved, seconded by Dr. Connell, that it be adopted. The motion was carried. The report follows:

Your Committee on the President's address beg to report as follows: Re the Joint Advisory Committee, it is our opinion, in view of our legislative responsibilities, we feel the Council representatives should be in a majority, and that they be members of and appointed by the Legislative Committee, and that this Council consider its duties as purely advisory, and not legislative.

The Committee endorses the opinion of the President, that a new list of licentiates be prepared, in accordance with the suggestions of the address.

Registration Committee's Report

The Registration Committee's Supplemental Report was read, with the following recommendations:

"Re candidate Number 124—the requesting for her, that she be granted a license, after having taken a three months' training in a Teaching Hospital in Ontario, be not granted."

The report was adopted on motion of Dr. Connell, seconded by Dr. Hardy.

Supplemental Report of Finance Committee

The Supplemental Report of the Finance Committee, as submitted by Dr. Becker, Chairman of the same, was then taken up.

Upon motion of Dr. Brodie, seconded by Dr. Kellam, the report was adopted.

The Report follows:

We are submitting statement of the assets and liabilities of the College.

The assets of the College consist of its property and equipment, of cash on deposit, long term bonds, overdue assessment fees, students' notes and unexpired portion of fire insurance premium.

The value of the property is unknown. It cost when purchased in 1908, the sum of eighteen thousand, and fifty-three dollars and seventy-five cents.

Its present assessed value, as ascertained today at the City Hall, is $23,250,00.

As the property will not again be used for residential purposes, the building situated on it cannot be regarded as having any appreciable value. There have not been many sales of land on the Avenue recently, so that no means is afforded of determining even its approximate value.

The cash on deposit, as of June 21st inst., was $45,366,57.

The bonds held by the College consist of $25,000,00 of the Province of Ontario, purchased in 1909, and carrying four per cent. interest. They do not mature until the year 1939. Owing to the recent issue by the Province of bonds carrying six per cent., the value of earlier issues, carrying four per cent., has materially decreased.

The other bonds held by the College consist of $10,000.00 of one of the earlier Dominion War Loan issues, bearing five per cent., and $15,000,00 of the last Victory Loan issue, bearing five and a half per cent. The market value of these bonds is less than par, and fluctuating from day to day.

Up to June 21st 1921, there is accumulated interest on these bonds, amounting to $142.65.

The overdue assessment fees, which can be collected, might be estimated to be as of the value of fifteen hundred dollars.

The students' notes have a value of two hundred and twenty-five dollars.

The furniture of the College might be put down as of the value of from five hundred to eight hundred dollars.

The unexpired portion of the fire insurance premium would be of the value of about thirty dollars.

The Assets of the College might be thus represented:—
The College property,

170 University Avenue, assessed value	$23,250	00
Cash on deposit	45,366	57
Long term Provincial and Dominion bonds, face value	50,000	00
Accrued interest thereon	142	65
Overdue assessment fees, approximately	1,500	00
Students' notes	225	00
Furniture, approximately	600	00
Unexpired portion of fire insurance premium, approximately	30	00
	$121,114	22

The Liabilities of the College consist of:—

Current obligations, incurred largely since the date of issue of the Annual Statement, June 21st 1921, and amounting approximately to	$ 8,000	00
Apparent surplus of Assets over Liabilities	113,114	22
	$121,114	22

(Sgd.) H. BECKER,
Chairman, Finance Committee.

Report of Rules and Regulations Committee

The Report of the Rules and Regulations Committee was then considered.

The by-laws contained in the report were taken as read in Council a first time. On motion of Dr. Jarvis, seconded by Dr. Horton, the Council went into Committee of the Whole, to consider the report clause by clause. At the request of the President, the Chair was taken up by Dr. King.

The report was then read clause by clause, considered and adopted in the Committee of the Whole.

On motion of Dr. Arthur, seconded by Dr. Jarvis, the Committee rose, the President took the chair and the Chairman reported the by-laws as adopted in Committee of the Whole.

Dr. Cruickshank moved, seconded by Dr. Ferguson, that the report of the Rules and Regulations Committee, as adopted by in Committee of the Whole, be now read a third time, adopted in Council, signed by the President and sealed with the seal of the College. (Carried.)

(For by-laws, see page 27 of the Annual Announcement.)

Miscellaneous

Dr. Walters moved, seconded by Dr. King, "That a Committee, consisting of Drs. Argue, Kellam and Hardy, with the mover and seconder, be appointed, to take up the matter of a new College building, to get sketch plans prepared for presentation to the Council at the next annual meeting, and a sum not exceeding five hundred dollars be placed at the disposal of this Committee for the above purpose." (Motion declared lost.)

Dr. Becker moved, seconded by Dr. Ferguson, "that a bonus of fifty dollars to each Examiner be allowed, and that the question of the investment of surplus funds be referred to the Executive Committee." (Carried.)

The following motion was also declared as carried:

Moved by Dr. J. C. Connell, seconded by Dr. E. T. Kellam, "That the Council desires to express, and have conveyed to Dr. Spankie its sympathy with him in his illness and that no deduction be made from the usual sessional indemnity, payable to members of the Council, in his case."

Dr. Ferguson moved, seconded by Dr. King, a vote of thanks to Dr. Argue for his ability, courtesy and urbanity, in the discharge of his duties as presiding officer of the Council in its daily sessions. (Carried.)

Dr. Argue graciously responded to the vote of thanks.

The Council adjourned for a ten-minute interval to allow the Legislative Committee to meet for organization purposes. Upon reassembling, Dr. King reported the Committee as having carried a resolution appointing Drs. King, Farncomb, Noble and Brodie as representatives of the Legislative Committee on the Joint Advisory Committee.

The minutes of this session of the Council were then read, and formally approved.

Dr. Horton moved the adjournment of the Council. (Carried.)

(Sgd.)   J. FENTON ARGUE, President.

June 30th, 1921.

TREASURER'S REPORT

To the Members of the Council of the College of Physicians and Surgeons of Ontario:

Gentlemen,—I beg to submit herewith Financial Statement for the Council Year, 1920-1921, just ended.

Receipts

Balance in Bank, June 21st, 1920, as audited		$30,043 27
Assessment Dues—		
Paid direct to Registrar	$5,011 50	
Collected by Bank	2,903 00	
		7,914 50
Examination Fees—		
Fall Examinations, 1920	1,775 00	
Spring Examinations, 1921	12,905 00	
		14,680 00
War License Fees		300 00
Matriculation Registration Fees		6,275 00
Registration Fees of Applicants, qualifying under Canada Medical Council certificates		1,650 00
Fees of Ontario Council Licentiates, for Certificates of Standing, when applying to the Canada Medical Council		105 00
Fees of Ontario Council Matriculants, for Certificates of Standing, when applying to the Canada Medical Council		1,150 00
Registration Fees of Licentiates of the British Medical Council, registering in Ontario		2,400 00
Fines		850 00
Rebate on Guarantee Bond		4 15
Repayment of Costs, in cases where names of members have been restored to the Register		400 00
Interest on Bonds—		
Province of Ontario	$1,000 00	
Dominion of Canada	1,325 00	
		2,325 00
Interest on Current Bank Account		472 34
		$68,569 26

Expenditures

Council Meeting, June, 1920—		
Members' Allowance	$4,195 05	
Stenographic Report of Proceedings, etc.	123 00	
		4,318 05
Officers' Salaries—		
Registrar	3,591 66	
Assistant Secretary	1,200 00	
Prosecutor	1,475 00	
		6,266 66
Legal Services, General		100 00
Prosecutions—Legal Charges, Witness Fees, Court Charges, Travelling Expenses, etc.		521 21
Executive Committee		677 70
Discipline Committee		314 90
Discipline Procedure		42 83
Printing Diplomas, Examination Papers, etc.		1,242 60

Printing Annual Announcement, Lists of Licentiates, etc........ 1,017 30
Telephone Service 97 62
Holding Professional Examinations—
  . General Expenses 316 75
  Examiners' Fees—
    Spring, 1920 .... $2,663 30
    Fall, 1920 .... 894 60
                                    ————————— 3,557 90
                                                          ————————
                                                          3,874 65
Fees Refunded 344 00
.Audit of Books, Vouchers, etc., of Registrar's Office 75 00
Rental of Safety Deposit Box 3 00
Registrar's Office—Supplies (This item includes postage, $659.84,
  on Announcements, Assessment Notices, etc.) 1,027 14
Stenographer 595 00
Treasurer's Bonds 30 00
Assistant Secretary's Bond 10 00
Prosecutor's Bond 5 00
Council Election, Quadrennial 700 20
Bank Charges, re Collection of Assessment Dues, Exchange on
  Cheques, etc. 326 12
Duncan, Mrs. J., Honorarium voted by Council :.............. 200 00
Advances made to Candidates (Returned Soldiers) to meet Exam-
  ination Fees, under instruction of Executive Committee
  (secured by approved notes) 225 00
Floral Wreath—late Dr. M. O. Klotz 25 00
Property and Building Maintenance—
  Painting, Plumbing, Carpentering, Furnace and
  Roof Repairs, Care of Grounds, Building, etc..... $265 30
  Electric Light 25 45
  Gas 67 92
  Fuel 403 00
  Water 24 42
  Fire Insurance (Three Year Term) 41 85
                                              ————————— 827 94
Miscellaneous 335 77
Balance on deposit in Sterling Bank 45,366 57
                                                          ————————
                                                          $68,569 26

All of which is respectfully submitted,
                H. WILBERFORCE AIKINS, Registrar-Treasurer.

Having audited the books and accounts of the Treasurer of the College
of Physicians and Surgeons of Ontario—including Bank and Cash Books, and
Vouchers thereto, for the Council year 1920-1921, I hereby certify that I
find the same correct and complete, and that the above Statement of Receipts
and Expenditures agrees therewith.
                HENRY J. WELCH, Chartered Accountant,
                                                    Auditor.
Toronto, June 21st, 1921.

COUNCIL MEETING, JUNE, 1920

NAME	Sessional Indemnity	Travel Time Allowance	Mileage	Total
Addison, Dr. W. L. T.	$125 00	$.....	$.....	$125 00
Argue, Dr. J. F.	125 00	50 00	26 20	201 20
Arthur, Dr. R. H.	125 00	50 00	26 00	201 00

NAME	Sessional Indemnity	Travel Time Allowance	Mileage	Total
Becker, Dr. H.	125 00	.....	.....	125 00
Brodie, Dr. G. M.	125 00	25 00	8 80	158 80
Connell, Dr. J. C.	125 00	37 50	16 50	179 00
Dales, Dr. F. A.	125 00	25 00	2 90	152 90
Eccles, Dr. F. R.	125 00	25 00	12 00	162 00
Emmerson, Dr. A. T.	125 00	25 00	13 40	163 40
Farncomb, Dr. T. S.	125 00	25 00	10 10	160 10
Ferguson, Dr. R.	125 00	25 00	12 00	162 00
Griffin, Dr. H. S.	125 00	25 00	4 00	154 00
Hardy, Dr. E. A. P.	125 00	.....	.....	125 00
Horton, Dr. R. N.	125 00	37 50	20 80	183 30
Jarvis, Dr. C. E.	125 00	25 00	12 00	162 00
Johnson, Dr. A. J.	125 00	.....	.....	125 00
Kellam, Dr. E. T.	125 00	25 00	8 20	158 20
King, Dr. E. E.	125 00	.....	.....	125 00
MacCallum, Dr. J. M.	125 00	.....	.....	125 00
McCallum, Dr. S.	125 00	25 00	10 70	160 70
Noble, Dr. R. T.	125 00	.....	.....	125 00
Routledge, Dr. G. A.	125 00	25 00	12 10	162 10
Spankie, Dr. W.	125 00	50 00	16 50	191 50
Stewart, Dr. A. D.	125 00	87 50	81 50	294 00
Walters, Dr. J. J.	125 00	25 00	6 25	156 25
Young, Dr. T. W. H.	125 00	25 00	7 60	157 60

EXECUTIVE COMMITTEE

Three Meetings in all

NAME	Attendance and Travel Time Allowance	Mileage	Total
Argue, Dr. J. F.	$150 00	$78 60	$228 60
Ferguson, Dr. R.	75 00	36 00	111 00
MacCallum, Dr. J. M.	25 00	.....	25 00
Routledge, Dr. G. A.	75 00	36 30	111 30
Young, Dr. T. W. H.	75 00	22 80	97 80
And by invitation:—			
King, Dr. E. E.:	37 50	.....	37 50
Noble, Dr. R. T.	12 50	.....	12 50
Connell, Dr. J. C.	37 50	16 50	54 00

DISCIPLINE COMMITTEE

Meeting, June 25th, 1920.

NAME	Attendance and Travel Time Allowance	Mileage	Total
Arthur, Dr. R. H.	$40 00	$26 00	$66 00
Becker, Dr. H.	10 00	.....	10 00
McCallum, Dr. S.	20 00	10 70	30 70
Walters, Dr. J. J.	20 00	6 25	26 25

Meeting, May 26th, 1921.

	Attendance and Travel Time Allowance	Mileage	Total
Arthur, Dr. R. H.	50 00	26 00	76 00
Becker, Dr. H.	12 50	.....	12 50
Griffin, Dr. H. S.	25 00	4 00	29 00
Kellam, Dr. E. T.	25 00	8 20	33 20
Walters, Dr. J. J.	25 00	6 25	31 25

EXAMINERS—SPRING, 1920

NAME	Retaining Fee	Examining and Travel Time Allowance	Mileage	Total
Gibson, Dr. W..............	$20 00	$375 00	$28 50	$423 50
Hodgins, Dr. E. L..........	20 00	400 00	40 50	460 50
Machell, Dr. H. T..........	20 00	362 50	28 50	411 00
Vrooman, Dr. J. P..........	20 00	400 00	31 40	451 40
Williams, Dr. E. L..........	20 00	400 00	52 50	472 50
Wilson, Dr. G. E...........	20 00	362 50	28 50	411 00

EXAMINERS—FALL, 1920

NAME	Retaining Fee	Examining and Travel Time Allowance	Mileage	Total
Connell, Dr. W. T..........	20 00	125 00	16 50	161 50
Gallie, Dr. W. E.	20 00	87 50	.....	107 50
McKay, Dr. D.	20 00	100 00	18 80	138 80
Middlebro, Dr. T. H........	20 00	100 00	24 20	144 20
Vrooman, Dr. J. P..........	20 00	125 00	16 50	161 50
Williams, Dr. E. L..........	20 00	100 00	24 00	144 00

RÉSUMÉ

To the Members of the College:

Under direction of the Council of the College, I am submitting rèsumè of proceedings of its ànnual meeting, and, associated with same, brief reference to matters of moment of joint public and professional interest, occurring in the interval-period between the last and the present meeting of the Council.

Dr. Routledge's Presidential Address

The members of the College will read with profit the annual address of the President.

Apart from its references to public questions affecting the College, it contains much of interest to the members of the College relating to the internal economy of the same.

For address, see page 47.)

Quadrennial Elections

The quadrennial elections of the College were held in October 1920.

Of the eighteen territorial representatives, seventeen, who had been members of the retiring Council, were again candidates, and were all re-elected. There were contests in five constituencies only, without change in representation.

In Division No. 3, Dr. A. S. Thompson, of Strathroy, was elected by acclamation, to succeed the late Dr. Eccles, resigned.

Dr. A. S. Cody, of Hamilton, was elected to fill the vacancy created by the resignation of Dr. A. E. Wickins, resigned. This was the only change in the Homeopathic section of the Council, the other members being re-elected.

The Universities reappointed their former representatives, to sit in the new Council. The Council, as thus elected, is made up as follows:—

Territorial representatives:— Drs. J. F. Argue, R. H. Arthur, G. M. Brodie, G. R. Cruickshank, F. A. Dales, A. T. Emmerson, T. S. Farncomb, H. S. Griffin, R. N. Horton, E. T. Kellam, E. E. King, S. McCallum, R. T. Noble, W. Spankie, A. D. Stewart, A. S. Thompson, J. J. Walters, T. W. H. Young.

Homeopathic representatives:—Drs. H. Becker, A. S. Cody, E. A. P. Hardy, C. E. Jarvis, G. A. Routledge.

University representatives:—Drs. W. L. T. Addison, J. L. Chabot, J. C. Connell, R. Ferguson; A. J. Johnson, J. M. MacCallum.

Medical Legislation

The Council of the College has for many years consistently sought to bring about accomplishment, inter alia, of two very laudable aims, the one, that of exhausting every means available to force candidates for its license to qualify under the highest standards, the other, that of impressing upon the authorities the necessity of eliminating through legislative action the practice of cults, which call for little or no knowledge of the human body, of its varied activities in health and disease.

The one object has been accomplished, as far at least, as it is possible to reach finality in anything which may be held to offer illuminating illustration of "eternal process moving on." There is probably no higher standard set anywhere for license to practice medicine, than in the Province of Ontario.

The other object has not been accomplished. Under the law, as interpreted in our Courts, men who have not shewn themselves in any way qualified to meet the requirements associated with the granting of a license to practice medicine in the Province of Ontario are apparently free to do so. Long periods of study and rigid examinations constitute in the minds of the public safeguards, wisely provided to guarantee efficiency and to assure service of a high order. No great flight of imagination is needed to picture the infinite harm which may result to the community in general, with the removal of these safeguards.

Specious representations always appeal to certain elements in the community. The law, in general, takes cognizance of such representations, where they concern financial transactions, but the same law makes quite inadequate provision, for dealing with representations, having definite relationship to questions of personal physical welfare and public health, embodying claims for which no basis in fact can be found, and which, for the most part, if not wholly untrue, are at least hopelessly misleading . These representations become positive menace to the community, when they openly disregard and seek to nullify all the teachings of modern preventive medicine.

The mass of the people is in academic sympathy with every legitimate move having for object the solution of problems affecting public health, and this sympathy is expressed in the shape of public grants and private benefactions, but the mass of the people, at the same time, lays to its soul the flattering unction, that, having ex-

pressed sympathy and provided endowment, its duty ceases. Pos-
sibly, no task in life is less burdensome, or more agreeable, than that
of relegating duties to others. The public passes on to the Legislature the task of making due provision for its own physical welfare.

Democratic institutions line up with the spirit of the age, but
democratic institutions do not always attain the ideal in their
practical evolution. One looks in vain for explanation of the
dual phenomenon of raising the standard and lowering the bars.
Millions of money freely devoted to aiding science to unfold the
secrets of nature, with the benificent purpose of alleviating suffer-
ing and banishing disease, marching with tacit recognition of cults,
whose disciples make light of the marvellous attainments of science,
and whose literature abounds with appeals to all that is sordid and
venal.

This anomaly is one, which cannot continue indefinitely. Pure
science and crass ignorance have nothing in common. The medical
profession holds itself in duty bound, through its representative
bodies, to direct the attention of the Government, to the hopelessly
illogical admixture of scientific exploring with scientific exploiting,
as found to exist today in the Province of Ontario.

With this object in view, a Joint Committee, selected from the
Executives of the College of Physicians and Surgeons of Ontario
and the Ontario Medical Association, waited upon the Honourable
the Premier of Ontario, and the Honourable the Minister of Education, following prorogation of the House.

The Committee sought to make it apparent to the Ministers in
question, that the interests of the public must suffer through any
policy permitting continued perpetuation of impossible relationships,
with the definite settlement of which earlier administrations had
been confronted, but had not deemed to be of moment sufficient to
demand immediate or imperative action.

Exception could not be taken to the courtesy, with which the
Committee was received, nor to the expression of sympathy
graciously extended to it. The Premier was absolutely frank, in
admitting that the situation was unsatisfactory, but, while assuring
the deputation that he was personally kindly disposed, he made it
quite clear, that, in a question of this nature, involving widely
diverging interests, he could not assume the responsibility of undertaking to commit the individual members of the House to approval
of the views submitted to him.

No definite undertaking was accordingly given by him, beyond
a promise to have the Cabinet give the medical situation careful
consideration, with the added hope, that the House might find ways
and means to meet the views of the profession, as presented to him
by the Joint Committee, representing it.

The aim of preventive medicine is to eradicate disease. The best brains of the most intelligent peoples of the world are concentrated to-day upon the problems of unravelling the cause of disease. The solution of the problem will not come through "drawing a bow at a venture," but through unremitting laboratory and bedside research, and the profession is directing its energies to conducting this colossal task along lines purely logical and scientific.

The concrete results of such intensive studies enure directly to the benefit of the people itself. Is it not reasonable, is it not logical, to suppose, that the people who thus directly benefit from scientific research should be the first to accord to it the recognition it deserves, and the first to discountenance specious representations, and spurious claims?

Where it concerns the best interests of the community, should any legislative body hesitate to choose between facts, ascertained to rest upon established foundations, and claims which are unproven and chimerical, and which, moreover, are not shewn to be wholly divorced from suspicion of an element of self-interest?

The obvious duty of the profession is to sound the alarm. Beyond this, it should not be called upon to pass. It would be guilty of wanton discourtesy, if it were to assume a need to intimate to those in charge of legislation, that toleration of conditions known to exist, inimical to the welfare of the community as a whole, is quite inconsistent with reasonable interpretation of the duties and responsibilities of high office.

More should not be asked of the medical profession than dignified presentation of facts.

Responsibility for providing appropriate remedy for ills, known to exist, and known to operate adversely to the attainment of the lofty ends contemplated in the well conceived and honestly directed efforts of modern medical science to eliminate chance and chicanery, and to seek solution of problems of health and disease, through employment of scientific methods only, rests with the Legislature.

Physical Therapy

Some years ago, while still a member of the Council, Dr. John S. Hart, representing the District of West Toronto, advocated the claims of Physical Therapy, and asked for it the wider recognition which he felt that it deserved in the curriculum of studies. Since then, increasing attention has been given to the subject, and at the recent Council Meeting, Dr. Edmund E. King moved a resolution, of which the Council approved, affirming the necessity of making a larger place for the study of this department of medical science.

The teaching of Physical Therapy has been for a long period of time carried on in connection with the general teaching of medicine, but the discovery of phenomena in the world of the natural sciences, until recently unknown, and improved methods devised for the purpose of its better practical application, have served to widen its sphere of usefulness, and the Council by its recent action has set its seal once more upon the value it attaches to this branch of medical science.

Medical Council of Canada

The report of the proceedings of the annual meeting of the Canada Medical Council, as presented by Drs. Emmerson and Farncomb, representatives therein of the College of Physicians and Surgeons of Ontario, contains the interesting announcement. that the Medical Council of British Columbia has effected arrangements with the Canada Medical Council, to have the latter body's qualifying examinations supersede those of the Provincial Council, so that candidates hereafter seeking licentiate standing in British Columbia by examination, must pass the examinations of the Canada Medical Council.

Hope was expressed by the Canada Medical Council, that ''in due season'' the other Provincial Councils would ''fall into line.'' The College representatives did not feel, that it would be opportune, at the present juncture, for the Ontario Medical Council to subordinate its powers in the matter of holding qualifying examinations in Ontario, in favour of the Medical Council of Canada.

The Council found itself in sympathy with the views of its representatives in this regard.

Action of the Council upon the Report of its Discipline Committee

Four cases came before the Discipline Committee for investigation.

In one of these, a member of the College was asked to explain why a Police Court conviction had been registered against him, in connection with excessive prescription of narcotic drugs.

The straightforward manner in which he gave his evidence, and his absolute candour, convinced the Committee of the truthfulness of his statements, and the Committee recommended that no adverse action be taken. Acting upon advice, the soundness of which he had not called in question, and for the purpose of avoiding publicity, he had pleaded guilty in private audience, where it was well within reason to believe that a conviction would not have been recorded against him in open court.

In the other three cases, the Committee held that the charges had been proven, and recommended suspension of the members in question.

Each of the charges involved a police court conviction, for contravention of the provisions of the Ontario Temperance Act.

The Council, in sustaining the recommendation of the Committee, once more placed itself on record, as determined to lend its aid to the authorities in their attempt to secure enforcement of the Act, and as equally determined to make it apparent to any member of the College, who, for reasons of his own and not disclosed, appears to regard as matter of indifference the discredit which his own misconduct brings upon the profession as a whole, that the College is official representative of the profession in Ontario, under sacred obligation to regard as inviolable the sense of honour, inherited by it as birthright, and to maintain without dimming, the lustre attaching to its high achievments of the past.

Government Analysis of Pharmaceutical Preparations

Dr. G. M. Brodie, of Woodstock, has urged for some years back the wisdom of having the Federal Government institute a laboratory for analysis of pharmaceutical preparations.

The President of the College, in his annual address, (see page — of the annual announcement) refers at length to this subject. He quotes a passage from a communication of the Chief Officer of Health for Ontario, to the effect that assurance was given him by the Deputy Minister of Health at Ottawa, that "he expected to have a laboratory established, and when it was established, it was proposed to carry on therein the examination of the various drugs and other products used in the treatment of disease."

The need for such analysis must be apparent to all who handle these preparations, and the thanks of the medical profession are due to Dr. Brodie, for his persistent endeavours in this connection.

Register of the Members of the College, known to be Resident and Practicing in Ontario

For the convenience of members of the College, of the various Boards, whose activities are more or less interwoven with those of the College, and for the use of the public, there is being published in this year's Annual Announcement a list of licentiates, known to be engaged in the practice of medicine in the Province of Ontario.

The list does not include those of the licentiates, practicing in other Provinces of Canada, or abroad.

The Council in annual session deferred for the present publication of a Register, containing the Ontario Medical Act, in view of changes in the same, which are looked for as likely to be made in the early future.

University of Ottawa

Dr. J. L. Chabot of Ottawa, graduate in Arts of the University of Ottawa, and graduate in Medicine of McGill University, has been selected by the University of Ottawa, to represent it in the Council of the College of Physicians and Surgeons of Ontario, to succeed the late Sir James Grant.

Obituary

During the course of the Council year, Dr. M. O. Klotz, a former president of the Council, died, following a brief attack of pneumonia.

Dr. Klotz had had as a student a distinguished career at the University. He located in Ottawa, and in a very short time assumed a leading position in the profession there. Returning a few years ago from an extended period of study abroad, he devoted himself largely to consultation and surgical work, and was at the height of his career, when the call came. He was electric with energy, clear in conception, brilliant in execution.

The College mourns his loss, as one of her brightest younger sons, who had "won his path upward and prevailed," and one for whom the future seemed to have in store abiding laurels.

Shortly before the Council met in annual session, Dr. Arthur Jukes Johnson passed away, after a prolonged illness. Dr. Johnson had for many years represented Trinity University, in the Council of the College. The University could not have made a happier selection. No one ever sat in the Council Chamber, who could establish better claim to equilibrium and poise, with well-balanced judgment, fortified by long, varied and rich experience.

Throughout a long and useful life, he was always a student, very generously endowed by nature with a faculty for keen analysis, which served him in good stead, when called upon to meet the demands of the community, in which he resided, for exercise of clear reasoning and sound judgment, in the various directions, in which his public activities were engaged.

In his personal relationships, he was felicitous to a degree, and those who were privileged to enjoy his more immediate acquaintance can never forget his personal charm, and the warmth and sincerity of his friendship.

Dr. H. S. Griffin, of Hamilton, a member of the Council, was not able to attend the Council Meeting, as he passed away in the evening of the day, in the afternoon of which the Council held its opening session.

Dr. Griffin was the most gifted member of his University class, and was conspicuous for scholarship. He was gold medallist of his year—facile princeps.

In point of service, he was one of the oldest of the Council members, representing in succession for long periods of time first Victoria University and later Division No. 7. For one year he was President of the Council.

Dr. Griffin was always willing to lend himself to a life of sacrifice, in season and out of season, whether at the bedside, in the operating room, or in his relationship to public service. In his long membership in the Council, he never failed to place at its disposal, in abounding measure, those abilities and faculties, with which nature had so generously endowed him, and which made him conspicuous among his fellows.

He had the happy faculty of exhibiting at one and the same the "fortiter in re" and the "suaviter in modo."

His personality—everybody loved him.

As well as the above, there were matters of less concern, and of routine character, engaging the attention of the Council in its annual session, to which reference need not be had.

Respectfully,

H. WILBERFORCE AIKĪNS, Registrar.

July 1921.

This list comprises names of those obtaining licentiate standing in the college since date of publication of announcement of 1920-1921, together with names of college members, at present engaged in practice in the province of Ontario.

```
1920 Abbott, Charles F., M.D., C.M. ....Dunnville
1879 Abbott, Rodney H., M.D., C.M..Amherstburg
1904 Abbott, S. F., M.D. ... .....Toronto, 179 Dowling Ave.
1887 Acheson, George, M.A., M.B. ...Hamilton, 9Proctor Blvd.
1904 Adams, Allan H., B. A., M.B. ...Toronto, 335 Jarvis St.
1890 Adams, E. H., M.D., C.M. .....Toronto, 325 College St.
1911 Adams, Frederick, M.B. ... ...Windsor
1869 Adams, Henry .............Embro
1917 Adams, H. R. ..............Long Branch
1916 Adams, J. F., M.B. ..........Hanover
1876 Adams, W. A., M.B. ..........Sault Ste. Marie
1910 Adams, W. F. M., M.B. .......Toronto, 1192 Gerrard St. E.
1913 Adams, William, Phm.B., M.B. ..Toronto, 267 Queen St. W.
1884 Addison, J. L., M.D., C.M. ....St. George
1895 Addison, W. L. T., B.A., MB. ..Toronto, 431 Broadview Ave.
1898 Addy, A. H., M.B. ...........Jordan
1890 Agar, J. S., M.B. ...........Chatham
1890 Agar, Mary Louisa, M.D., C.M. .Chatham
1918 Agnew, G. Harvey, M.B. ......Toronto, 290 High Park Ave.
1914 Aiken, L. R., M.D. ... .......Courtright
1915 Aikenhead, J. W., M.D. ... ...Toronto, 119 Howard Park Ave.
1881 Aikins, H. W., B.A., M.D., C.M. ..Toronto, 264 Church St.
1866 Aikins, M. H., B.A., M.B. .....Burnhamthorpe
1883 Aikins, W. H. B., M.D.. C.M. ...Toronto, 134 Bloor St. W.
1869 Aikman, P. A., M.D. ........Windsor
1918 Aitchison, W. S., M.B. ........Toronto, 1265 Dundas St. W.
1915 Altken, G. W. A., M.D. .......Shedden
1890 Aldrich, A. G., M.D., C.M .....Port Hope
1912 Alexander, Charles C., M.B. ....Brantford
1899 Alexander, G. W., M.D., C.M. ...Beachburg
1899 Alexander, N. B., M.D. .......London, 473 Clarence Ave·
1871 Alexander, R. A., M.D., C.M. ...Grimsby
1913 Alexander, S. L., M.D. ·.......Toronto, 152 Bloor St. W.
1894 Alexander, W. H., M.D.. C.M. ..Toronto, 238 Carlton St.
1919 Alexander, W. P. J., M.B. .....Madoc
1905 Alford, J. H., M.D., C.M. ........Ottawa, 179 O'Connor St.
1893 Alger, H. H., M.D., C.M ......Stirling
1878 Algie, James, MB. ..........Toronto, 1155 King St. W.
1906 Alguire, A. R., M.D., C.M. ·.....Cornwall
1873 Alguire, D.O. .................Cornwall
1871 Allan, Edward, M.B. .........Arthur
1882 Allan, William, M.B., C.M·. ....Toronto, 39 Woodlawn Av. W.
1887 Allen, Norman, M.D., C.M. ....Toronto, 108 Carlton St.
1911 Allison, Duncan, M.B. ........Welland
1915 Allison, H. C., M.D. .........Lakeside
1866 Allison, Samuel, M.D. .........Caledon East
1901 Allison, T. W., M.D., C.M. ......Caledon East
```

1869 Alway, E. A,, M.D., C.M. . . . . . . .Bartonville
1897 Alway, W. R., M.D., C.M. . . . . . .Waterford
1918 Ames, CA., M.D., C.M. . . . . . . .Newmarket
1895 Amyot, H J., M.B. . . . . .Windsor
1891 Amyot, J. A., M.B. . . . . .Ottawa, Dept. of Health.
1900 Amys, C. H., Phm.B., M.D., C.M.Peterboro
1921 Anderson, A. L. B. A., M.B. . . . . .Saskatoon, Sask.
1888 Anderson, C. N., M.D., C.M. . . . .Sandwich
1913 Anderson, F. C., B.A., M.D., C.M.. . .Ottawa, 169 Lisgar St.
1910 Anderson, G. W., M.B. . . . . . . .Toronto, 132 Eglington Ave. W
1892 Anderson, H.B., M.D., C.M. . . . .Toronto, 184 Bloor St. E.
1870 Anderson, H. L., M.B. . . . . .Toronto, 55 Walker Ave.
1904 Anderson, J. A., M.D., C.M. . . . . .Smith's Falls
1875 Anderson, J. R., M.D. . . . . .Ailsa Craig
1884 Anderson, J. E., M.D., C.M. . . . .Scotland
1920 Anderson, J. P., M.B. . . . . .Toronto, General Hospital
1907 Anderson, J. S., M.B. . . . . .Wooler
1893 Anderson, Norman, M.D., C.M.. . .Toronto, 659 Huron St.
1905 Anderson, R. W., M.B. . . . . . . .New Hamburg
1889 Anderson, R. K., M.D., C.M. . . .Milton
1894 Anderson, W. J., M.D., C.M. . . .Jasper
1914 Anglin, George C., M.B. . . . . . . .Toronto, 233 Annette St.
1883 Anglin, W. G., M.D., C.M. . . . .Kingston, 52 Earl St.
1916 Angrove, H. S., M.B. . . . . .Kingston, 93 Wellington St.
1887 Appelbe, James, M.D., C.M. . . . . .Parry Sound
1920 Archer, C. D., M.D., C.M. . . . . :. .Fort William
1890 Archer, David, M.B. . . . . .Port Perry
1892 Archer, Robert, M.D., C.M. . . . .Port Perry
1918 Archibald, Cedric H., B.A., M.B..Toronto, 127 Stibbard Ave.
1902 Archibald, T. D., B.A., M.B. . . .Toronto, 112 College St.
1890 Ardagh, A. P., M.D., C.M. . . . . .Orillia
1888 Ardagh, A. E., M.D., C.M. . . . . .Orillia
1913 Argue, H. H., M.B. . . . . .Mount Forest
1896 Argue, J. Fenton, M.D., C.M.. . .Ottawa, 116 Nepean St.
1896 Arkell, H. E., M. B. . . . . .London, 317 Piccadilly St.
1921 Armour, J. C., M.D., C.M. . . . . . .Perth
1877 Armour, J. P., M.B. . . . . .St. Catharines
1908 Armour, Robert G., M.B. . . . . . .Toronto, 98 St. George St.
1867 Armstrong, Albert, M.D. . . . . . . .Arnprior
1921 Armstrong, A. G., M.B. . . . . . . .Warkworth
1899 Armstrong, C. C., M.D., C.M . . .Warkworth
1918 Armstrong, Ernest L., M.D. . . . . .Baden
1919 Armstrong, G. W., B.A., M.B. . . . . . .Toronto, 142 Broadview Ave.
1920 Armstrong, H. G., M.B. . . . . .Brussels
1889 Armstrong, H. W., M.D., C.M. . .Fergus
1919 Armstrong, L. Noble, M.D., C.M..Hamilton, 95 Bay St. S.
1916 Armstrong, R. H., M.B. . . . . . . .Kirkland Lake
1866 Armstrong, Thomas . . . . .Toronto, 79, Farnham Ave.
1889 Armstrong, W. J., M.D. . . . . . . .Mitchell
1890 Arnall, H. T., M.D., C.M. . . . . . .Barrie
1911 Arnold, W. C., M.B. . . . . .Haileybury
1900 Arnott, D. H., M.D. . . . . .London, 226 Queen's Ave.

1902 Arnott, H. G., M.D. ....Hamilton, 26 Emerald St. S.
1894 Arrell, William, M.B. ....Hamilton, 317 Main St. E.
1912 Arseneau, J. C. E., B.S., M.D. ..Fort William
1891 Arthur, J. R., M.B. ....Collingwood
1886 Arthur, R. H., M.D., C.M. .....Sudbury
1878 Ashby, T. Harry, M.D. ....Toronto, 175 Roxborough St. W
1899 Ashton, E. C., M.D., C.M. .....Ottawa, 198 Somerset St. W.
1920 Asselstine, S. M., M.D., C.M. ...Kingston, 318 Earl St.'
1910 Atkinson, C. F., M.B. ....Tillsonburg
1905 Atkinson, E. T., M.D., C.M. ....Port Dalhousie
1921 Atwell, W. C., M.B. ....Toronto, 162 Mavety St.
1917 Aubin, A. J., M.D. ....Sturgeon Falls
1914 Austin, J. P., M.B. ....Windsor
1920 Austin, L. J., M.B.. B.C, ...Kingston
1915 Avery, W. H., M.D. ....Toronto, 29 Springrove Ave.
1912 Axford, E. C. ....Alvinston
1921 Ayer, Isabel T., M.B. ....Toronto General Hospital
1904 Aylesworth, F. A., M.D., C.M. ......Toronto, 112 College St.
1870 Aylesworth, G. M., M.D. ....Collingwood
1915 Ayotte, Joseph, M.D. ....Plantagenet
1904 Babb, W. F. ....London, 205 Queen's Ave.
1915 Baby, G. R., M.D., C.M. ......Hamilton, 475 Main St. E.
1907 Backus, Annie A. ....Port Rowan
1906 Bagshaw, Elizabeth C., M.B. ..Hamilton, 608, King St. E.
1908 Baillie, Wm., B.A., M.B. ......Toronto, 320 Rushton Rd'.
1916 Baillie, W. H. T., M.A., M.B. ..Toronto, 53 Boon Ave.
1878 Baines, A M., M.D., C.M. ......Toronto, 228 Bloor St. W.
1915 Baker, D. MacTavish, M.B. ....Keewatin
1911 Baker, E. S., M.B. ....Haliburton
1899 Baker, E., M.D., C.M. ....Springfield
1920 Baker, H. E., M.B. ....Toronto, 747 Lansdowne Ave.
1909 Baker, H. W. M.B. ....,....Toronto, 606 Spadina Ave.
1899 Baker, J. A., B.A., M.B. ......Gore Bay
1900 Baker, J. Y., B.A., M.D., C.M. ...Dalhousie Mills
1920 Baker, R. H., M.B. ....Harrow
1890 Baker, W A., M.D.; C.M. ....Peterboro
1903 Baldwin, J. M., B.A., M.D., C.M..Toronto, 95 Lyndhurst Ave.
1911 Balfour, E. B., M.B. ....Lucknow
1911 Ball, H. D., M.B. ....Toronto, 178 Sherbourne St.
1915 Ball, R. B., M.B. ....Toronto, 1799 Dufferin St.
1915 Ball, S. S., M.B. ....Stouffville
1914 Ballantyne, C. C., M.B. ....Galt
1903 Ballantyne, C. T., M.D., C.M. ..Ottawa, 199 Rideau
1917 Ballantyne, E. N., B.A., M.D. ......London, 20 Elmwood Ave.
1916 Ballantyne, T W., M.B. ....Kitchener
1907 Ballantyne, W. H., M.D., C.M. ..Ottawa, Plaza Building
1899 Balmer, George, M.B. ....Toronto, 323 Margueretta St.
1906 Banghart, P. C., M.D. ....London, 477 Dundas St.
1916 Banting, F. G., M.B. ....London, 442 Adelaide St.
1918 Banting, O. Fenton, M.B. ......Granton
1901 Banting, W. T., M.D. ....Lucan
1896 Barber, G. W., M.D., C.M. ......Brantford
1892 Barber, H. L., M.D., C.M. ......Burk's Falls
1888 Barber, W C., M.D., C.M. ......Allandale
1910 Barclay, G. O., M.B. ....:.....Ottawa, 104 Rochester St.
1911 Barker, R. R., M.D., C.M. ......Westport

1918 Barnes, H. M., B.A., M.D., C.M. .Ottawa, 46 Carlyle Ave.
1918 Barnes, W. B., M.B. ....Toronto, 1247 King St. W.
1887 Barnet, A D., M.B. ....Fergus
1915 Barnett, J. W., M.B. ....Toronto, 248 Danforth Ave.
1919 Barnhart, W. S., M.D., C.M. ....Ottawa, 239 Florence St.
1917 Barolet, L. J., M.D. ....Montebello, P.Q.
1915 Barrett, H. M., M.D. ....Salford
1916 Barry, J. E., M.B. ....Burlington
1921 Bartley, K. M., M.B. ....Toronto, General Hospital
1907 Barton, J. W. ....Toronto, 318 Palmerston Blvd.
1886 Bascom, Horace, M.D. ....Whitby
1866 Bascom, Joseph, M.B. ....Newton Brook
1896 Basken, J. T., M.D., C.M. ......Ottawa, 350 Somerset St.
1914 Bastedo, A. F., M.B. ....Bracebridge,
1921 Bastow, Douglas C., M.B. .....Toronto, 171 Howland Ave.
1889 Bateman, F. J., M.D. ....Strathroy
1886 Bateman, R. M., M.D., C.M. ...Toronto, 361 Danforth Ave.
1912 Bateman, W. R., M.D., C.M. ...Toronto, 34 Glenholme Ave.
1908 Bates, G. A., M.B. ....Toronto, 169 Bay St.
1909 Bates, Kendall, M.B. ....Toronto, 169 Bay St.
1889 Bateson, U. E., M.D., C.M. .....London, 234 Central Ave.
1919 Battley, Sinclair, M.B. ....Sarnia
1899 Bauer, J. A., M.B. ....Hamilton, 238 East Main St.
1921 Beamish, Oswald F., M.D., C.M. .Ottawa, 285 Fifth Ave.
1920 Beamish, W. F., M.B. ....Belwood
1914 Bean, S. J. T., M.D. ....London, 228 Wharncliffe Rd.
1895 Bean, S. B., M.B. ....Parry Sound
1896 Beasley, W. J., M.B. ....Sandwich
1906 Beattie, A. W., M.D. ....Belmont
1896 Beatty, A. A., M.D., C.M. ......Toronto, 201 Bloor St. E.
1890 Beatty, A. C., M.D., C.M. .....Garden Hill
1884 Beatty, Elizabeth R., M.D., C.M.Lansdowne
1901 Beatty, H. A., M. B. ....Toronto, 52 Howland Ave.
1896 Beatty, W. J., M.D., C.M. .....Keewatin
1920 Beaudoin, L. P., M.D. ....Hawkesbury
1914 Beaven, J. R., M.B. ....Galt
1916 Beaver, G. W., M.B. ....Niagara Falls
1906 Becker, Charles W., M.D. .....Toronto, 349 Sherbourne St.
1889 Becker, Henry, M.D., C.M. ....Toronto, 1330 King St. W.
1916 Becker, Mary B., M.B. ....Toronto, 1330 King St. W.
1895 Beckett, James, M.B. ....Toronto, 20 Avoca Ave.
1882 Bedard, Eugene ....Pembroke
1890 Bedard, J. A., M.D. ....North Bay
1896 Bedell, T. C. D., M.B. ....Kingston, Sydenham Hospital
1889 Beeman, T. A., M.D., C.M. ....Bancroft
1886 Beemer, Frank, M.D., C.M. ....Toronto, 37 Sussex Ave.
1874 Beemer, N. H., M.B. ....Mimico
1919 Beer, E. C., M.D., C.M. ....Toronto, 2212 Queen St. E.
1921 Belanger, J. E., B.A., M.D., C.M..Hull, Que.
1919 Belanger, P. B., M.D., C.M. ....Ottawa, 822 Somerset St.
1910 Belfie, Gerald, M.B. ....Ottawa, 238 Gilmour St.
1911 Belfry, R. A., M.B. ....Toronto, 445 Broadview Ave.
1907 Bell, A. M., M.D., C.M. ....Toronto, 140 Danforth Ave.
1915 Bell, A. M., M.B. ....Toronto, 74 Hilton Ave.
1898 Bell, B. C., B.A., M.B. ....Brantford
1900 Bell, Charles C., M.A., M.B. ...Chatham

```
1915 Bell, D. E., M.D., C.M. ........Toronto, 11 Nanton Court Apts.
1870 Bell, F. F. .................Windsor
1919 Bell, F. J., B.A., M.B. .........Haliburton
1919 Bell, G. Leslie, M.D., C.M. .....Binbrooke
1920 Bell, G. L., M.B. ............Sioux Lookout
1886 Bell, J. C., M.D., C.M. ........Merlin
1890 Bell, J. C., M.D., C.M. .......Simcoe
1890 Bell, John H, M.D., C.M. .....Hamilton, 156 James St. S.
1897 Bell, J. A., M.D. ..............Sarnia
1874 Bell, R. W., M.D., C M .......Toronto, Prov. Bd. of Health
1883 Bell, William D. M., C.M.M.D. ..Ottawa, 151 Stanley Ave.
1906 Bell, W. J., M.B. ...........Toronto, Prov. Board of Health
1883 Belt, R. W., M.D., C.M. .......Oshawa
1883 Belton, C. W., M.B. ...........Ottawa, Ont.
1906 Bennett, A. C., M.B. .........Toronto, 1326 King St. W.
1905 Bennett, Eleanor F., M.D., C.M. .Toronto, 1326 King St. W.
1905 Bennett, J. H., M.B. ..........Copper Cliff
1891 Bennett, T. E., M.B. .........Meaford
1899 Bennett, W. H., M.B. .........Tillsonburg
1908 Bennetto, F. R., M.B. ..........Guelph
1919 Benny, J. J,. M.D., C.M. ......St. Catharines
1912 Benson, H. W., M.D. .........Port Hope
1889 Berdan, O. L., M.D., C.M. .....Strathroy
1913 Bergeron, J. A., M.D. .........Mattawa
1911 Beroard, L. C. E., M.D., C.M. ..Ottawa, 565 Somerset St.
1917 Berry, Grant, M.B. .........Toronto, 55 Dixon Ave.
1890 Berry, J. D., M.D., C.M. ......Willowdale
1917 Berry, W. E., B.A., M.D., C.M. .West Hamilton
1887 Bertram, T. A., M.D., C.M. .....Dundas
1905 Berwick, M. W., M.B. .........Grand Valley
1898 Bethune, F. H., M.D., C.M. ....Emo
1916 Bethune, H. N., M.B. .........Toronto, 344 Shaw St.
1908 Bethune, W., M.B. ..........Hamilton, Main & Sherman Av.
1888 Bibby, F. T., M.B. ...........Flesherton
1915 Bice, Ernal, M.D. ............Clandeboye
1908 Bice, J. G., M.D. ............Delaware
1920 Bicknell, N. J., M.B. .........Toronto, 103 Rose Ave.
1896 Bier, T. H., M.B. ............Brantford
1904 Biggar, J. L., M.B. ..........Ottawa, B.P.C.C.
1905 Biggs, G. M., M.B. ..........Toronto, 341 Bloor St. W.
1884 Bingham, G. A., M.D., C.M. ....Toronto, 610 Church St.
1881 Bingham, G. S., M.D., C.M. ....Hamilton, 27 Wellington St. S.
1907 Binns, E. E., M.B. ...........Welland
1893 Bird, C. H., M.D., C.M. .......Gananoque
1921 Bird, Grant L., M.B. ..........Brighton
1889 Birdsall, W. W., M.D., C.M. ...Port Arthur
1899 Birnie, Jessie A., M.D., C.M. ...Peterboro
1921 Birrell, R. G., B.A., M.B. ......Pinkerton
1911 Bissell, E. S., M.D., C M ......Mallorytown
1892 Bissonette, J. D., B.A., M.D., C.M.Stirling
1916 Black, C. N. M., M.B. .........Toronto, 201 Howard Park Av.
1908 Black, H. Homer, Phm.B., M.D. .London, 469 King St.
1890 Black, M. C., M.D. ...........Hespeler
1919 Black, W. N. D., M.B. ........Toronto, 37 Roselawn Ave.
1907 Blackwell, B. A., M.D. ........Penetanguishene
```

1892 Blain, E. B., M.D., C.M. .... Hamilton, 684 Main St. E.
1904 Blair, H. G. F. .... North Gower
1907 Blair, J. K., M.B. .... Arthur
1919 Blair, W. G., M.B. .... Perth
1906 Blake, M. R., M.D., C.M. ...... Winnipeg, Man.
1916 Blake, W. A., M.B. .... Hamilton, 952 East Main St.
1919 Blakely, A. M., M.B. .... Ford City
1904 Blakeman, F. W. .... Ottawa, 300 Cooper Ave.
1916 Blakslee, Vanarsdale, M.D., C.M.Belleville
1908 Blanchard, E., M.B. .... Cannington
1893 Blanchard, Fabian, M.B. .... Lindsay
1921 Blatz, W. E., M.A., M.B. ..... Hamilton, 187 Charlton Ave. E.
1920 Bleakley, T. W., M.B. .... Toronto, 233 Delaware Ave.
1906 Boddington, D. H., M.B. ...... Toronto, 81 Willcocks St.
1913 Bodkin, W. A. T., M.D. .... Burlington
1902 Bogart, I. G., M.D., C.M. ..... Kingston, 102 Wellington St.
1919 Bohemier, C. A., M.D. .... Bourget
1918 Boles, W. P., M.B. .... Arkona
1891 Bolster, L. E., M.D., C.M. ..... Goderich
1919 Bond, C. E., M.B. .... Weston
1914 Bond, J. E., M.B. .... Toronto, 535 Broadview Ave.
1915 Bond, R. A., M.B. .... Toronto, 18 College St.
1890 Bond, W. L., M.B. .... Toronto, 2317 Yonge St.
1921 Bonfield, John P., M.B. .... Ottawa, 48 College Ave.
1914 Bonin, Adrien, M.D. .... Embrun
1877 Bonnar, H. A. .... Toronto, 296 Bathurst St.,
1916 Boone, Frank H., M.B. .... Toronto, 173 Avenue Road.
1911 Booth, Gordon E. .... Ottawa, 243 Laurier Ave., W.
1892 Bourns, W. H., M.D., C.M. ... Frankville
1901 Bourque, Edmond, B.A., M.D., C.M.. Ottawa, 212 Bronson Ave.
1909 Bowen, H. M., M.D., C M ..... Toronto, 302 Bloor St. W.
1890 Bowie, E. F., M.D., C.M. ...... Toronto, 191 Spadina Ave.
1902 Bowie, H. A., M.D., C.M. ...... Essex Centre
1893 Bowie, T. I., M.D., C.M. .... Streetsville
1879 Bowlby, D. A., M.B. .... Simcoe
1901 Bowles, C. T., M.D., C.M. ..... Ottawa, 153 First Ave.
1892 Bowles, G. H., M.D., C.M. ..... Toronto, 476 Dovercourt Rd.
1912 Bowman, F. B., M.B. .... Hamilton, 134 James St. S.
1880 Bowman, George, M.B. .... Penetanguishene
1915 Bowman, J. Thornley, M.D. .... London, 138 Wortley Rd.
1919 Box, J. H., M.B. .... Kitchener
1917 Boyce, A. J., B.A., M.B. ...... Turbine
1908 Boyce, H. A., M.D., C.M. ...... Kingston, 93 Wellington St.
1917 Boyce, H A., M.B. .... Deseronto
1880 Boyce, W. W., M.D., C M ..... Belleville
1908 Boyd, Edmund, B.A., M.B. .... Toronto, 143 College St.
1891 Boyd, Geoffrey, B. A., M.B. ..... Toronto, 48 Bloor St. E.
1898 Boyd, H. O., M.D. .... Bobcaygeon
1915 Boyd, J. R., M.B. .... Welland
1910 Boyd, J. S., M.B. .... Simcoe
1904 Boyd, R. M., M.D., C.M. ...... Fort William
1906 Boyd, S. J., M.B. .... Newmarket
1894 Boyd, W. Brown, M.D., C.M. ... Coldwater
1908 Boyer, G. F., M.B. .... Toronto, 143 College St.
1920 Boyes, J. G., M.D. .... London, 150 Central Ave.
1890 Boyes, E. T., M.D., C.M. .... Hamilton, 17 East Ave. S.

1898 Boyle, J. P., B.A., M.D., C.M. .. Casselman
1901 Boynton, W. J., M.D., C.M. ..... Pefferlaw
1921 Bracken, E. J., M.D., C.M. .... Gananoque
1912 Bradley, J. C., M.B. .... Westmeath
1894 Bradley, J. L., M.D., C.M. ..... Toronto, 312 Brunswick Ave.
1898 Bradley, T. P., M.D., C.M. .... Sarnia
1916 Bragg, N, W., M.B. .... Brantford
1902 Brand, C. W., M.D.. C.M. ..... Toronto, 1036 Bloor St. W.
1903 Brandon, Edgar, M.D., C.M. ... North Bay
1883 Bray, James, M.B. .... Toronto, 288 Gerrard St. E.
1916 Bray, Mabel .... Hamilton, The Mountain San.
1890 Bray, Reginald V., M.D., C.M. .. Chatham
1919 Breen, Adrian L. .....:..... Espanola
1919 Bremner, A. G., M.D. .... Guelph
1914 Bremner, J. M., M.B. .... Toronto, 387 Indian Grove
1918 Brennan, E. J., M.D., C.M. ..... North Bay
1914 Brereton, C. H., M.D. .... Toronto, 287 Oakwood Ave.
1912 Breslin, L. J., B.A., M.B. ...... Toronto, 405 Dundas St. W.
1911 Breuls, R. W., M.B. .... Toronto, 845 Bloor St. W.
1911 Brewster, F. A., M.B. .... Owen Sound
1909 Bricker, J. G., M.B. .... Cargill
1905 Brien, J. W., M.B. .... Windsor
1895 Brien, J. W., M.D., C.M. .... Essex
1913 Brisco, C. A., M.B. .... Timmins
1915 Broad. C. O.. M.B. .... Toronto, 480 Danforth Ave.
1889 Broad, J. J., M.D., C.M. ...... Wellington
1913 Brockenshire, F. A., M.B. ..... Windsor
1908 Broddy, W. A., M.B. .... Port Rowan
1913 Brodey, Abraham, B.A., M.B. .. Toronto, 307 Palmerston Blvd.
1921 Brodie, A. W., M.D., C.M. ..... Blaine Lake, Sask.
1886 Brodie, G. M., M.D., C.M. ..... Woodstock
1921 Bromley, A. J., M.B. .... Toronto, 1201 Bathurst St.
1886 Bromley, Edwin. B.A., M.D., C.M. Sault Ste. Marie
1915 Brooke, R. J. W., M.B. .... Toronto, 469 Pape Ave.
1919 Broome, A. E., M.D., C.M. ..... London, Byron Sanitarium
1910 Brown, A. G., M.B. .... Toronto, 423 Avenue Road.
1903 Brown, Andrew, M.B. .... Markdale
1919 Brown, A. H., M.D .... Brockville
1918 Brown, B. A., M.D., C.M. ..... Oshawa
1909 Brown, Caroline S., M.D., C M . Toronto, 601 Ossington Ave.
1918 Brown, C. C., M.B. .... Toronto, 1978 Dufferin St.
1921 Brown, Clara A., B.A., M.B. ... Toronto, 285 Pacific Ave.
1899 Brown, C. H., B.A., M.D., C.M. .. Ottawa, 222 Somerset St.
1901 Brown, E. L., M.D., C.M. ..... Aultsville
1920 Brown, E. W., M.D. .... Neustadt
1895 Brown, G. W., M.D., C.M. .... Port Arthur
1914 Brown, H. E., M.B. .... Toronto, 223 Westmoreland Ave.
1912 Brown, Hubert A. W., B.A.. M.B. Queensville
1905 Brown, J. A., M.D., C.M. ...... Colborne
1909 Brown, J. B., M.B. .... Toronto, 131 Oakwood Ave.
1879 Brown, J. L. .... New Hamburg
1903 Brown, Jonathan, M.D., C.M. .. Toronto, 901 College St.
1892 Brown, J. N. E., M.B. .... Toronto, 238 Bloor St. W.
1869 Brown, J. Price, M.D. .... Toronto, 106 South Drive
1904 Brown, J. V., M.B. .... Orillia
1920 Brown, Michael J., M.B. ...... Toronto, 970 Queen St. E.

1871 Brown, Miles, M.D. . . . . Chesterville
1919 Brown, M. G., M.B. . . . . Hamilton General Hospital.
1916 Brown, P. Beckett, B.A., M.B. . . Toronto, 142 Broadview Ave.
1909 Brown, P. G., M.B. . . . . Toronto, 101 Bay St.
1889 Brown, Peter, M.D., C.M. . . . . . Toronto, 970 Queen St. E.
1892 Brown, P. M., M.B. . . . . Camlachie
1914 Brown, W. A., M.D., C.M. . . . . . Douglas
1919 Brown, W. J. B., M.B. . . . . Niagara Falls
1906 Brown, W Chapman, M.D., C.M. Toronto, 386 Bloor St. W.
1907 Brown, W. E. . . . . Orillia
1893 Brown, W. F., M.B. . . . . St. Mary's
1891 Brown, W. A., M.D., C.M. . . . . . Chesterville
1916 Brown, W. Easson, M.B. . . . . . . Toronto, 10 Carlton St.
1902 Brown, W. J., M.D., C.M. . . . . . London, 472 Clarence St.
1884 Brown, W. M., M.D., C.M. . . . . . Neustadt
1868 Browning, J W., M.D. . . . . Exeter
1880 Brownlee, Milne, M.D. . . . . Woodstock
1892 Bruce, H. A., M.B. . . . . Toronto, 64 Bloor St. E.
1893 Bruce, R. F., M.D., C.M. . . . . . . Port Perry
1910 Brunet, Ernest . . . . Ottawa, 232 St. Patrick St.
1905 Bryan, Herman, M.B. . . . . Port Arthur
1920 Bryans, E. E., M.D. . . . . Hamilton
1912 Bryans, F. T., M.B. . . . . Toronto, 160 Bloor St. W.
1890 Bryans, W. F., M.B. . . . . Toronto, 230 Carlton St.
1908 Brydon, W. H., M.B. . . . . Brampton
1866 Buchanan, C. W., M.D. . . . . Toronto, 715 Bloor St. W.
1896 Buchanan, Daniel, M.B. . . . . Galt
1871 Buchanan, George, M.B. . . . . . . Toronto, 628 Manning Ave.
1905 Buchanan, N. D., M.B. . . . . Peterboro
1908 Buck, G. S., M.B. . . . . Toronto, 1266 College St.
1911 Buck, Harold, M.B. . . . . St. Thomas
1913 Buck, L. L., M.D., C.M. . . . . . . Grimsby
1906 Bucke, R. W., M.D. . . . . London, 293 Wolfe St.
1890 Bueglass, A. S., M.D., C.M. . . . . . Hamilton, 88 Jackson St. W.
1903 Buell, J. B., M.D. . . . . Stevensville
1889 Bull, Emerson, M.D., C.M. . . . . . Lambton Mills
1894 Bull, J. H., M.B. . . . . Chatsworth
1921 Bulmer, F. M. R., M.B. . . . . Toronto, 592 Ossington Ave.
1918 Bulmer, Mabelle Audrey, C., M.B. Aurora
1919 Bunt, M. H., M.B. . . . . Everett
1898 Burdon, F. L., M.D. . . . . London, 461 Waterloo St.
1899 Burgess, A M., M.B. . . . . Bala
1906 Burgess, H. W., M.D., C.M. . . . . Toronto, 2 Glen Manor Drive
1911 Burgess, W. A., M.D. . . . . Ottawa, 254 Wilbrod St.
1912 Burke, F. S., M.B. . . . . Toronto, 11 Edgedale Rd.
1866 Burnham, E. L., M.B. . . . . Millbrook
1875 Burnham, G. H., M.D. . . . . Toronto, 128 Bloor St. W.
1914 Burnham, H. H., M.B. . . . . Toronto, 128 Bloor St. W.
1909 Burns, H. S., M.B. . . . . Hamilton, 1010 Barton St. E.
1908 Burns, J. L., M.B. . . . . Toronto, 693 Broadview Ave.
1888 Burns, R. A. E., M.D., C.M. . . . . Inglewood
1901 Burns, W T., B.A., M.B. . . . . . . Toronto, 256 Dunn Ave.
1905 Burr, W A., M.D. . . . . Toronto, 479 Roncesvalles Av.
1916 Burroughs, C. M., M.B. . . . . Sudbury
1893 Burrows, F. J., M.D., C.M. . . . . . Seaforth
1892 Burrows, J. G., M.D., C.M. . . . . Marlbank

```
1918 Burrows, Newton S, M.D., C M  . Guelph
1905 Burson, E. C., M.B. ........... Toronto, 110 St. Clair Ave. W.
1896 Burt, G. S., M.B. ............... Owen Sound
1915 Burwell, G. B., B.A., M.D., C.M. .... Renfrew
1919 Butler, A J., M.B. .......... Burwash
1897 Butler, J A., M.D., C.M. ...... Newcastle
1912 Butt, W. H., M.B. .......... Toronto, 864 Keele St.
1915 Buttle, W. W., M.B. ......... Pakenham
1919 Byers, D. P., M.B. .......... Toronto, 62 Danforth Ave.
1911 Byers, J. C., M.D., C.M. ....... Metcalfe
1911 Byrne, E. P., M.D., C.M. ....... Ottawa, 460 Somerset St.
1899 Cahoon, Frank, M.B. ......... Bloomfield
1918 Cain, R. F., M.B. ............ Sault Ste Marie
1898 Cairns, George, M.D., C. M. .... Mount Bridges
1920 Cairns, James W., M.D. ...... Pipestone, Man.
1915 Cairns, R. M., M.B. ........... Ottawa, 87 Nepean St.
1908 Calder, Margaret Cowan, M.B. . Wingham
1893 Calder, R. M., M.B. .......... St. Catharines
1914 Caldwell, G. L., M.B. ......... Windsor
1911 Caldwell, R. A. .............. Port Arthur
1907 Calhoun, J. C., M.B. ......... Toronto. 155 Bloor St. E.
1908 Callahan, T. H., M.B. ........ Toronto, 92 College St.
1920 Cameron, A. A., M.D., C.M. ... Toronto, 227 Western Ave.
1896 Cameron, D. A., M.D., C.M. ..... London, 301 Picadilly St.
1912 Cameron, D R. ............. Oshawa
1906 Cameron, D. G., M.D., C.M. .... Windsor
1896 Cameron, G. S., M.D., CM. ..... Peterboro
1920 Cameron, G. C., M.B. ........ Toronto, 65 Hilton Ave.
1874 Cameron, I. H.. M.B. ........ Toronto, 307 Sherbourne St.
1914 Cameron, K. W., M.B. ......... Perth
1906 Cameron, Malcolm H. V., M.B. . Toronto, 11 Prince Arthur Av.
1916 Cameron, Olive G. P., M.A., M.B. Toronto, 11 Prince Arthur Av.
1906 Cameron, W. H., M.B. ......... Coniston
1911 Campbell, A. A., M.B. ........ Toronto, 96 College St. Room 2
1901 Campbell, A. C., M.B. ........ St. Thomas
1880 Campbell. A. W., M.D. ........... Prince Albert
1894 Campbell. Byron, M.B. ........ Toronto, 50 Lauder Ave.
1900 Campbell, C. A., B.A., M.B. ... Kirkton
1869 Campbell, C. T., M.D., C.M. .... London, 327 Queen's Ave.
1899 Campbell, C A.. M.D., C.M. ... Toronto, 172 Bloor St. E.
1920 Campbell, D. M., M.D., C.M. ... Toronto, 166 Northcliffe Blvd.
1911 Campbell, D. A., M.B. ........ North Bay
1885 Campbell, Frank, M.D., C.M. ... Hepworth
1921 Campbell, F. C. B., M.B. ...... Hepworth
1917 Campbell, Fred J. H., B.A., M.D. London, 541 Dundas St.
1889 Campbell, James. M.D., C.M. ... Tottenham
1913 Campbell, J. A., M.D. ......... St. Thomas
1911 Campbell, J. P., M.B. ........ Toronto, 207 Bloor St. E.
1891 Campbell, James W., M.D.. C.M. .... Kingston. 150 Clergy St.
1909 Campbell, J. A. M., M.B. ...... London, Westminster Hospital
1909 Campbell, J. deL. ............ Lansdowne
1906 Campbell, J. F., M.D., C.M. ... Windsor
1911 Campbell, George A., M.B. ..... Ottawa, 424 Jackson Bldg.
1907 Campbell, K.. M.B. .......... Toronto, 147 Bloor St. W.
1893 Campbell, L. H., M.D., C.M. .... Bradford
```

1893 Campbell, Neil, M.D., C.M. ... Thorold
1911 Campbell, Roscoe, M.B. ...... Hanover
1915 Campbell, Walter R., M.B. .... Toronto, 1 Queen's Park
1912 Campbell, W. C., M.B. .... Copper Cliff
1920 Campbell, William N., M.D., C.M. Hastings
1888 Campeau, W. J., M.D., C.M. ... Harrow
1885 Cane, F. W., M.B. .... Allandale
1904 Canfield, A. W., M.D., C.M. ... Toronto, 462 Avenue Rd.
1884 Canfield, F. D., M.D., C.M. ..... Ingersoll
1908 Cannon, O. A., M.B. .... Hamilton, 576 Main St. E.
1889 Carbert, G. B., M.D., C.M. ..... Campbellville
1914 Cardwell, W. A., M.B. .... Toronto, 1208 Dufferin St.
1919 Carleton, E. A., M.B. .... New Toronto
1912 Carleton, G. W., M.B. .... Toronto, 1222 Gerrard St. E.
1919 Carlisle, Vernon, M.B. .... Mount Dennis
1887 Carlyle, J. C., M.B. .... Toronto, 417 Sherbourne St.
1884 Carmichael, D. N., M.D., C.M. . Peterboro
1915 Carpenter, T. A., M.B. .... Mildmay
1887 Carr, Leeming, M.B. .... Hamilton, 415 King St. E.
1915 Carr, L. A., M.B. .... Hamilton, 415 King St. E.
1919 Carr, O. E., B.A., M.B. .... McKellar
1906 Carrick, W. M., M.B. .... Hamilton, 119 Main St. E.
1896 Carron, F. B., M.D., C.M. ..... Brockville
1920 Carrothers, W. W., M.D. ...... London, 441 Pall Mall St.
1889 Carruthers, John, M.D., C.M. .. Little Current
1920 Carruthers, W. B., M.D., C.M. . Jellicoe
1901 Carscadden, R. H., M.D., C.M. . Lindsay
1906 Carson, R. J., M.D., C.M. ...... Orillia
1904 Carson, T. A., M.B. .... Toronto, 200 Howard Park Av.
1893 Carter, Charles, M.D., C.M. .... Hamilton, 70 West Main St.
1919 Carter, T. P., M.B. .... Bolton
1907 Cartwright, V. E., M.B. ...... Pickering
1884 Carveth, G. H., B.A., M.D., C.M. .... Toronto, 178 Huron St.
1905 Carveth, W. H .,M.B. .... Toronto, 178 Huron St.
1914 Cascaden, J. H., M.D., C.M. .... Toronto, 256 Dundas Crescent
1883 Case, T. E., M.D., C.M. .... Dungannon
1883 Casgrain, H. R., M.D., C.M. ... Windsor
1901 Casselman, C. C., M.D., C.M. ... Huntsville
1910 Casselman, S. B., M.D., C.M. .. Sault Ste. Marie
1914 Casserly, M. J., M.B. .... Toronto, 147 Springhurst Av.
1886 Cassidy, J. I., M.D., C.M. ..... Toronto, 37 High View Cres.
1915 Cates, H. A., M.B. .... Weston
1913 Cathcart, J. P. S., M.B. .... Port Lambton
1915 Cathcart, W. A., M.B. .... Port Lambton
1883 Cattermole, J. F., M.B. .... Woodstock
1919 Cauley, A. A., M.D., C.M. ...... Hamilton, 405 King St. E.
1905 Caulfeild, A. H. W., M.B. .... Toronto, 13 Spadina Rd.
1895 Caven, J. G., B.A., M.B. .... Toronto, 88 Bloor St. E.
1912 Caven, W E., M.B. .... Ottawa, 143 Carling Ave.
1886 Caven, W. P., M.B. .... Toronto, 70 Gerrard St. E.
1899 Cawthorpe, F. J., M.B. .... Tavistock
1909 Cays, F. A., M.D., C.M. .... Kingston, 124 Wellington St.
1903 Cerswell, W. A., M.B. .... Toronto, 862 Dovercourt Rd.
1892 Chabot, J. L., M.A., M.D., C.M. . Ottawa, 170 Laurier Ave.
1913 Chalmers, A. B. .... Bridgeburg

1911 Chamberlain, H. W., M.B. ..... Scotland
1866 Chamberlain, T. F., M.D. ...... Morrisburg
1889 Chambers, Graham, B.A., M.D. ..... Toronto, 26 Gerrard St. East
1884 Chambers, W. J., M.D., C.M. ... Toronto, 285 Lauder Ave.
1889 Channonhouse, R. C., B.A., M.D., Richmond
1907 Chant, J., M.D., C.M. .... Belleville
1919 Chantal, Leonard E., M.D., C.M. Ottawa, 525 McLeod St.
1890 Chapin, Cecil D., M.B. .... Brantford
1907 Chapin, C. G., M.B. .... Toronto, 229 Danforth Ave.
1904 Chapman, G. E., M.D., C.M. ... Kitchener, 125 Frederick St.
1905 Chapman, Wm. J., M.D., C.M. ...... St. Catharines
1911 Charbonneau, J. E., B.A., M.D., C.M.. Sudbury
1910 Charlebois, J. A., M.D., C.M. ... Fournier
1899 Charlesworth, J. E., M.B. ..... Harriston
1907 Charlton, Robert M., M.D. .... Hamilton, 490 York St.
1900 Charlton, S. E., M.B. .... Galt
1882 Charlton, W. J., M.D., C.M. .... Weston,
1921 Charteris, Walter F., M.B. ..... Chatham
1915 Chassels, John M.B. .... Toronto, 131 Eglinton Ave. E.
1918 Cherniak, I. M., M.D. .... Windsor
1901 Chevrier, F. X. A., M.D. .... Ottawa, 193 Waller St.
1892 Chevrier, R., M.D. .... Ottawa, 168 Daly Ave.
1910 Childs, J. R. N., M.D. .... London, 221 Queen's Ave.
1918 Christian, J. R., M.B. .... Toronto, 866 Keele St.
1910 Christie, J. D., M.B. .... Toronto, 831 Danforth Ave.
1898 Church, F. W. H. .... Aylmer, P. Q.
1905 Church, H. C. .... Ottawa, 14 Powell Ave.
1913 Clairoux, J. A., M.D. .... Loiselleville
1896 Clare, Harvey, M.D., C.M. ..... Toronto, 183 Geoffrey St.
1892 Clark, A. M., M.B. .... Toronto, 232 Shaw St.
1869 Clark, C. W., M.D. .... Toronto, 455 Huron St.
1912 Clark, C. W. L., M.D. .... Toronto, 112 College St.
1905 Clark, C. W., M.D. .... Toronto, 1986 Queen St. E.
1892 Clark, D. A., M.D., C.M. ...... Ottawa, 8 Broadway Ave.
1909 Clark, D. W., M.D. .... Pontypool
1869 Clark, G. F., M.D. .... Aylmer .
1921 Clark, H. G., M.B. .... Toronto, 806 Keele St.
1911 Clark, R. W., M.B. .... Kingston, 130 Bagot St.
1917 Clark, T. Crossan, M.B. .... Hamilton, 115 Herkimer St.
1918 Clark, Walter T., M.D. .... Toronto, 1591 Dufferin St.
1898 Clark, W. J., M.B. .... Toronto, 867 College St.
1875 Clarke, C. K., M.D. .... Toronto, 34 Roxborough St. E.
1919 Clarke, E. K., M.B. .... Toronto, 34 Roxborough St. E.
1914 Clarke, Harold, M.B. .... Brighton
1881 Clarke, J. G., M.D., C.M. ...... Meaford
1887 Clarke, W. H., M.D., C.M. .... Lindsay .
1901 Clarkson, F. A., M.B. .... Toronto, 421 Bloor St. W.
1907 Cleaver, E. E., B.A., M.B. .... Toronto, 155 Bloor St. E.
1914 Clegg, Frank R., M.D. .... London, 688 Dundas St.
1919 Clegg, G. G., M.B. .... London, 115 Royal Bank Bldg.
1901 Cleland, F. A., B.A., M.B. ..... Toronto, 131 Bloor St. W.
1915 Clement, F. W., M.B. .... Toronto, 440 Shaw St.
1897 Clemes, S. R., M.D., C.M. ...... Toronto, 1918 Queen St. E.
1882 Clendenan, G. W., M.D., C.M. .. Toronto, 417 Pacific Ave.
1914 Clifford, E. J., M.B. .... Ayr
1889 Cline, C. A., M.D. .... London, 507 Queen's Ave.

1888 Cline, L. F., M.D., C.M. .... Kitchener
1878 Clinton, George, M.D. .... Toronto, Prov. Board of Hea'h
1920 Clouse, E. B., M.B. .... Toronto, 384 Bloor St. W.
1887 Clouse, Elias, M.D., C.M. ...... Toronto, 384 Bloor St. W.
1901 Clutterbuck, H. E., M.D., C.M. ... Toronto, 148 Grace St.
1902 Coates, F. P., M.D. .... Toronto, 1989 Queen St. E.
1912 Coates, L. H., M.B. .... Brantford
1915 Coatsworth, R. C., M.A., M.B. . Toronto, 296 Parliament St.
1900 Cockburn, Harriet, M.D., C.M. . Toronto, 100 Walmer Rd.
1912 Cody, M. G., M.D. .... Mount Albert
1912 Cody, W. M., M.B. .... Hamilton, 55 Wentworth St. S.
1905 Cody, W. S., B.A., M.D. .... Hamilton, 55 Wentworth St. S.
1919 Cohen, Benjamin, B.A., M.B. ... Toronto, 885 Dundas St. W.
1917 Cohen, Isaac. M.B. .... Sault Ste Marie
1903 Colbeck, O. W., M.B. .... Niagara Falls
1905 Colbeck, W. K., M.B. .... Welland
1907 Cole, C. E. C., B.A., M.B. ..... Toronto, 53 Indian Rd. Cres.
1871 Cole, H J., M.B. .... Brantford
1894 Coleman, Frank, M.B. .... Hamilton, 48 Holton Ave. S.
1906 Coleman, H. B., M.B. .... Palmerston
1898 Coleman, Theobald. M.D. ...... Hamilton, 137 Main St. E.
1902 Colling, F. J., M.B. .... Toronto, 460 College St.
1918 Coiling, J. F. G., M.D. .... Lambeth
1910 Collins, Albert, M.B. .... Bridgeburg
1912 Collins, J. D., M.D. .... Harrow
1898 Collison, George W. .... Brinston
1900 Collison, W. G., M.D., C.M. ... Lindsay
1915 Collver, Bessie L., M.B. ...... Simcoe
1899 Colville, J., M.D., C.M. .... Northwood
1900 Colville, Neil, M.B. .... Orono
1921 Colvin, W. G., M.D. .... Komoka
1904 Conboy, R. S., M.D., C M ..... Toronto, 1045 Bloor St. W.
1886 Conerty. J. M,. M.D., C.M. ... Smith's Falls
1914 Conn, Hartly, M.B. .... Mimico Beach
1918 Connell, H. C., B.A., M.D., C.M. Kingston, 265 King St.
1888 Connell, J C., M.A., M.D., C.M. . Kingston, 265 King St.
1894 Connell, W. T., M.D., C.M. .... Kingston, 11 Arch St.
1919 Connell, W. M., M.B. .... Blind River
1919 Connell, W. S. T., M.D., C.M. ... Hamilton, 433 King St.
1914 Connelly, H. E., M.B. .... Ottawa, 577 McLaren St.
1920 Conner, F. E., M.D., C.M. ..... Toronto, 7 Roslin Ave.
1896 Connolly, B. G., M.B. .... Ottawa, Roxborough Apts.
1900 Connolly, E. L., M.B. .... Collingwood
1903 Connor, Emma, M.B. .... Belleville
1919 Connors, R. V., M.B. .... Ottawa, 54 Primrose Ave.
1907 Consitt, E. C. V., M.D., C.M. ... Perth
1866 Constantinides, Petros, M.D. ... Toronto, 56 Gerrard St. E.
1905 Cook, A. H., M.D. .... Port Dover
1875 Cook, A. B., M.D., C.M. .... Toronto, 87 Roxborough St. W.
1904 Cook, J. W., M.B. .... Fort William
1914 Cook, Lorne H., M.B. .... Toronto
1905 Cook, W. J. .... Sudbury
1901 Cook, W. R., M.B. .... Toronto, 1088 Bloor St. W.
1909 Cooke, H. M., M.B. .... Toronto, 38 Carlton St.
1913 Cooke, K. E., B.A., M.B. ...... Hamilton, 26 Emerald St. S.
1869 Cooke, Sidney P., M.D., C.M. ... Ottawa, 445 Albert St.

1890 Coon, D. A., M.D., C.M. .... Elgin
1907 Cooper, George, M.D. .... Englehart
1886 Cooper, R. E., M.B. .... Seaforth
1890 Copeland, E. M., M.D. .... London, 591 Hamilton Rd.
1911 Copeland, G. G., B.A., M.B. .... Toronto, 2 St. Clair Ave. W.
1899 Copp, C. J., M.D., C.M. .... Toronto, 96 Wellesley St.
1918 Copp, J. C., M.B. .... Toronto, 358 Runnymeade Rd.
1919 Corbett, C. B., M.B. .... Ottawa, 81 Ossington Ave.
1916 Corcoran, D., M.B. .... Elmvale
1916 Cornell, B. S., M.B. .... Toronto, 91 Dupont St.
1872 Cornell, C. M. B. .... Brockville
1915 Cornish, C. C., M.D. .... Ingersoll
1889 Cornu, Felix, M.D. .... Ottawa, 150 Metcalfe St.
1907 Corrigan, W. J., M.D., C.M. .... Toronto, 544 St. Clair Ave. W·
1915 Cosbie, W. G., M.B. .... Toronto, 30 Douglas Drive
1913 Costain, W. A., M.B. .... Toronto, 64 Bloor St. E.
1909 Cotnam, I. D., M.D., C.M. ..... Morrisburg
1915 Cotton, J. H., M.A., M.D. ..... Toronto, 24 Bloor St. E.
1918 Couch, Albert E. H., M.B. .... Tiverton
1885 Couch, J. A., M.D., C M ...... Toronto, 697 Euclid Ave.
1890 Coughlin, C. B., M.D., C M .... Belleville
1911 Coulombe, P. O., B.A., M.D., C.M. Sturgeon Falls
1919 Coulson, E. G., M.B. .... Leamington
1920 Coulter, J. W., M.B. .... Dover Centre
1882 Coulter, R. M., M.D. .... Ottawa, 190 Cooper St.
1909 Coulter, W. G. G., M.D. .... Windsor
1907 Counter, J. W., M.D. .... Ingersoll
1918 Courtenay, H. D., B.A., M.D. .. Ottawa, 189 Metcalfe St.
1885 Courtenay, J. D., M.B. .... Ottawa, 189 Metcalfe St.
1915 Courtice, J. T., M.D. .... Toronto, 27 Sandford Ave.
1901 Coutts, Edgar N., M.B. .... Agincourt
1915 Coutts, Eldon, D., B.A., M.B. .. Toronto, 65 Gothic Ave.
1918 Coutts, Roy, M.B. .... Toronto, 533 College St.
1918 Couture, Ernest, M.D., C.M. .... Ottawa, 573 St. Patrick St.
1875 Cowan, G. H., M.B. .... Napanee
1920 Cowan, R. D., M.B. .... Galt
1906 Cowper, H. D., M.D. .... Welland
1918 Cox, M. A., M.B. .... Toronto, 34 St. Clair Ave. W·
1921 Coyle, R. J., M.D, C.M. .... Kingston, Hotel Dieu Hospital
1919 Crack, Isaac E., B.A., M.D.C.M.. Hamilton, 970 King St. E.
1921 Craig, Edward, M.D., C.M. .... North Gower
1900 Craig, J. E., M.D.C.M. .... Ottawa, 342 McLaren St.
1914 Craig, V. H., M.D.C.M. .... Ottawa, 1108 Somerset St.
1894 Crain, W. E., M.B. .... Cttawa, 239 O'Connor St.
1888 Craine, A. D., M.D.C.M. ...... Smith's Falls
1908 Crann, G. R., M.B. .... Gowganda
1896 Cranston, J. G. M.D.C.M. ...... Arnprior
1909 Crassweller, Henry, M.B. ...... Windsor
1901 Crawford, A. H., B.A., M.D.C.M.. Marmora
1918 Crawford, E. C. A., M.D.C.M... Madoc
1917 Crawford, J. S., M.B. .... Toronto, 515 West Marion St.
1899 Crawford, M.M., M.B. .... Toronto, 39 Roxborough St. W.
1892 Crawford, William, M.B. ...... Hamilton, 52 Main St. W.
1889 Creasor, John A., B.A., M.D.C.M. North Cobalt
1921 Crehan. W. H. K., M.B. .... Toronto, 118 St. George St.
1915 Crews, T. Harold, M.B. .... Windsor

1892 Crichton, A., B.A. .... Castleton
1904 Croft, L. V. .... Middleville
1919 Cronk, G. S., M.B. .... Belleville
·1901 Cronyn, W. H., B.A., M.B. .... Ottawa, The Air Board
1905 Crosby, G. W., M.D. .... Toronto, 2 College St.
1919 Cross, J. S., B.A., M.D.C.M. .... Ottawa, 374 Rideau St.
1920 Cross, W. D. S., M.B. .... Gravenhurst
1911 Crowe, H. S., B.A., M.D.C.M. .. Schreiber
1899 Crowe, W. B. .... Trenton
1913 Crowley, L. E., M.D.C.M. ..... Kingston, 110 Ordnance St.
1902 Crozier, J. A., B.A., M.D.C.M. .. Port Arthur
1886 Cruickshank, G.R., B.A., M.D.C.M. Windsor
1919 Cruikshank, H. C., M.B. ...... Toronto, 20 Chestnut Park
1911 Cruise, W. W., M.B. .... Toronto, 251 Gladstone Ave.
1904 Cryan, J. H., M.D.C.M. .... Demorestville
1921 Cryderman, W. J., M.B. .... Niagara Falls
1904 Cullen, E. K., M.B. .... Detroit, Mich.
1913 Cumberland, Thomas D., M.B... Kingston. Rockwood Hosp.
1907 Cumming, C. R, M.B. .... Galt
1919 Cumming, John R., M.D.C.M. .. Cornwall
1897 Cummings, J. A., M.B. .... Bond Head
1888 Cummings, Samuel, M.D. ...... Toronto, 3 Queen's Park
1910 Cunningham, J. D., M.B. ...... Alliston
1915 Cunningham, J. G., B.A., M.B.. Toronto, 1034 Bathurst St.
1912 Cunningham, S. A., M.B. ...... Toronto, 329 Bloor St., West
1918 Cunningham, W. H., M.B. .... St. Catharines
1910 Currey, D. V., M.B. .... St. Catharines
1901 Currie, C. J., M.B. .... Toronto, 175 College St.
1895 Currie, Morley, M.B. .... Picton
1916 Curry, P. W. M., M.B. .... Toronto, 10 Maynard Ave.
1920 Curtin, Agnes A., M.B. .... Kemptville
1894 Curtis, J. D., M.B. .... St. Thomas
1886 Cuthbertson, C. R., M.D.C.M. .. Toronto, 114 Madison Ave.
1908 Dafoe, A. R., M.B. .... Callander
1920 Dafoe, W. A., Jr., M.B. .... Toronto, 196 Glenholme Ave.
1878 Dafoe, W. A., Sr., M.B. .... Madoc
1915 Dale, Gordon McI., B.A., M.B... Toronto, 591 Church St.
1906 Dale, J. M., M.D.C.M. .... Toronto, 685 Pape Ave.
1897 Dales, F. A., M.B. .... Stouffville
1885 Dales, John R., M.D.C.M. ...... Dunbarton
1916 Dales, L. W., B.A., M.B. ...... Aurora
1906 Dales, Walter, M.D.C.M. ...... Sudbury
1906 Dalrymple, J. M., M.B. .... Toronto, 1032 College St.
1915 Daly, Joseph, B.A., M.B. ...... Belleville
1913 d'Amours, J. E., M.D. .... Papineauville, P. Q.
1894 Danard, A. L., M.D.C.M. .... Owen Sound
1891 Danby, J. J., M.D.C.M. .... Ottawa, 375 Gilmour St.
1893 Darling, R. E., M.D.C.M. ...... Goodwood
1903 Davey, J. E., M.B. .... Hamilton, 146 King St. West
1877 Davidson, Alexander, M.B. .... Toronto. 286 Russell Hill Rd.
1909 Davidson, R. E., M.B. .... Toronto, 1980 Queen St. E.
1912 Davies, A. P., M.D.C.M. .... Ottawa, 287 MacLaren Ave.
1905 Davies, T. Alex., M.B. .... Toronto, 578 Sherbourne St.
1920 Davies, T. B., M.D.C.M. .... Ottawa, 162 Clemow Ave.
1920 Davis, D. I., M.B. .... Toronto, St. Michael's Hosp.
1907 Davis, E. G., M.D. .... Ottawa, Dept. S.C.R.

1914 Davis, F. G., M.B. . . . . Birch Cliff
1916 Davis, G. Albert, B.A., M.B. . . . . Toronto, 10 The Oaks, Bain Av.
1897 Davis, J. J., M.D. . . . . Gananoque
1903 Davis, N. A., M.D.C.M. . . . . Madawaska
1911 Davis, R. E., M.B. . . . . Toronto, 2469 Queen St. E.
1910 Davis, Robert W., M.B. . . . . . . Mindemoya
1892 Davis, S. Nixon, M.D.C.M. . . . . . Welland
1910 Davis, Walter, M.B. . . . . Toronto, 244 Bathurst St.
1921 Davison, G. R., M.D.C.M. . . . . . . Merrickville
1888 Dawson, J. F., M.B. . . . . Toronto, 548 Bathurst St.
1910 Dawson, L. M., M.D.C.M. . . . . . . Ottawa, 83 Second Ave.
1918 Day, A. W., B.A., M.D. . . . . Hamilton, 229 Locke St. S.
1920 Day, E. A. F., M.D. . . . . Timmins
1902 Day, H. E., M.D.C.M. . . . . Kingston, 271 Alfred St.
1910 Day, W. E. C., M.B. . . . . Sioux Lookout
1896 Deacon, G. R., M.D.C.M. . . . . . . Stratford
1896 Deacon, J. D., M.D.C.M. . . . . . . Pembroke
1915 Deadman, William J., B.A., M.B. . . . Hamilton, General Hospital
1918 Dean, K. C. W., M.D.C.M. . . . . Ste. Anne de Bellevue, P. Q.
1899 Dean, M. B., M.B. . . . . Fort William
1900 Dean, W. E., M.D.C.M. . . . . Toronto, 38 Gerrard St. East
1912 Defries, Robert D., M.D. . . . . . Toronto, 135 Collier St.
1911 Defries, W. J., M.B. . . . . Toronto, 30 Bloor St., West
1904 DeHaitre, J. E. N., M.B. . . . . . . Ottawa, 110 Stewart St.
1895 Delahey, F. C., M.B. . . . . Pembroke
1915 De La Matter, Ira, M.B. . . . . . . Hastings
1917 Delaney, Thomas F., M.B. . . . . Ottawa, 880 Somerset St.
1919 Delisle, J. B., M.D. . . . . Ottawa, 12 Spadina Ave.
1905 Demary, A. F., M.B. . . . . Toronto, 2 Lyall Ave.
1917 Denney, Wilmer L., M.D. . . . . . London, 260 Queen's Ave.
1921 Dennison, N. M., B.A., M.D.C.M. . . Kingston, 365 Brock St.
1919 Denyes, G. F., M.D.C.M. . . . . . . Shannonville
1912 Derby, L. L., M.D.C.M. . . . . Westboro
1916 Desorcy, C. A. M.D. . . . . Sault Ste. Marie
1913 DesRosiers, Arthur . . . . Eastview Centre
1914 Detweiler, H. K., M.B. . . . . Toronto, 33 Regal Rd.
1919 Devins, C. J., M.B. . . . . Aurora
1889 Dewar, M. C., M.D.C.M. . . . . . . London, 202 Hamilton Rd.
1885 Dewar, P. A., M.D.C.M. . . . . . . Windsor
1909 Dewar, R. D. . . . . Melbourne
1875 Deynard, A. B., M.D.C.M. . . . . . Owen Sound
1919 Diamond, F. W., M.D. . . . . Coldsprings
1904 Dickey, J. S., M.D.C.M. . . . . . . Newington
1919 Dickie, J. K. M., M.B. . . . . Ottawa, 196 Elgin St.
1889 Dickinson, G. A., M.D.C.M. . . . . Port Hope
1920 Dickson, C. S., B.A., M.B. . . . . . Barrie
1899 Dickson, J. A., B.A., M.D.C.M. . . Hamilton, 130 Main St. E.
1920 Dickson, W. B., B.A., M.B. . . . . Sault Ste. Marie
1912 Digby, Reginald W., M.D.C.M. . . Brantford
1900 Dillane, M. K., M.D.C.M. . . . . . Schomberg
1907 Dillane, R. H., M.B. . . . . Powassan
1910 Dingwall, D. G., M.D.C.M. . . . . Dryden
1918 Dion, Emile H., M.D. . . . . Ottawa, 105 Rideau St.
1905 Dixon, E. C., M.D.C.M. . . . . Toronto, 197 Dundas St., E.
1919 Dixon, H. A., M.B. . . . . Toronto, 122 Bloor St., W.
1908 Dixon, J. A., M.D.C.M. . . . . Sudbury

1893 Doan, Warren, M.D.C.M. ...... Harrietsville
1914 Dobbie, J. A., B.A., M.B. ...... Ottawa, 138 O'Connor St.
1906 Dobbie, W. J., M.A., M.D.C.M. ... Weston
1919 Dobson, H. V., M.B. .... Stayner
1920 Docherty, J. F., M.B. .... Seaforth
1904 Dodd, F. J., M.D.C.M. .... Pembroke
1902 Doherty, F. J., M.D.C:M. ...... Toronto, 32 Orchardview Blvd.
1921 Dolan, D. J., M.D.C.M. .... Pakenham
1921 Dollar, G. L., M.B. .... Toronto, 7 Dundonald St.
1908 Donevan, F. J., M.D.C.M. ...... Oshawa
1920 Donnelly, F. J., M.D.C.M. ...... Iroquois Falls
1885 Doolittle, P. E., M.D.C.M. ...... Toronto, 619 Sherbourne St.
1884 Dorland, S. M., M.D.C.M. ...... Rodney
1915 Dougan, J. A., M.D.C.M. ...... Lindsay
1913 Douglas, C. L., M.D. .... London, 544 Dundas St.
1914 Douglas, H. T., M.D.C.M. ...... Ottawa, 226 MacLaren St.
1916 Douglas, John ᴐ., M. B. .... North Bay
1910 Douglas, L. A., M. B. .... Windsor
1907 Douglas, L. H., M.D. .... London, Dept. S.C.R.
1870 Douglas, William, M.B. ...... Fort Erie
1914 Dover, Harry, M.D.C.M. .... Ottawa, 450 MacLaren Street
1891 Dow, James, M.B. .... Toronto, 188 St. John's Road
1886 Dow, W. G., M.D.C.M. .... Owen Sound
1919 Dowd, R. Allan, M.B. .... Osgoode
1918 Dowd, W. Ritchie, B.A., M.D.C.M. Ottawa, 13 Third Avenue
1919 Dowler, V. B., B.A., M.B. ..... Fort William
1879 Dowling, J. F. .... Ottawa 84 Fourth Avenue
1918 Downes, W. P., B.A., M.D.C.M. . Hamilton, 250 Hughson Drive
1918 Downham, W. S., M.D. .... London, 288 St. James Street
1895 Downing, A., M.B. .... Carlton Place
1901 Downing, H. G., M.B. .... Otterville
1909 Downing, J. H., M.D. .... Toronto, 1239 Gerrard St. E.
1896 Downing, J. J. B., B.A., M.D.C.M. Chesley
1900 Dowsley, G. W. C., M.B. ..... Toronto, 147 Cowan Avenue
1917 Doyle, J F., M.B. .... Tweed
1902 Doyle, W.C., M.D. .... Windsor
1920 Draper, T. F., M.D.C.M. ...... Glenburnie
1906 Driscoll, A. C., M.D.C.M. ...... Trenton
1920 Drouin, Adolphe, M.D. .... Ottawa, 95 Rideau Street
1920 Drury, W. Herbert, M.D.C.M. .. Kitchener
1914 Duck, J. A., M.B. .... Toronto, 158 Roncesvalles Ave.
1907 Dudley, W. H., M.D.C.M. ...... Sault Ste. Marie
1917 Duffett, W. H., M.D.C.M. ...... Adolphustown
1904 Duggan, C. E., M.D.C.M. ...... St. David's
1871 Dumble, W. C. .... Toronto, 121 Ann Street
1911 Duncan, A. S., M.D. .... London, 849 Dundas Street
1881 Duncan, J. H., M.B. .... Chatham
1908 Duncan, John, M.B. .... Toronto, 294 Roncesvalles Ave.
1915 Duncan, J. H., M.A., M.B. ..... Sault St. Marie
1921 Duncan, W., M.B. .... Port Credit
1913 Dunfield, Charles F., M.D. ..... Petrolia
1878 Dunfield, J., M.B. .... Petrolia
1906 Dunn, J. F., M.D.C.M. .... Almonte
1911 Dunn, J. M., M.D.C.M. .... Elgin
1919 Dunning, C. S., M.D.C.M. ...... Toronto, 147 Bloor Street West
1886 Dunton, Daniel, M.D.C.M. ..... Paris
1914 Dure, F. M., M.B. .... Brighton

```
1911  Durocher, U. J., M.D. ........Windsor
1885  Dwyre, A. W., M.D.C.M. ......Perth
1921  Dymond, W. A., M.D.C.M. ....Ottawa, 53 Argyle Avenue
1886  Eadie, A. B., M.D.C.M. ........Toronto, 899 Queen St. West
1921  Eadie, G. S., B.A., M.B. ......Toronto, 899 Queen St. West
1911  Eager, J. C., M.B. ...........Hamilton, 8, Glendale Crescent
1912  Eagles, A. S., M.B. .............Meaford
1920  Eagles, G. H., M.B. .............Toronto, General Hospital
1899  Eagleson, Samuel, M.D.C.M. ...Madoc
1906  Eakins, G. E., M.B. ...........Port Arthur
1915  Earl, A. B., M.B. ........... Athens
1910  Earle, G. N., M.B. ...........Omemee
1892  Earle, W. M., M.D.C.M. .......Avonmore
1906  East, H. M., M.D.C.M. ........Toronto, 955 Queen St. East
1887  Easton, C. L., M.D.C.M. .......Smith's Falls
1899  Easton, J. L., M.B. ...........Ayton
1887  Eastwood, J. H., M.B. ........ Peterboro
1914  Eberhart, F. L., M.B. ........Meaford
1915  Eby, Wilbert H., B.A., M.B. ...Toronto, 520 St. Clair Ave. W.
1869  Eccles, F. R., M.D. ...........London, 228 Princess Avenue
1910  Ecclestone, W. M., M.B. ......Toronto, 284 St. Clair Ave. W.
1891  Edgar, J. W., B.A., M.B. ......Hamilton, 16 Bay St. South
1916  Edis, J. F., M.B. ............Larder Lake
1886  Edmison, A. H., M.D.C.M. .....Kenora
1905  Edmison, T. B., M.B. .........Toronto, 250 Merton St.
1918  Edmonds, L. C., M.B. ........Toronto, 1981 Queen St. East
1921  Edmonds, W. B., M.B. ........Toronto, 165 Roxborough St. W
1921  Edwards, J. Charles R., M.B. ...Cannington
1907  Edwards, R. G., M.B. ........Brampton
1918  Eede, J. R. L., M.B. ..........Leamington
1886  Ego, Angus, M.B. ............Markdale
1919  Elgie, W. A., M.D. ...........Chatham
1916  Elkerton, Frank J., M.B. .....Toronto, 2 College Street
1889  Elliott, H. C. S., M.D.C.M. ....Toronto, 234 Bloor St. East
1916  Elliott, H.A., B.A., M.B. ......Toronto, 11 Broadway Avenue
1884  Elliott, A. G., M.B. ...........Lucknow
1919  Elliott, C. H., M.B. ...........Kingston, 362 Brock Street
1895  Elliett, George, M.D.C.M. ......Toronto, 219 Spadina Rd.
1896  Elliott, G. A., M.B. ..........Toronto, 81 Queen St. E.
1903  Elliott, H. R., M.B. ..........Niagara Falls
1898  Elliott, J. H., M.B. ..........Toronto, 11 Spadina Rd.
1884  Elliott, J. E., M.D.C.M. .......Toronto, 69 Bloor St. E.
1921  Ellis, Ernest W., B.A., M.B. ...Toronto, 31 Antler Ave.
1920  Ellis, Harold L., M.D.C.M. .....New York, 2149 7th Ave.
1911  Ellis, Stayner, M.B. ..........Windsor
1920  Ellis, T. A., M.B. ............Niagara Falls South
1904  Ells, R. H., B.A., M.B. ..........Ottawa, 270 Lisgar St.
1909  Elmore, C. W., M.B. .........Beamsville
1896  Embury, A. T., M.D.C.M. ......Bancroft
1888  Embury, Elizabeth, M.D.C.M. ..Ottawa, 179 Frank St.
1910  Emerson, H. G., M.B. .........Comber
1889  Emmerson, A. T., M.D.C.M. ...Goderich
1909  Emmett, H. L., M.B. ........Fonthill
1886  English, W. M., M.D. .... ....Hamilton, The Ontario Hospital
1918  Erb, I. H., M.B. .............Toronto, 1549 Bloor St. West
1919  Esser, D., M.B. .............Toronto, 324 Dundas St. West
1911  Etherington, Frederick, M.D.C.M.Kingston, King & William Sts.
```

1920 Ettinger, G. H., B.A., M.D.C.M..Kingston, 437 King St. West
1912 Evans, D. T., M.B. ....Kapuskasing
1912 Evans, E. G., M.B. ....Huntsville
1921 Evans, E. D. ....Owen Sound
1892 Evans, J. A. C., M.B. ....Toronto, 23 Roselawn Ave.
1908 Evans, J. A., M.B. ....Toronto, 309 Avenue Rd.
1869 Evans, L. Hamilton, B.A., M.D..Toronto, 197 College St.
1904 Evans, Stuart, M.D.C.M. ......Ottawa, 677 McLaren St.
1919 Evelyn, S. J., M.B. ....Toronto, 19 Summerhill Ave.
1906 Ewin, D. L., M.D. ....St. Thomas
1911 Eyres, H. H., M.B. ....Burlington
1909 Fader, W. R., M.B. ....Toronto, 1589 Dufferin St.
1914 Faed, P. E., M.B. ....Toronto, 1087 Bathurst St.
1890 Fairfield, C. A. D., B.A., M.D.C.M.Beamsville
1919 Fallis, L S., M.D.C.M. ....Burlington
1915 Fallis, L C., M.B. ....Shelburne
1919 Falls, Franklin N., M.D.C.M. ...Ottawa, 454 Gilmour St.
1866 Fares, O. W., M.D ....Port Colborne
1874 Farewell, Adolphus, M.D. ......Walkerton
1911 Faris, M. N., M.B. ....Brantford
1894 Farley, F. J., M.D.C.M. ....Trenton
1877 Farley, John J. M.D.C.M. ......Belleville
1920 Farlinger, A. C., M.D.C.M. ....New Liskeard
1891 Farmer, G. D., M.D.C.M. ......Ancaster
1919 Farmer, Roy J., M.D. ....London, 419 Princess Ave.
1884 Farncomb, Alfred, M.D.C.M. ...Newcastle
1894 Farncomb, T. S., M.D.C.M. ....Trenton
1916 Farquharson, C. D., M.D.C.M. ..Agincourt
1902 Farrell, A. R., M.D.C.M. ......Toronto, 1459 Danforth Ave.
1875 Faulkner, G. W. ....Belleville
1905 Faulkner, J. A., B. A., M.D.C.M.Belleville
1919 Favier, P. M., M.D. ....Ottawa, 224 Dalhousie St.
1921 Fawcett, J. P., M.D.C.M. ......Hamilton, 24 Bay St. South
1904 Fawns, W. S., M.B. ....Toronto, 1209 College St.
1918 Feader, Harry, M.B. ....Toronto, 186 Simcoe St.
1895 Feader, W. A., M.D.C.M. ......Dickinson's Landing
1895 Featherstone, H. M., M.D.C.M. .Prescott
1911 Fee, Donald L., M.D.C.M. ......Allston
1909 Feldhans, H. W., M.B. ....Copper Cliff
1916 Fenwick, C. P., M.B. ....Niagara Falls
1909 Ferguson, A. D., M. B. ....Kenora
1905 Ferguson, B. J., M.B. ....Teeswater
1917 Ferguson, D. D., M.D. ....London, Queen Alexandra, San.
1919 Ferguson, F. C., M.D. ....London. Victoria Hospital
1920 Ferguson, Harold, M.B. ....Uxbridge
1909 Ferguson, H. J., M.D. ....London, 228 Oxford St.
1914 Ferguson, H. E., M.B. ....Toronto, 371 Spadina Rd.
1904 Ferguson, J., M.B. ....Kincardine
1920 Ferguson, J. Y., B.A., M.D.C.M. .Toronto, 6 Aberdeen Club
1882 Ferguson, John, M.A., M.D. ...Toronto, 264 College St.
1895 Ferguson, J. H., M.D.C.M. .....Springfield
1901 Ferguson, J. I., M.D.C.M. .....London, 141 Wortley Rd.
1921 Ferguson, J. S., M.B. ....Chatham
1892 Ferguson, Malcolm, M.D.C.M. ..Ethel
1890 Ferguson, R., B.A., M.D. ....London, 141 Wortley Rd.
1911 Ferguson, R. M., M.D.C.M. ....Smith's Falls

1913 Ferguson, W. D., M.B. ....Hamilton. 839 Main St. East
1911 Ferguson, W. E., M.B. ....Toronto, 264 College St.
1912 Ferrier, D. J. N., M.B. ....Drayton
1915 Ferrier, Gordon, M.B. ....Mimico
1903 Ferrier, G. C., M.D.C.M. ......South Mountain
1920 Ferrill, C. W., M.D.C.M. ......Beachburg
1894 Ferris, G. M., M.D.C.M. ....Cobourg
1907 Fidlar, Edward, B.A., M.B. ....Toronto, 310 Huron St.
1877 Field, Byron, M.B. ....Pickering
1894 Field, G. H., M.D.C.M. ....Cobourg
1909 Fielding, W. M., M.B. ....Consecon
1884 Fierheller, George, M.D.C.M. ...Toronto, 535 Sherbourne St.
1869 File, A. J., M.D. ....Ameliasburg
1919 Filson, Ralph M., B.A., M.B. ...Kingston, 172 Alfred St.
1916 Findley, Douglas G., M.B. .....Toronto, 649 Church St.
1916 Finlayson, D. R., M.B. ....Ripley
1906 Finnigan, J. F., M.D.C.M. ......Oshawa
1887 Fish, W. A., M.D.C.M. ....Toronto. 678 Broadview Ave.
1893 Fisher, Eva R., M.D.C.M. ......Arthur
1920 Fisher, John H., M.B. ....Kingston, 524 Princess St.
1882 Fisher, Richard M., M.D.C.M. ..Wiarton
1919 Fisher, R. H., M.B. ....Sarnia
1904 Fisher. R. O., M.B. ....Toronto. 343 Sherbourne St.
1910 Fisher, S. M., M.D. ....London, 787 Richmond St.
1899 Fissette. C. C., M.B. ....Brantford
1920 Fitzpatrick. C. P., M.B. ......Napanee
1895 Flaherty, T. F., M.D. ....Massey Station
1901 Flath, Everon, M.B. ....Toronto, 128 Lauder Ave.
1908 Flegg, R. F., M.D.C.M. ....Ottawa. 333 McLaren Ave.
1908 Fleming, A. Grant, M.B. ......Toronto, 182 Dupont St.
1914 Fleming, R. H., B.A., M.B. ....Toronto, 1105 Broadview Ave.
1918 Fleming, Mortimer. M.B. ......Toronto, 535 King St. East
1895 Fleming, S. E., M.B. ....Sault St. Marie
1916 Fleming, Victor P., M.B. ......Toronto, 525 Dovercourt Road
1913 Fletcher. A. Almon, M.B. ......Toronto, 143. College St.
1894 Fletcher, A. G. A., M.D.C.M. ...Toronto, 37 Auburn Ave.
1920 Fletcher, D. R., M.D.C.M. .....Toronto, 999 Queen St. W.
1890 Fletcher. W. J., M.D.C.M. .....Toronto. 415 Euclid Ave.
1914 Flock, G. M., M.B. ....Windsor
1886 Foley, Declan E., M.D.C.M. ....Westport
1919 Foley, S. I., M.B. ....Howe Island
1919 Foote, W. S., M.B. ....Port Elgin
1878 Forbes, J. M., M.D. ....Caledonia
1898 Ford, A. B., M.A., M.D.C.M. ....Oshawa
1869 Ford, S. P., M.D. ....Norwood
1890 Forfar, J. E., M.D.C.M. ......Toronto, 212 Carlton St.
1919 Forge, F. W., M.B. .. ..Lion's Head
1892 Forrest, James, M.B. ....Toronto, 165 Dowling Ave.
1892 Forrest, R. F., M.D.C.M. ....Port Hope
1884 Forrester, E. L., B.A., M.D.C.M..Toronto. 416 Concord Ave.
1897 Forster, F. J. R., M.B. ....Stratford
1911 Forster, G. J., M.B. ....Belleville
1886 Forster, J. M., M.D.C.M. ......Whitby
1921 Forsyth, K. C., M.D.C.M. .....Ottawa, 458 Laurier Ave. W.
1898 Foster, A. L. ....Ottawa, 329 Kent Street
1884 Foster, C. M., M.D.C.M. ......Toronto, 34 Roxborough W.
1903 Foster, R. F., M.B. ....Highland Park, Mich.

1891 Fotheringham, J. T., B.A., M.D. .... 20 Wellesley St.
1919 Found, Norman, B.A., M.B. .... Bowmanville
1921 Fournier, D., M.D.C.M. .... Sudbury
1892 Fowler, R. V., B.A., M.D.C.M. . Perth
1916 Frain, Charles E., M.B. .... Minden
1904 Fraleigh, A. J., B.A., M.D.C.M. . Toronto, 149 Broadview Ave.
1892 Fraleigh, A. E., M.D. .... St. Mary's
1907 Frankish, E. R., M.D.C.M. ..... Toronto, 398 Bloor St. West
1921 Fraser, Donald, M.D.C.M. ..... Stratford
1921 Fraser, G. Murray, M.B. .... Toronto, 123 Sheldrake Blvd.
1919 Fraser, James E., B.A., M.D.C.M. Toronto, Western Hospital
1889 Fraser, J. B., M.D.C.M. .... Toronto, 414 Sherbourne St.
1878 Fraser, J. R. .... Lakefield
1916 Fraser, J. W., M.D.C.M. ...... Cochrane
1910 Fraser, M. J. .... Stratford
1915 Fraser, Robert H., B.A., M.B. ... Battle Creek, Mich., Sanitarium
1884 Fraser, R. N., M.D.C.M. ...... Thamesville
1889 Fraser, S. M., M.D. .... Ottawa, 188 Wellington St.
1911 Fraser, W. G., M.D.C.M. ...... Ottawa, 176 Metcalfe St.
1907 Frawley, N. D., M.B. .... Toronto, 503 Markham St.
1874 Frazer, D. B., M.B. .... Stratford
1904 Frederick, E. V., M.B. .... Peterboro
1887 Free, E. J., M.D.C.M. .... Campbellford
1919 Free, F. deF., M.B. .... Campbellford
1887 Freeborn, J. S., M.D. .... Magnetawan.
1916 Freel, H. B., M.B. .... Stouffville
1882 Freel, I. A., M.B. .... Stouffville
1918 Freele, L. W. M., M.D. .... Glencoe
1887 Freeman, A. E., M.D.C.M. ..... Inverary
1915 Freeman, W. P., M.D. .... Listowel
1910 Fripp, G. D., B.A., M.D.C.M. ... Sault Ste. Marie
1899 Frizzell, W. T., M.B. .... Owen Sound
1913 Frost, R. O., M.B. .... Toronto, 5 Raglan Ave.
1883 Frost, R. S., M.D.C.M. .... Kinmount
1912 Fuller, C. L. R., M.B. .... Windsor
1915 Furlong, H. G., M.D.C.M. ...... Ingersoll
1921 Gaboury, Hector, M.D., C.M. ...... Alfred
1875 Gaboury, Ulric .... Alfred
1909 Gaby, Robert E., B.A., M.D. ... Toronto, 662 Bathurst St.
1905 Gage, H. E., M.D.C.M. .... Paisley
1912 Galbraith, D. J., M.B. .... Dutton
1905 Galbraith, Malcolm, M.B. ..... Sarnia
1910 Galbraith, T. M., B.A., M.D.C.M. Napanee
1906 Gallagher, J. A., M.D.C.M. .... Toronto, 1061 Gerrard St. E.
1921 Gallaugher, Leonard C., M.B. ...... Mansfield
1910 Gallie, J. G., M.B. .... Toronto, 143 College St.
1904 Gallie, W. E., M.D. .... Toronto, 143 College St.
1919 Galligan, J. B., B.A., M.D. ..... Pembroke
1886 Galligan, T. D., M.D.C.M. ...... Eganville
1905 Gallivan, J. V., M.D.C.M. .... : . Peterboro
1896 Gallow, W. F., M.B. .... Goderich
1894 Galloway, Artemas, M.D.C.M. .. Woodville
1887 Galloway, James, M.B. .... Beaverton
1889 Gamble, J. B., B.A., M.B. ...... Brantford
1909 Gandier, J. C., B.A., M.B. ..... Clinton

1918 Garbutt,. C. T. P., M.B. .... Toronto, 816 Danforth Ave.
1907 Gardiner, G. H., M.B. .... Toronto, 123 Annette St.
1911 Gardiner, J. N., B.A., M.D.C.M. Toronto, 206 Bloor St., West
1891 Gardiner, R. J., M.D.C.M. ..... Kingston, 68 Johnson St.
1914 Gardiner, W. J., M.B. .... Mount Dennis
1911 Gardner, Percy N., M.B. .... Ford City.
1902 Gardner, R. L., B.A., M.D.C.M. . Ottawa, 328 Waverley
1882 Garrett, R. W., M.A., M.D.C.M. . Kingston, 52 Johnson St.
1919 Gauthier, L. P., M.D. .... Ottawa, 364 Chapel St.
1906 Gaviller, C. A. F., M.D.C.M. ... Owen Sound
1892 Gear, Henry, M.B. .... Erin
1918 Geddes, W. A. S., M.B. .... Pakesley
1905 Geddes, W. J., M.D.C.M. ...... Verona
1890 Gee, J. J., M.D.C.M. .... Toronto, 214 Wellesley St.
1911 Geiger, William, M.B. .... Waterloo
1879 Geikie, A. J., M.D. .... Toronto, 52 Maitland St.
1876 Geikie, W. W., M.D. .... Toronto, 274 Huron St.
1916 Geldert, G. M., M.D.C.M. ...... Ottawa, 445 Daly Ave.
1904 Gemmell, W. T., M.D.C.M. .... Stratford
1889 Gemmill, E. W. .... Toronto, 299 Kingswood Rd.
1902 Genge, T. S., M.D.C.M. .... Verona
1910 George, Nelson, M.D. .... London, 427 Waterloo St.
1916 George, Ruggles, B.A., M.B. ... Toronto, 121 St. Clair Ave., W.
1907 Gesner, D. H., M.D.CM. .... Grimsby
1920 Gibb, W. B., M.B. .... Haverstraw, N. Y.
1895 Gibson, Allen, M.B. ......:...... Hillsburg
1921 Gibson, Charles C., M.D. ...... Allandale
1892 Gibson, James C., M.D.C.M. .... Detroit, Mich., 3518 Baldwin Ave.
1893 Gibson, J. L., M.D.C.M. ...... Lynden
1910 Gibson, J. R., M.B. .... Toronto, 82 Westmount Ave.
1920 Gibson, M. J., M.B. .... Hamilton, Main & Kensington
1897 Gibson, Thomas, M.A., M.B.C.M. Ottawa, 164 Metcalf St.
1905 Gibson, W., M.D.C.M. .... Kingston, 85 William St.
1921 Gibson, W. J., M.D.C.M. ...... Gananoque
1914 Giguere, J. P., M.D. .... Blind River
1906 Gilbert, W. L. C., M.B. .... Toronto, 236 Sherbourne St.
1906 Gilchrist, A. J., M.B. .... Toronto, 455 Palmerston Ave.
1916 Gilchrist, J. A., B.A., M.B. .... Toronto, 455 Palmerston Ave.
1889 Gilchrist, W. C., M.D.C.M. .... Orillia
1911 Gillespie, A. T., M.B. .... Fort William
1920 Gillespie, J. H., M.D.C.M. ..... Morrisburg
1910 Gillespie, William, M.D. ...... Kitchener
1911 Gillie, J. C., M.D.C.M. .... Fort William
1916 Gillies, A. E., M.B. .... Toronto, 655 Broadview Ave.
1897 Gillies, M. H., B.A., M.B. ...... Teeswater
1916 Gillies, J. Z., B.A., M.B. ...... Toronto, 1435 Lansdowne Ave.
1907 Gillis, E. D., M.B. .... Ridgetown
1915 Gillrie, F. R., M.B. .... Hamilton, 320 Barton St.
1889 Gillrie, M. E., M.D.C.M. ...... Hamilton, 255 King St. W.
1921 Gillrie, R. B., M.B. .... Drayton
1904 Gilmour, C. H., M.B. .... Toronto, 116 St. George St.
1882 Gilpin, William, M.D.C.M. ..... Brechin
1919 Gimby, J. E., M.B. .... Sault Ste. Marie
1890 Gimby, W. E., M.D.C.M. ...... Sault Ste. Marie
1916 Givens, W. C., M.B. .... Toronto, 1622 Danforth Ave.

1893 Glaister, William, M.D.C.M.   ...Wellesley
1916 Glancy, J. A. R., M.D. ....Toronto, 56 Pleasant Blvd.
1908 Glanfield, W. J., M.A., M.B. ....Wallacetown
1921 Glasgow, Gordon K., M.B. .....Tupperville
1893 Glassco, G. S., M.B. ....Hamilton, 235 Queen St.
1906 Glendenning, Henry, M.D.C.M. .Toronto, 199 Bloor St. E.
1907 Glendinning, E. F., M.D.C.M. ...Hamilton, 307 Grosvenor Ave.
1915 Glenn, L. A., M.D. ....Chatham
1906 Glenn, O. J., M.D.C.M. ....Wardsville
1913 Gliddon, R. W., M.B. ....St. Thomas
1912 Gliddon, W. O., B.A., M.D.C.M.Ottawa, 201 O'Connor St.
1911 Glionna, G., M.B. ....Toronto, 606 Bathurst St.
1913 Glover, T. J., M.B. ....Toronto, 538 Jarvis St.
1889 Godfrey, Forbes, M.B. ....Mimico
1915 Godfrey, W. Harry, M.D.C.M. ..Hamilton, 270 Ottawa St.
1896 Goldie, William, M.D. ....Toronto, 86 College St.
1896 Goldsmith, P. G., M.D.C.M. ...Toronto, 84 Carlton St.
1918 Gooch, Chilvers, M.B. ....Hamilton, 762 King St. E.
1904 Goodchild, J. F., M.D.C.M. .....Toronto, 33 Bloor St. E.
1920 Goodfellow, F. R., M.D.C.M. ..McDonald's Corners
1896 Goodfellow, J. S., M.D.C.M. ....Morrisburg
1890 Goold, A. J., B.A. ....Waterford
1921 Gordon, A. C., M.B ....Toronto, 70 Bartlett Ave.
1896 Gordon, Emma L. Skinner, M.B.Toronto, 467 Spadina Ave.
1919 Gordon, E. J., M.B. ....St. George
1877 Gordon, George, M.B. ....London, 130 Langarth St.
1917 Gordon, G. D., M.D.C.M. ....Kemptville
1912 Gordon, H. H., M.B. ....Ottawa, 27 Willard St.
1893 Gordon, J K. M., M.D.C.M. ...Ottawa, 172 Fourth Ave.
1899 Gordon, Margaret, M.D.C.M. ...Toronto, 726 Spadina Ave.
1919 Gordon, Roderick J., M.D. .....London, 509 Ontario St.
1915 Gorman, M. E., M.B. ....Preston
1905 Gormley, J. C., M.D.C.M. .....Crysler
1879 Gould, D. H., M.B. ....Fenelon Falls
1906 Gould, W. J. H., M.D. ....Paris
1919 Goulding, Arthur M., B.A., M.D.Toronto, 88 Warren Rd.
1900 Gow, James, M.B. ....Windsor
1892 Gowan, T. J., M.D. ....Horning's Mills
1905 Gowland, M. E., M.A., M.B. ...Milton
1919 Grace, N. M., M.B. ....Arnprior
1921 Grady, Lilian R., M.B. ....Peterborough
1919 Graef, F. W., M.B. ....Clifford
1885 Graham, Angus, M.D.C.M. .....London, 510 King St.
1887 Graham, A. D., M.D.C.M. .....Bothwell
1912 Graham, C. R., B.A., M.D.C.M. ....Kearney
1906 Graham, Duncan, M.B. ....Toronto, 1 Queen's Park
1894 Graham, E. D., M.D.C.M. .....Keswick
1905 Graham, G. W., B.A., M.B. ....Toronto, 255 Avenue Rd.
1913 Graham, G. C., M.B. ....Fenelon Falls
1884 Graham, H. H., M.D.C.M. .....Fenelon Falls
1910 Graham, J. Lorne, M.B. ....Ottawa, 202 Laurier Ave. W.
1887 Graham, John, M.D.C.M. .....Pembroke
1905 Graham, John, M.D.C.M. .....Bolton
1921 Graham, John A., M.B. ....Toronto, 213 Davenport Rd.
1903 Graham, Joseph S., M.B. ....Toronto, 55 College St.
1914 Graham, M. D., B.A., M.D.C.M. .Ottawa, 251 Creighton St.

1917 Graham, M. G., M.B. .... Exeter
1907 Graham, M. R., M.B. .... Toronto, 1487 Danforth Ave.
1920 Graham, N. F. W., B.A., M.B. ... Allandale
1877 Graham, P. L., M.B. .... Lobo
1915 Graham, P. V., M.B. .... Toronto, 16 Ranleigh Ave.
1911 Graham, Roscoe R., M.B. ..... Toronto, 112 College St.
1916 Graham, Stanley G., M.B. ..... Toronto, 31 Oriole Rd.
1903 Graham, W. A., M.D.C.M. ..... Ottawa, 297 Sunnyside Ave.
1904 Graham, W. A, M.B. .... Toronto, 104 Wells Hill Ave.
1902 Grant, A. J., M.D. .... London, 205 Queen's Ave.
1877 Grant, Andrew, M.B. .... Beaverton
1901 Grant, C. C., M.D.C.M. .... Woodville
1898 Grant, James, M.B. .... Bracebridge
1895 Grant, J. A. C., B.A., M.D.C.M. . Gravenhurst
1919 Grant, W. R., M.D.C.M. ...... Hamilton, 437 Maple Ave.
1888 Grasett, J. C. C., M.D.C.M. ... Simcoe
1897 Gray, Andrew, M.B. ....,..... Chippawa
1903 Gray, E. A., B.A., M.B. .... Toronto, 124 Gothic Ave.
1892 Gray, Eliza R., M.D.C.M. ..... Toronto, 98 Carlton St.
1892 Gray, Jennie, M.D.C.M. ..,... Toronto, 98 Carlton St.
1898 Gray, T. L., M.D. .... St. Thomas
1890 Gray, W. A., M.D.C.M. .... Smith's Falls
1881 Gray, W. L., M.D.C.M. .... Pembroke
1917 Graydon, W. L., M.B. .... Toronto, 64 Awde St.
1916 Greaves, A. Vernon, M.B. ..... Bruce Mines
1921 Green, Percy, Phm.B., M.B. .... Port Hope
1919 Green, J. T., M.D. .... Hamilton, 777 King St. E.
1892 Green, R. H., M.B. .... Embro
1890 Greene, E. H., M.D.C.M. ...... Toronto, 58 Avenue Rd.
1892 Greene, F. T., M.B. .... Stoney Creek
1889 Greenlaw, J. A., M.D.C.M. ..... Palmerston
1910 Greenleese, J. C., M.D.C.M. .... Ottawa, 70 Argyle Ave.
1904 Greenway, G. E., M.B. .... Hamilton, 346 Main St. E.
1895 Greenwood, A. B., M.B. .... Ohsweken
1920 Greenwood, F. C., M.D.C.M. ... St. Catharines
1878 Greenwood, F. S., M.D.C.M. ... St. Catharines
1905 Greenwood, W. T., M.D.C.M. ... St. Catharines
1913 Greer, G. Garnet, M.B. .... Kingston, 254 King St.
1880 Greer, T. Newton, M.B. .... Peterborough
1919 Gregory, A. W., M.B. ....:.... Lawrence Station
1891 Griffith, R. C., M.B. .... Toronto, 212 Jamieson Ave.
1902 Grimshaw, W. S., M.D., C.M. ... Toronto, 306 St. Clair Ave. W.
1871 Groves, Abraham, M.D. .... Fergus
1878 Groves, J. W., M.B. .... Ottawa, 295 Clemow Ave.
1889 Groves, W. H., M.D., C.M. ..... Dixie.
1889 Grundy, Henry, M.D. .... Toronto, 460 King St. E.
1911 Guest, Edna M., M.B. .... Toronto, 467 Spadina Ave.
1915 Guest, F. R., M.D. .... Blyth
1887 Guinane, Joachim, M.B. .... Toronto, 152 Dundas St. E.
1883 Gullen, Augusta S., M.D. ..... Toronto, 461 Spadina Ave.
1883 Gullen, J. B., M.D., C.M. ..... Toronto, 461 Spadina Ave.
1895 Gunn, Arthur, M.D., C.M. ...... Toronto, 436 Yonge St.
1911 Gunn, C. G., M.B. .... Ottawa, 297 Laurier Ave. E.
1905 Gunn, J. G., M.D. .... London, 36 Hayman Court
1882 Gunn, William, M.D., C.M. ..... Clinton
1919 Gunne, L. G., M.D. .... Kenora

1885 Gunne, W. J., M.D., C.M. ...... Kenora
1915 Guy, D. H., M.B. .... Maxwell
1914 Guyatt, B. L., M.B. .... Toronto, Prov. Brd. Health
1912 Guyatt, R. E., M.A., M.B. ..... Hamilton, 683 Barton St. E.
1896 Gwyn, Norman B., M.B. ...... Toronto, 48 Bloor St. E.
1907 Hacking, Roy, M.B. .... Tara
1888 Haentschel, C. W., M.D., C.M...... Haileybury
1910 Haffey, M. J., M.B. .... Toronto, 152 Carlton St.
1919 Haffner, A. B., M.D., C.M. ..... Kingston, 409 Johnston St.
1895 Hagar, F. C., M.D., C.M. ...... Ottawa, 201 Cooper St.
1919 Hagerman, A. R., M.B. .... Toronto, 105 Dewson St.
1912 Hagmeier, J. Edwin, M.B. .... Kitchener
1912 Hagmeier, L. G., M.B. .... Kitchener
1920 Hague, O. G., M.B. .... Toronto, 158 Borden St.
1916 Hagyard, H. C., M.B. .... Perth
1892 Haig, Andrew, M.A., M.D., C.M. Campbellford
1921 Haight, W. R. W., M.B. ...... Gelert
1904 Hair, C. H., M.D., C.M. .... Toronto, 545 Palmerston Blvd.
1898 Haist, E. A., M.B. .... Ottawa, 362 Rideau St.
1902 Haist, O. W., M.D., C.M. ...... Hamilton, 214 Wentworth St. N.
1910 Hale, G. C. .... London, 20 Hayman Ct. Apts.
1911 Hale, Wm., Jr., B.A., M.D. .... Gananoque
1920 Hall, C.M., M.D., C.M. .... Kenmore
1906 Hall, F. W., M.B. .... Chatham
1895 Hall, G. W., M.D., C.M. .... Little Britain
1900 Hall, Janet, M.D., C.M. .... Woodstock
1920 Hall, R. C., B.A., M.B. .... Toronto, General Hosp.
1919 Hall, Wilbert, M.B. .... Mitchell
1887 Hall, William, M.D., C.M. ..... Brampton
1913 Halliday, A. A., M.B. .... Toronto, 143 College St.
1920 Halliday, C. W., B.A., M.D. .... Chatham
1905 Halliday, R. W. .... Toronto, 320 Palmerston Blvd.
1911 Hambly, W. R., M.D., C.M. .... Wingham
1904 Hamilton, B. H., M.D., C.M. ... Sault Ste. Marie
1879 Hamilton, Charles J., M.D. .... Cornwall
1868 Hamilton, C. S., M.D., C.M. ... Cobourg
1911 Hamilton, G. H., Ross, M.B. ... Petrolia
1915 Hamilton, H. P., M.B. .... Kitchener
1907 Hamilton, J. J., M.B. .... Bethany
1909 Hamilton, Laura S. M., M.B. ... Richmond Hill
1909 Hamilton, R. J., M.B. .... Ailsa Craig
1889 Hamilton, Walter, M.D., C.M. .. Toronto, 308 Bathurst St.
1914 Hamilton, W. G., M.D., C.M. ... Westport
1902 Hamilton, W. T., M.B. .... Toronto, 301 Broadview Ave.
1906 Hamlin, F. V., M.B. .... Toronto, 954 Dundas St. W.
1905 Hammond, E. A., M.D., C.M. ... Peterboro
1912 Hand, W. T., M.D., C.M. ...... Hamilton, 32 Sherman Ave. S.
1915 Haney, W. C., M.B. .... Welland
1885 Hanks, A. R., M.D., C.M. ...... Blenheim
1920 Hanley, G. J., M.B. .... Kingston, 73 Gore St.
1915 Hanley, J. B. .... Midland
1919 Hanley, J. Swift, B.A., M.D., C.M. Kingston, 81 Wellington St.
1911 Hanley, T. R., B.A., M.B. .... Toronto, 124 Bloor St. W.
1890 Hanly, J. F. .... Almonte

1920 Hanna, Charles E., M.D., C.M. .. Toronto, 203 Dawlish Ave.
1879 Hanna, Frank .... Brantford
1911 Hanna, G. M., M.B. .... Brantford
1886 Hanna, J. E., M.D., C.M. ...... Ottawa, 2 Dorothy Ave.
1914 Hannah, Beverley, M.B. ...... Toronto, 155 Bloor St. E.
1886 Hansler, J. E., M.B. .... Fonthill
1896 Harcourt, G. V., M.D., C.M. ... Powassan
1912 Harcourt, W. V., M.D. .... Guelph
1919 Hardiman, B. C., M.D., C.M. ... Fort William
1921 Harding, Andrew W., M.D. ..... Mitchell
1889 Harding, W. Ernest, M.D., C.M. Brockville
1897 Hardy, E. A. P., M.D. .... Toronto, 333 Bloor St. W.
1906 Hardy, E. B., M.B. .... Toronto, 88 Dunvegan Road
1900 Hargrave, H. G., B.A., M.B. ..... Toronto, 325 Parliament St.
1918 Hargrave, H. R., M.B. .... Toronto, 254 Withrow Ave.
1909 Harkness, J. Graham, M.B. ..... St. Catharines
1911 Harper, F. S., M.B. .... Hamilton, 557 King St. E.
1896 Harper, W. S., M.D., C.M. .... Ottawa, 274 Friel St.
1890 Harrington, A. J., M.D., C.M. .. Toronto, 813 Bathurst St.
1915 Harris, C. A., M.D. .... London, 421 Dundas St.
1921 Harris, Charles W., B.A., M.B. . Toronto, 1276 King St. W.
1921 Harris, Chester, B.A., M.B., Ch.B. Toronto, 166 Oakwood Ave.
1920 Harris, E. C., M.B. .... Walkerville
1904 Harris, R. B., M.B. .... Copper Cliff
1915 Harris, R. I., M.B. .... Toronto, 311 Avenue Rd.
1888 Harris, W. H., M.D., C.M. ..... Toronto, 1276 King St. W.
1918 Harris, William, B.A., M.B. ... Toronto, 391 Dundas St. W.
1903 Harris, W. J., M.D., C.M. ...... Toronto, 365 Danforth Ave.
1921 Harrison, Esther D., M.B. ..... Toronto, 137 Bloor St. W.
1908 Harrison, F. C., B.A., M.B. .... Toronto, 29 Roxborough St. W.
1914 Harrison, H. M., M.D., C.M. ... Toronto, 280 Roncesvalles Ave.
1909 Harrison, J. P., M.B. .... Dunnville
1881 Harrison, W. T., M.D. .... Keene
1912 Hart, A. P., M.B. .... Wilfred
1921 Hart, Hugh, B.A., M.B. .... Harriston.
1886 Hart, J. W., M.D., C.M. ...... Huntsville
1888 Hart, J. F., M.D., C.M. .... Athens
1889 Hart, J. S., M.D., C.M. .... Toronto, 179 Dowling Ave.
1887 Hart, M. W., M.D., C.M. ...... Prescott
1901 Hart, V. A., M.D., C.M. .... Barrie
1914 Hartry, R. E., M.B. .... Byng Inlet
1893 Harvey, E. E., M.B. .... Peterboro
1911 Harvey, F. R., M.B. .... Kitchener
1885 Harvie, A. R., M.D., C.M. ..... Orillia
1910 Harvie, C. A., M.B. .... Orillia
1912 Harvie, H. H., M.B. .... Coldwater
1886 Harvie, J. A., M.D., C.M. ...... Coldwater
1893 Harvie, J. N., B.A., M.B. ...... Orillia
1919 Harvie, R. M., M.B. .... Coldwater
1912 Hassard, F. R., B.A., M.B. .... Toronto, 1361 King St. W.
1886 Hastings, C. J., M.D., C.M. .... Toronto, 252 Russell Hill Road
1913 Hastings, E. R., M.B. .... Toronto, 791 Queen St. E.
1883 Hawk, Albert, M.B. .... Galt
1916 Hawkey, R. J., M.D. .... Hamilton, 395 Barton St. E.
1916 Hawkings, J. E., B.A., M.D. .. Galt

1907 Hawkins, C. S., M.B. ....Toronto, 611 Spadina Ave.
1887 Hay, H. R., M.D., C.M. ....Wiarton
1885 Hay, S. M., M.D., C.M. ....Toronto, 2 Spadina Road
1886 Hay, W. W., M.D., C.M. ....Wallaceburg
1899 Hayden, E. W. ....Cobourg
1890 Hayes, A. N., M.D. ....Sarnia
1912 Hayes, Ethel M., B.A., M.B. ... Toronto, 467 Spadina Ave.
1919 Hayes, J. V., M.B. ....Peterboro
1908 Hazelwood, J. F., M.B. ....Toronto, 122 Beach Ave.
1919 Hazlett, J. M., B.A., M.D., C.M. Collingwood
1903 Hazlewood, B. J., M.D., C.M. ... Bowmanville
1915 Hazlewood, H C. P., M.B. ..... Sanitarium
1910 Healy, J. J. ....Toronto, 574 Sherbourne St.
1915 Hearn, Percival, M.B. ....Toronto, 65 Runnymede Rd.
1883 Hearn, Richard, M.D., C.M. ..... Toronto, 249 Dovercourt Rd.
1891 Heaslip, Andrew W., M.B. ..... Picton
1914 Heffering, H., M.B. ....Toronto, 425 Broadview Ave
1892 Heggie, D. L., M.B. ....Brampton.
1886 Heggie, W. C., M.D., C.M. ..... Toronto, 116 Dovercourt Rd.
1915 Helliwell, Maurice R., M.B. ... Toronto, 130 Glenholme Ave
1892 Heming, F. H., M.B. ....Meaford
1918 Henderson, D. A., M.B. ....Toronto, 1259 Danforth Ave.
1907 Henderson, E. M., B.A., M.B. ... Toronto, 9 Bedford Rd.
1897 Henderson, N. R., M.D., C.M. ... London, 479 Clarence St.
1915 Henderson, R. Hartley, M.B. ... Guelph
1902 Henderson, Velyien E., M.A., M.B. Toronto, 111 Admiral Rd.
1916 Henderson, W. I., M.B. ....Depot Harbour
1896 Henderson, W. J., M.B. ....Cannington
1900 Hendrick, A. C., M.A., M.B. .... Toronto, 20 Bloor St.. E.
1920 Hendry, H. W., M.B. ....Toronto, 86 Amelia St.
1904 Hendry, W. B., M.B. ....Toronto, 112 College St.
1892 Henry, A. E., M.D., C.M. ....Ignace
1918 Henry, George A., M.B. ....Sudbury
1870 Henry, S. M., M.D. ....Toronto, 138 Howard Park Ave.
1921 Henry, S. G., M.D. ....London, 463 Maitland St.
1891 Henry, T. H., M.B. ....Orangeville
1905 Henry, T. R., M.B. ....Norwich
1919 Henry, W. J., M.B. ....Flesherton
1920 Henry, W. E., B.A., M.B. ......Markdale
1882 Henwood, A. J., M.D., C.M. .... Brantford
1889 Henwood, J. M., M.D., C.M. .... Toronto, 62A Charles St. E.
1921 Hepburn, John, M.B. ....Toronto, 105 Robert St.
1902 Herod, John, M.D., C.M. ......Thorold
1890 Herriman, W. C., M.B. ....Orillia
1892 Hershey, J. A., M.B. ....Owen Sound
1904 Hess, L. R. N., M.B. ....Hamilton, 44-56 Hughson St.
1919 Hession, H. A., M.B. ....Toronto, 1030 Dovercourt Rd.
1891 Hett, J. E., M.B. ....Kitchener
1920 Hewett, C. D., M.B. ....Dunnville
1914 Hewitt, S. R. D., M.B. ... .Toronto, 14 Inglewood Drive
1896 Hicks, Everett S., M.D., C.M. ... Brantford
1920 Hicks, W. H., M.B. ....Kingston, 632 Princess St.
1893 Higbee, Annie Carveth, M.D., C.M. Toronto, 180 Huron St.
1919 Higginson, W. L., M.D., C.M. ..Westmeath
1889 Hilker, A. E., M.D., C.M. .....Hamilton, 352 Barton St. E.
1921 Hill, Carl E., M.B. ....Richmond Hill

1909	Hill, C. E., M.B.	Toronto, 160 Bloor St. W.
1904	Hill, F. W., M.D.	Belleville
1915	Hill, H. W., M.D.	London; Inst. Public Health
1919	Hill, James C., M.B.	Foleyet
1916	Hill, L. R., M.B.	Toronto, 264 Wright Ave.
1890	Hillary, R. M., M.D., C.M.	Aurora
1891	Hilliard, W. L., M.B.	Waterloo
1886	Hillier, Riel, M.D., C.M.	Leamington
1869	Hillier, S C., M.D.	Bowmanville
1919	Hillis, L. C., M.D.	Oil Springs
1907	Hincks, C. M., M.B.	Toronto, 735 Bloor St. West
1916	Hipwell, F. W. W., M.B.	Toronto, 240 Danforth Ave.
1895	Hird, William, B.A., M.B.	Wallaceburg
1900	Hiscock, R. C., M.A., M.D., C.M.	Verdun, P.Q.
1888	Hoare, C. W., M.D., C.M.	Walkerville
1890	Hobbs, A T., M.D.	Guelph
1921	Hobson, W. J., M.B.	Milford
1915	Hodge, W. R., B.A., M.B.	Toronto, 68 South Drive
1890	Hodgetts, C. A., M.D., C.M.	Ottawa, Dept. of Health
1904	Hodgins, E. L., M.B.	London, 312 Oxford St.
1916	Hodgins, W. E., M.B.	London, 165 Ridout St.
1908	Hodgson, E. G., M.D., C.M.	Toronto, 48 Bloor St. E.
1906	Hogan, J. T., M.D., C.M.	Smith's Falls
1920	Hogarth, W. P., M.B.	Fort William
1894	Hogg, D. H., M.D., C.M.	London, 116 York St.
1899	Hogg, J. S., M.D., C.M.	Preston
1903	Hoidge, E. T., M.B.	Toronto, 547 Palmerston Blvd.
1880	Hoig, D. S., M.B.	Oshawa
1889	Holdcroft, Joseph, M.D., C.M.	Havelock
1915	Hollis, K. E., M.D., C M	Toronto, 495 Annette St.
1909	Holme, H. R., B.A., M.B.	Toronto, 695 Broadview Ave.
1918	Holmes, Arthur, M.B.	Bracebridge
1877	Holmes, F. S. L., M.D., C.M.	Kemptville
1900	Holmes, G. W., M.B.	Chatham
1904	Holmes, K. H., M.B.	Chatham
1907	Holmes, L. S., M.D.	London, 344 Richmond St., W.
1908	Holmes, R. E., M.D.	Windsor
1911	Holmes, Shirley, M.B.	Chatham
1867	Holmes, T. K., M.D.	Chatham
1918	Holmes, W. H., M.B.	Toronto, 378 Roncesvalles Ave.
1887	Honsberger, J. F., M.D., C.M.	Kitchener
1887	Hood, F. C., M.D., C.M.	Toronto, 720 Spadina Ave.
1898	Hooper, E. R., B.A., M.B.	Toronto, 415 Bloor St. W.
1896	Hooper, Edward M., M.B.	Toronto, 87, Forest Hill Road
1920	Hooper, George, M.D., C.M.	Ottawa, 196 Metcalfe St.
1887	Hoover, J. H. M.D., C.M.	Tillsonburg
1902	Hope, J. T., M.D., C.M.	Alexandria
1910	Hopkins, B. H., M.B.	Kingston, 25 West St.
1921	Hopkins, H. E., M.B.	Toronto, 338 Pacific Ave.
1887	Hopkins, R. R., M.D., C.M.	Toronto, 338 Pacific Ave.
1886	Hopkins, W. B., M.D., C.M.	Hamilton, 158 Mary St. N.
1911	Hopper, D. A., M.B.	Waterdown
1905	Hore, A. L., M.B.	Markham
1920	Horne, S. J. W., M.D., C.M.	London, Westminster Hospital
1909	Horton, B. B., M.B.	Thornton
1911	Horton, E. M., M.B.	Enterprise

1879	Horton, R. N., M.D., C.M.	Brockville
1899	Hossack, J. G., M.B.	Innerkip
1888	Hotson, Alexander, M.D., C.M. .	Parkhill
1888	Hotson, A. N., M.D., C.M.	Innerkip
1892	Hough, A. H., M.D.C.M.	Wiarton
1919	Houghton, C. L., M.D.	Wyoming
1907	Houston, G. W., Phm.B., M.B.	Hamilton, 902 King St., E.
1919	Houston, J. F., M.B.	Carleton Place
1905	Houston, P. J. F., M.B.	Toronto, 34 Hurndale Ave.
1912	Howard, C. A., M.D., C.M.	Kingston, 199 Brock St.
1907	Howard, E. A. E., M.B.	Toronto, 102 Avenue Road
1878	Howe, F. M.	Blackstock
1917	Howell, J. H., M.A., M.B.	Galt
1885	Howell, J. H .,M.B.	Welland
1890	Howell, R. G., M.D., C.M.	Jarvis
1899	Howey, R., M.B.	Owen Sound
1880	Howey, W. H., M.D., C.M.	Sudbury
1874	Howitt, H., M.D.	Guelph
1905	Howitt, H. O., M.D., C.M.	Guelph
1915	Howitt, John R., M.B.	Hamilton, 104 George St.
1875	Howitt, W. H .,M.D., C.M.	Toronto, 100 Carlton St.
1900	Howland, G. W., B.A., M.B.	Toronto, 147 Bloor St. W.
1909	Howlett, G. P., M.D., C.M.	Ottawa, 430 Somerset St.
1920	Howson, A. G., M.B. .,.......	Peterborough
1893	Hubbard, J. P., B.A., M.B.	Forest
1908	Huehnergard, H. H., M.B.	Kitchener
1920	Huether, Leslie, B.A., M.B.	Guelph
1903	Huffman, J. L., M.D.	Arkona
1905	Hughes, F. N., M.D., C.M.	Toronto, 1357 Bathurst St.
1894	Hughes, F. W., M.D.	London, 234 Queen's Ave.
1918	Hughes, J. Vernon, M.B.	London, 234 Queen's Ave.
1900	Hume, Rowena, M.D., C.M.	Toronto, 226 Carlton St.
1914	Humphrey, J. N., M.B.	Toronto, 468 Church St.
1920	Hunt, B. V., M.D., C.M.	Kingston, 18 Earl St.
1879	Hunt, Henry	Toronto, 20 Brunswick Ave.
1904	Hunt, J. G., M.B.	London, Queen's Ave., & Queen
1907	Hunt, J. W., M.B.	Toronto, Dom. Orthopedic Hosp
1904	Hunt, W. B. S., M.B.	Port Arthur
1888	Hunter, A. J., M.D., C.M.	Woodstock
1891	Hunter, A C., M.D., C.M.	Goderich
1875	Hunter, John, M.B.	Toronto, 268 Roncesvalles Ave.
1921	Hurdman, A. G., M.D., C.M. ...	Ottawa, 73 Cartier St.
1914	Hurley, John J., M.B.	Toronto, 995 Bathurst St.
1909	Hurtubise, J..R., B.A., M.D., C.M.	Sudbury
1910	Husband, G. L.	Hamilton, 129 Main St. W.
1916	Hutchinson, E. D., M.B. ...,...	Windsor
1912	Hutchinson, Fred, B.A., M.B. ...	Sarnia
1919	Hutchinson, William, M.D., C.M.	Ottawa, 75 Sparks St.
1901	Hutchison, H. S., M.B.	Toronto, 96 College St.
1895	Hutchison, J. C., B.A., M.D.; C.M.	Grafton
1910	Hutchison, W. G., M.D.	Hespeler
1888	Hutton, J. G., M.D., C.M.	Durham
1919	Hutton, R. L., M.B.	Brantford
1915	Hutton, W. L., M.B.	Brantford
1911	Huxtable, E. W., M.B.	Newburgh

1911	Huyck, P. H., M.D., C.M.	Kingston, 120 Wellington St.
1916	Hyndman, A. B., M.D., C.M. ...	Carp
1893	Hyndman, H. K., M.D.	Exeter
1888	Hyttenrauch, L. J. A., M.D. ...	Windsor
1904	Ingram, Robert, M.B.	Windsor
1890	Inksetter, W. E., M.D., C.M. ...	Dundas
1908	Innes, J. C.	Port Credit
1921	Ireland, A. J., M.D.	St. Catharines
1919	Irvine, H. J., M.B.	Camp Borden
1920	Irvine, P. L,. M.B.	Drayton
1913	Irwin, D. C., M.D., C.M.	Navan
1890	Irwin, E. F., M.D., C.M.	Weston
1921	Irwin, G. A. L., M.D., C.M.	Halifax, N. S.
1890	Irwin, Houston	Pembroke
1906	Irwin, J. R., M.B.	Cobourg
1916	Isaacson, Arthur, M.B.	Toronto, 583 Dundas St.
1889	Ivy, J. A., B.A., M.D.	Cobourg
1916	Jackson, A. B., M.B.	Simcoe
1905	Jackson, A. A., M.B.	Toronto, 250 Symington Ave.
1897	Jackson, G. H., M.B.	Union.
1902	Jackson, G. F., M.D., C.M. .;...	Haileybury
1910	Jackson, G. P.|, M.B.	Toronto, 1543 Queen St., W.
1873	Jackson, W. .F.	Brockville
1916	Jaffrey, W. R., M.D., C.M.	Hamilton, 64 Hughson St., S.
1911	James, Arthur B., M.B.	Toronto. 48 College St.
1921	James, Ivan W., M.D., C.M.	Carp
1895	James, J. F., M.D.	Sarnia
1887	James, M., M.D., C.M.	Mattawa
1892	Jamieson, Alison, M.D., C.M. ...	London, 369 Queen's Ave.
1887	Jamieson, Archibald, M.D., C.M.	Arnprior
1911	Jamieson, D. B., M.B.	Durham
1902	Jamieson, G. B., M.D., C.M. ...	Edgar
1911	Jamieson, Ross A., B.A., M.B. .	Toronto, 155 Bloor St., E.
1888	Jamieson, T. J., M.D., C.M. ...	Cardinal
1910	Jamieson, William, M.B.	Hamilton, 246 James St., S.
1916	Jamieson, W. G., M.B. ......,.	Cobourg.
1916	Janes, R. M., M.B.	Toronto, Sick Children's Hosp.
1883	Jaques, William, M.D., C.M. ...	Jarvis
1882	Jarvis, Charles E., M.D., C.M. ..	London, 715 Dundas St.
1915	Jeffrey, F. H., B.A., M.B.	Paris
1916	Jeffrey, A. M., M.B.	Toronto, 107 Carlton St.
1915	Jeffrey, E. S., M.B.	Toronto, 107 Carlton St.
1920	Jeffrey, G. S., M.B.	Burwash
1916	Jeffs, G. D., B.A., M.B.	Toronto, 2761 Yonge St.
1884	Jenner, J. E., M.B.	Kingsville
1911	Jepson, G. L., M.D.	London, 405 Dundas St.
1900	Johns, C. P., B.A., M.D., C.M. ..	Thornhill
1911	Johnson, H. E., M.B.	Mount Albert
1887	Johnston, D. J., M.B.	Iroquois
1884	Johnston, F. H., M.D., C.M. ...	Burford
1921	Johnston, Harold W., M.B.	Drayton
1908	Johnston, H. B., M.B.	Fenelon Falls
1894	Johnston, H. A., M.B.	Port Burwell
1882	Johnston, J. M., M.D., C.M. ...	Toronto, 6 Washington Ave.
1907	Johnston, J., B.A., M.D., C.M. ..	Burgessville
1900	Johnston, Margaret M., M.D.C.M....	Toronto, 108 Avenue Rd.

1919 Johnston. R. A., M.D. .... London, 2 Carrothers Ave.
1911 Johnston, Robert E., M.B. .... Toronto, 589 Bathurst St.
1902 Johnston, Samuel, M.D., C.M. .. Toronto, 108 Avenue Rd.
1909 Johnston, T. J., M.B. .... Midland
1916 Johnston, W. J., M.B. .... Toronto, 29 Wellesley St.
1891 Johnston, W. J., M.D., C.M. ... Trenton
1920 Johnstone, Charles G., M.D., C.M. Port Arthur
1881 Jones, A. C .,M.D., C.M. ...... Hamilton, 215 Main St. W.
1885 Jones, Ogden, M.D., C.M. ...... Toronto, 126 Carlton St.
1887 Jones, G. F., M.D. ....·.... Webbwood
1920 Jones, G. Russell, M.B. .... Webbwood
1918 Jones, Howard O., M.B. ...... Toronto. 208 Dundas St., E.
1884 Jones, J. A., M.D. .... Ottawa, 206 James St.
1917 Jones, L. M., M.D. .... Thamesford
1907 Jones, Newbold C. .... Toronto. 43 Wellesley St.
1907 Jones, R. A., M.B. .... Toronto, 509 Broadview Ave.
1914 Jones, S. O. H., M.D. .... Strathroy
1887 Jones, S. J., M.D., C.M. .... Hamilton, 2 West Ave., N.
1915 Jones, W. A., M.D. .... Kingston, 251 University Ave.
1919 Jones, W. Ewart, M.B. .... Toronto, 50 Prescott Ave.
1896 Jones, W. W., B.A., M.B. ...... Toronto, 41 Avenue Rd.
1910 Jordan, Dennis, B.A., M.D., C.M. Toronto, 97 Danforth Ave.
1920 Jordan, Graham A., M.B. ...... Hamilton, General Hospital
1901 Jordan, Joseph, M.B. .... Toronto, 1369 Lansdowne Ave.
1894 Jory, J. M., M.D., C.M. .... St. Catharines
1882 Josephs, G. E., M.D., C.M. ..... Pembroke
1917 Jost, H. T., B.A., M.D., C.M. ... Ottawa. 258 Laurier Ave. W.
1915 Joyal, J. A.. Hector, M.D. ..... Haileybury
1921 Joyal, J. E. Ildor, M.D. .... Timmins.
1915 Joyce, H G. .... Freelton
1920 Joyce, R. E., M.B. .... Bronte
1905 Judson, A. H., M.D., C.M. .... Brockville
1880 Judson, G. W., M.D. .... Lyn
1911 Jupp, J. B., M.B. .... Woodstock.
1872 Kains, Robert, M.D. .... St. Thomas .
1919 Kaiser, N. W., M.D. .... London, 110 Wellington St.
1890 Kaiser, T. E., M.D., C.M. ..... Oshawa
1890 Kalbfleisch, F. H., M.D., C.M. . Kitchener
1905 Kane, J. A., M.B. ...·...... Cobalt
1915 Kane, J. E., M.D., C.M. .... Kingston, 136 Wellington St.
1904 Kappele, D. P., M.B. .... Hamilton 504 Main St.. E.
1888 Karn, C. J. W.; M.D., C.M. ..... London, 425 Richmond St.
1911 Kay, A. D. W., M.B. .... Ottawa. St. Luke's Hosp.
1908 Kay, A. F., M.B. .... Schomberg
1906 Keane, A. W., M.D., C.M. ..... Essex
1887 Keane, M. J., M.D., C.M. ...... Brantford
1909 Kearns, D. A., M.D., C.M. ..... Ottawa, 194 Wilbrod St.
1911 Kearns, J. A., M.B. .... Phelpston
1902 Kee, R. J., M.B. .... Ottawa, B.P.C., Canada
1919 Keefe, W. J., M.D., C.M. ..... Iroquois Falls .
1912 Keeley, J. A., M.B. .... Toronto. 2881 Dundas St.. W.
1880 Keffer, T. D., M.D. .... Maple
1913 Keillor, B. F., M.B. .... London. 46 Stanley St.
1915 Keillor, C. M., M.D. .... Kingsville
1902 Keith, J. P., M.B. .... Sault Ste. Marie
1919 Keith, N. M., B.A., M.D. .... Rochester, Minn., Mayo Clinic.
1895 Kellam, E. T., M.B. .... Niagara Falls

1911 Kelly, B. E., M.B. .... Peterborough
1900 Kelly, E. P., M.D., C.M. ...... Toronto, 177 Bloor St., E.
1920 Kelly, Faustina A., B.A., M.B. Sudbury
1896 Kelly, J. K., M.D., C.M. .... Almonte
1909 Kelly, J. M., M.D., C.M. .... Delta
1915 Kelly, T. F., M.B. .... Orillia
1901 Kelly, W. A., M.B. .... Florence
1899 Kemp, H. G., M.D., C.M. ...... Toronto, 39 Avenue Road
1920 Kemp, M. W., M.B. .... Nickelton
1907 Kendall, W. B., Phm.B., M.D., C.M.. Sanitarium P.O.
1911 Kendrick, Bryce, B.A., M.D., C.M. Leamington
1919 Kendrick, M. A., M.D., C.M. .... Leamington
1919 Kennedy, C. Irlma M., M.B. ... Wingham
1920 Kennedy, G. L. D., M.D., C.M. . Ottawa, Westminster Apts.
1919 Kennedy, M. J., M.D., C.M. ..... Cobourg
1921 Kennedy, O E., M.B. .... Ottawa, c|o Bank of Montreal
1887 Kennedy, R. A., B.A., M.D., C.M. Ottawa, 150 Metcalfe St.
1918 Kennedy, R. B., M.B. .... Essex
1907 Kennedy, W. B. D. .... Cameron Falls
1920 Kenner, H. B., M.D., C.M. ..... Stratford
1908 Kenny, R. Y., M.B. .... Sarnia
1884 Kent, F. D., M.B. .... Thornbury
1907 Kerfoot, H. Wilfred, M.D., C.M. . Smith's Falls
1904 Kerfoot, W. J., M.B. .... Prescott
1918 Kerr, M. R., M.D., C.M. .... Elgin
1919 Kerr, M. G., M.B. .... Toronto, 687 Lansdowne Ave.
1894 Kerr, Thomas, M.D., C.M. ..... Toronto, 675 Dovercourt Rd.
1889 Kerr, William, M.D., C.M. ..... Toronto, 687 Lansdowne Ave.
1900 Kerr, W. A., M.D., C.M. .... Elora
1909 Keyes, J. E. L., M.B. .... Toronto, 75 Bloor St., E.
1907 Keys, S. J., M.D., C.M. .... Kingston, 255 Queen St.
1888 Kidd, D. A., M.D., C.M. .... Atwood
1872 Kidd, Edward, M.D. .... Trenton
1910 Kidd, George C., M.B. .... Brockville
1910 Kidd, G. E., B.A., M.D., C.M. .. Ottawa, 360 Bay St.
1883 Kidd, J. F., M.D., C.M. .... Ottawa, 221 O'Connor Street
1921 Kilborn, Leslie G, M.A., M.B. .. Toronto, 79 Charles St. W.
1892 Kilbourn, Benjamin, B.A., M.B. Toronto, 236 Annette St.
1907 Kilgour, Donald McE., M.B. ......Toronto, 6 Ridout S.
1905 Killoran, J. F. L., M.B. ...... Toronto, 862 College St.
1906 Kindred, H. C., M.D., C.M. .... Tweed
1886 King, E. E., M.D., C.M. ...... Toronto, 61 Queen St. E.
1870 King, Frank, M.D. .... Toronto, 17 Warren Rd.
1893 King, James .... Leamington
1898 King, J. H., M.D. .... Morriston
1916 King, J. Leslie, M.B. .... Milton
1914 King, J. W. deC., M.D. .... Peterboro
1911 King, P. O., M.D. .... St. Thomas'
1893 King, R. B., B.A., M.D., C.M. ... Newboro
1920 Kingswood, R. C., M.D. ...... London, 383 Princess Ave.
1906 Kinnear, J. A., M.D., C.M. ...... Toronto, 267 Russell Hill Rd.
1912 Kinsella, M. D. B., M.D., C.M. .. Toronto, 84 College St.
1910 Kinsey, A. L., M.B. ...,..... Hearst.
1915 Kinsey, H. I., M.B. .... Toronto, 415 Bloor St. W.
1920 Kinsman, J. D., M.B. .... Fonthill
1880 Kippax, J. R., M.D. .... Brantford

1908 Kirby, P. J., M.B. .... Guelph
1911 Kirby, T. S., M.B. .... Kitchener
1912 Kirby, W. J., M.B. .... Toronto, 363 Danforth Ave.
1907 Kirkpatrick, C. G., M.B. .... Orillia
1919 Kirkup, N. N., M.B. .... South Porcupine
1914 Kister, C. O. E., B.A., M.B. .... St. Catharines
1919 Kiteley, Elizabeth, M.B. .... Espanola
1911 Kitt, A. N., M.B. .... Whitney
1898 Klotz, J. E., M.B. .... Westboro
1921 Kniewasser, A. V., M.D., C.M. . Ottawa, 667 King Edward Ave.
1904 Knister, C. E., M.B. .... Comber
1900 Knox, A. A., B.A., M.B. ...... St. Mary's
1914 Knox, J. E., M.B. .... Toronto, 53 College St.
1915 Koljonen, Heikki, B.A., M.B. .. Sudbury
1909 Krupp, Weston, M.B. .... Woodstock
1905 Kyle, N. D., M.B. .... Fergus
1902 Kyles, R. N., B.A., M.D., C.M. .. Orangeville
1899 LaBelle, James S., M.D., C.M. . Windsor
1915 Labelle, J A., M.B. .... Ottawa, 250 Somerset St.
1906 Labrosse, J.L.A., B.A., M.B., C.M. St. Eugene
1915 Lacasse, Gustave, M.D. .... Tecumseh
1908 Lackner, H. M., M.B. .... Kitchener
1876 Lackner, H. G., M.B. .... Kitchener
1919 Ladouceur, F., B.A., M.D., C.M. .... Casselman
1882 Lafferty, James, M.B. .... Hamilton, 24 Bay St. S.
1914 Laframboise, J. M., B.A., M.D., C.M.. Ottawa, 692 St. Patrick St.
1913 L'Africain, Eugene, M.D. .... Sudbury
1907 Laidlaw, C., B.A., M.D., C.M. .. Ottawa, 251 Elgin St.
1903 Laidlaw, J. H., B.A., M.D., C.M.... Ottawa, 295 Cooper St.
1909 Lailey, W. W., B.A., M.B. ...... Toronto, 43 Avenue Rd.
1911 Laing, A. V., M.D., C.M. ...... Port Colborne
1919 Laing, G. F., M.D., C.M. .... Windsor
1919 Laing, J. R., M.D., C.M. .... Hamilton, 288 Locke St. S.
1893 Laird, C. J., M.D., C.M. .... Southampton
1906 Laird, W S., M.B. .... Guelph
1899 Lake, E. J., M.D., C.M. .... Kingston, 258 Bagot St.
1869 Lake, S. K., M.D. .... Kingston, 357 Johnson St.
1910 Lake, W. E. .... Ridgetown
1905 Lalonde, A. J., M.D. .... Cornwall
1913 Lamy, J. L., M.D. .... Ottawa, 169 St. Patrick St.
1919 Lane, H. B., M.B. .... Toronto, 20 Alhambra Ave.
1910 Lane, R. D., M.B. .... Toronto, 1201 Bloor St.
1911 Lane, R. T., M.B. .... Sault Ste. Marie
1889 Lanfear, H. O., M.D., C.M. .... Melrose
1915 Lang, D. E., B.A., M.B. .... Nesterville
1910 Lang, O. K., M.B. .... Toronto, 90 Walmsley Blvd.
1888 Langford, C. B., M.D., C.M. .... Blenheim
1909 Langmaid, C. A., M.D., C.M. ... Windsor
1895 Langrill, A. S., M.B. .... Hamilton, 229 King St. W.
1866 Langrill, J. A., M.B. .... Hamilton, 229 King St. W.
1891 Langrill, W. F., M.B. .... Hamilton, General Hospital.
1904 Langs, M. H., M.B. .... Hamilton, 257 Main St. E.

1907 Langstaff, Lillian C., M.B. ..... Richmond Hill
1891 Langstaff, Rolph L., M.D., C.M. . Richmond Hill
1908 Lannin, G. E. J. .... Hamilton, 150 St. James St. S.
1920 Lanspeary, W. D., M.B. .... Windsor
1920 Lapointe, Hector, M.D. .... Ottawa, Buckingham Apts.
1893 Lapp, L. P., B.A., M.D., C.M. ... Toronto, 7.73 Dufferin St.
1886 Lapp, T. C., M.D., C.M. ...... Cobourg
1904 Large, Fred, M.B. .... Windsor
1915 Larocque, Edmond, M.B. ...... Plantagenet
1905 Laroque, J. B., B.A., M.D., C.M. . Alfred
1921 Latchford, J. K., B.A., M.B. ... Toronto, 151 St. George St.
1902 Latta, E. E., M.D., C.M. ...... Colborne
1906 Lauchland, L. C., B.A., M.D., C.M.... Dundas
1919 Laughlen, B. V. M., M.B. ..... Toronto, 495 Broadview Ave.
1917 Laughlen, G., M.B. .... Toronto, 495 Broadview Ave.
1921 Laughlin, E. R., M.B. .... Belleville
1895 Laurie, C. N., M.D., C.M. ...... Port Arthur
1919 Laurie, Wilfrid J., M.D. .... Niagara-on-the-Lake
1900 Lavine, Samuel, M.D., C.M. .... Toronto, 159 Beverley St.
1901 Law, Robert, M.D., C.M. ...... Ottawa, 190 Laurier Ave. E.
1920 Lawler, Ambrose B., M.D., C.M. Kingston, 218 Alfred St.
1887 Lawrence, F. O., M.D., C.M. ... St. Thomas
1911 Lawson, A. Smirle, M.B. ...... Toronto, 82 College St.
1894 Lawson, J. A., M.B. .... Brampton
1908 Lawson, J. H., B.A., M.B. ...... Toronto, 903 College St.
1885 Lawton, T. M., M.D., C.M. .... Ridgetown
1919 Lazenby, F. S., M.B. .... White River
1906 Leach, G. C., B.A., M.D., C.M. .. Hamilton, 409 King St. E.
1918 Leach, J. W., M.B. .... Rocklyn
1912 Leach, W. J., M.B. .... Manotick
1917 Leacy, P. A., M.B. .... Capreol
1902 Leader, R. W., M.B. .... Wheatley
1919 Leahy, W. H., M.D., C.M. ..... Sault Ste. Marie
1919 Leatherdale, I. J., M.D. ...... Jarvis
1920 Leavine, S. F., M.D., C.M. ..... Elgin
1921 Lee, Alder P., M.B. .... Kingsville
1912 Lee, J. G., M.B. .... Toronto, 650 Broadview Ave.
1896 Lee, J. P., M.D., C.M. .... Kingsville
1917 Leech, F. W., M.B. ..:....... North Bay
1916 Leeds, J. H., M.B. .... Wellandport
1919 Lees, H. Hislop, M.D., C.M. ... Windsor
1904 Leeson, J. D., M.B. .... Aylmer
1912 Legault, J. H., M.D., C.M. ..... Ottawa, 143 Murray St.
1917 Legault, Louis, M.D. .... Crysler
1902 Leggett, T. H., M.D., C.M. ..... Ottawa, 287 Elgin St.
1921 Lehman, E. J., M.B. .... North Bay
1875 Leitch, Archibald, M.B. .... St. Thomas
1920 LeMay, J. A., M.D., C.M. .... Ottawa, 142 St. Patrick St.
1911 LeMesurier, A. B., M.B. ...... Toronto, 310 Bloor St. W.
1879 Leonard, R. A., M.D., C.M. .... Napanee
1918 Leonard, S. C., M.B. .... Hanover
1883 Lepper, W. J., M.B. .... Toronto, 8 Lonsdale Rd.
1910 Leslie, N. V., M.B. .... Hamilton, 69 Main St. W.
1920 LeTouzel, J. Robert, M.D. ..... London, 382 Ontario St.
1919 Letts, Frank L., M.B. .... Mildmay

1916 Lewis, Charles T., M.B. .... Detroit, Mich.
1914 Lewis, E. P., B.A., M.B. ..... Toronto. 102 College St.
1916 Lewis, G. F., M.B. .... Windsor
1907 Lewis, W. A., M.D., C.M. ..... Barrie
1915 Ley, A. G., M.B. .... Toronto, 354 Danforth Ave.
1920 Leys, W. M., M.D., C.M. .... Montreal, P.Q.
1915 Lighthall, D. S., M.B. .... Picton
1905 Limbert, M. H., M.B. .... Parry Sound
1916 Lindsay, A. R., M.B. .... St. Catharines
1886 Lindsay, James, M.D., C.M. ... Guelph
1899 Lindsay, John C., M.B. .... London, 719 Dundas St.
1911 Linscott, Garretson, M.B. ..... Toronto, 288 Roncesvalles Ave.
1921 Linton, James A., M.B. .... Toronto, 567 Christie St.
1912 Lipman, Arthur, B.A., M.D., C.M. Richards Landing
1920 Lipsett, Henry, M.B. .... Toronto, 258 Simcoe St.
1894 Lipsey, R. M., M.B. .... St. Thomas
1920 Lipsitt, G. E., M.B. .... Marksville
1885 Little, A. T., M.D., C.M. ...... Barrie
1921 Little, George D., M.D., C.M. ... Outremont, Montreal, P. Q.
1906 Little, G. G., M.B. .... Walkerville
1920 Little, Harold S., M.B. .... Ridgetown
1915 Little, O. J. S., M.B. .... Toronto, Oakwood & Vaughan
1920 Little, T. R., M.B. .... Kingston, 95 Clergy St. W.
1920 Little, W. C., M.B. .... Barrie
1913 Livingston, F. J., B.A., M.B. ... Toronto, 53 College St.
1911 Livingston, J. M., B.A., M.B. .. Waterloo
1916 Livingstone, D. M., M.B. ...... Dundas
1915 Livingstone, G. C., M.B. .... Toronto, 457 Dovercourt Rd.
1911 Livingstone, H. D., M.B. ...... Listowel
1894 Livingstone, H. D., M.D., C.M. .. Toronto, 332 Bloor St. W.
1920 Lloyd, F. P., M.A., M.B. ...... Toronto, 34 Tennis Cres.
1918 Lloyd, I. M., M.B. .... Sault Ste. Marie
1918 Lloyd, W. H., M.D., C.M. ..... Chesterville
1921 Locke, Arthur C., M.D., C.M. ... Kingston, Queen's University
1918 Locke, H. W. B., M.B. .... Toronto, 159 Walmer Rd.
1906 Locke, M. W. .... Williamsburg
1913 Lockett, W. F., M.D., C.M. ..... Hamilton, 907 King St. E.
1893 Lockhart, A. S., M.D., C.M. .... Toronto, 3216 Dundas St. W.
1890 Lockhart, G. D., M.D., C.M. ... King
1920 Logan, F. A., B.A., M.B. .... Niagara Falls
1903 Logan, Harris, B. A., M.B. ..... Niagara Falls S.
1886 Logie, William, M.D., C.M. .... Sarnia
1919 Logie, W. D., M.B. .... Sarnia
1886 Logie, W. J., B.A., M.D., C.M. .. Paris
1907 Longmore, H. B., B.A., M.D., C.M. Campbellford
1887 Loucks, W. F., M.D., C.M. ..... Campbellford
1906 Loudon, J. D., B.A., M.B. ...... Toronto, 83 St. George St.
1921 Loudon, T. G., M.D., C.M. ..... Lindsay
1913 Lougheed, G. W., M.D. .... Toronto, 675 Bathurst St.
1919 Lougher, Fred, H., M.B. ...... Kingston, 283 Queen St.
1920 Loughlin, E. I., M.D. .... London, 757 Richmond St.
1870 Lovett, William, M.D., C.M. .... Woodstock
1918 Low, Donald M., M.B. .... Toronto, General Hospital
1916 Lowe, William A., M.B. .... Bruce Mines
1914 Lowrey, B. D., M.B. .... Toronto, 970 Ossington Ave.
1906 Lowrey, R. C., M.B. .... Toronto, 1847 Dufferin St.

1920 Lowrie, H. A., M.B. . . . . Toronto, 501 Markham St.
1902 Lowry, W. H., M.D., C.M. . . . . Toronto, 100 College St.
1874 Lowry, W. H., M.B. . . . . Guelph
1885 Lucy, Robert, M.D., C.M. . . . . . . Guelph
1897 Ludwig, A .G., M.D., C.M. . . . . St. Catharines
1919 Lumb, S. S., M.B. . . . . Eldorado
1919 Lunz, Gerald J. . .: . . . . Hamilton, 14 Cannon St. W.
1902 Lusk, C. P., M.D., C.M. . . . . Toronto, 250 Bloor St. W.
1908 Lyman, W. S., Phm.B., M.D., C.M. . . Ottawa, 292 Somerset St.
1921 Lynch, M. G., M.D., C.M. . . . . . . Kingston, 240 Johnston St.
1890 Lynd, Ida E., M.D., C.M. . . . . . . Toronto, 224 Dovercourt Rd.
1919 Lyon, Benjamin, M.B. . . . . Kingston, 447 Johnston St.
1920 Lyon, R. C., M.B. . . . . Kingston, 447 Johnston St.
1905 Lyon, S. Mortimer, M.D., C.M. . Toronto, 122 Bloor St. W.
1911 Mabee, H. C., M.D., C.M. . . . . . . Odessa
1887 Mabee, J. E., M.D., C.M. . . . . . . Odessa
1909 Mabee, O. R., M.D., C.M. . . . . . Toronto, 419 Bloor St. W.
1909 Mabee, W. J., M.B. . . . . Toronto, 468 Church St.
1911 Macallum, A. B., B.A., M.D. . . . . Toronto, 243 College St.
1891 Macartney, G. P., M.D., C.M. . . . Stratford
1913 Macauley, A. F., M.D. . . . . Ottawa, 22 Vittoria St.
1911 Macauley, B. N., M.B. . . . . Dunnville
1919 MacAvelia, M. T., M.D., C.M. . . . Fort William
1910 MacBeth, W. L. C., M.B. . . . . . Toronto, 160 Jamieson Ave.
1916 MacCallum, A. J., M.B. . . . . Windsor
1897 MacCallum, E. C. D., M.D., C.M. Kingston, 302 Barrie St.
1887 MacCallum, J. M., B.A., M.D., C.M. . Toronto, 13 Bloor St. W.
1894 MacCarthy, G. S., M.D., C.M. . . . Ottawa, 110 Lisgar St.
1919 MacDermott, W. B., M.B. . . . . . London, 695 Talbot St.
1872 Macdonald, Albert A., M.B. . . . . Toronto, 12 Bedford Rd.
1919 MacDonald, A. E., M.B. . . . . Brantford
1916 MacDonald, A. R., M.B. . . . . Toronto, 106 Runnymede Rd.
1901 MacDonald, F. C., B.A., M.B. . . . . . . St. Catharines
1919 MacDonald, H. M., M.D., C.M. . . . . . . Oshawa
1908 MacDonald, J. D., M.D. . . . . Huntsville
1919 MacDonald, J.D., M.B. . . . . Essex
1919 Macdonald, J. H., M.B. . . . . Smith's Falls
1920 Macdonald, J. O., B.Sc.; M.D. . . Kingston, 113 Johnston St.
1890 MacDonald, J. A., M.B. . . . . Markham
1907 MacDonald, J. D., M.D. . . . . Ingersoll
1898 MacDonald, John M., M.D., C.M. . . . . Toronto, 687 Pape Ave.
1915 MacDonald, J. A., M.D. . . . . Worthington
1912 MacDonald, Marshall, M.B. . . . . Thedford
1900 Macdonald, William, A., M.B. . . . . . . Windsor
1901 MacDonald, W. J., M.D., C.M. . . . . . . St. Catharines
1916 Macdougall, C. S., M.B. . . . . Toronto, 415 Bloor St. W.
1888 Macdougall, D. S., M.D., C.M. . . . . . Russell
1910 Macdougall, G. L., B.A., M.B. . . Harriston
1920 Macfarlane, D. A., M.B. . . . . . . Ste Agathe des Monts, P. Q.
1908 MacFarlane, P. B, B.A,. M.B. . . Hamilton, 152 James St. S.
1905 MacGillivray, T. D., B.A., M.D., C.M. Port Arthur
1921 MacGregor, D. A, M.D. . . . . . . Ottawa, 413 Jackson Building
1891 MacGregor, J. A., M.D. . . . . London, 496 Waterloo St.

1919 MacGregor, R. R., M.B. ...... Toronto, 13 Grosvenor St.
1912 MacHaffie, L. P., M.D., C.M. ... Ottawa, 251 Elgin St.
1873 Machell, H. T., M.D. .... Toronto, 459 Avenue Rd.
1919 MacIntyre, G. D., M.D., C.M. .. Vankleek Hill
1914 Macintyre, Horace, M.B. .... Toronto, 214 St. John's Rd.
1920 Mack, Harold J., M.D. .... Cornwall
1895 MacKay, Alexander, M.D., C.M. . Toronto, Prov. Brd. Health
1871 MacKay, Andrew, M.D. .... Woodstock
1916 MacKay, Angus, M.B. .... Toronto, 606 Spadina Ave.
1891 MacKay, Charles, M.D., C.M. .. Seaforth
1904 MacKay, C. M., M.B. .... Woodstock
1911 MacKay, Charles R., M.B. .... Unionville
1916 MacKay, W. M., M.D., C.M. ... Portsmouth
1895 MacKechnie, W. G., M.D., C.M. .... Toronto, 96 College St.
1893 MacKendrick, H. F., M.D., C.M. Galt
1900 MacKenzie, A. J., B.A., M.B. .. Toronto, 12 Avenue Rd.
1917 MacKenzie, A. E., M.B. .... Niagara Falls
1909 MacKenzie, C. R., M.B. ...... St. Thomas
1908 MacKenzie, D. W., M.B. ...... Victoria Harbor
1912 Mackenzie, E. A., M.B. .... Port Colborne
1917 Mackenzie, J. W., M.B. .... Weston
1919 Mackie, J. W., M.B. .... Lansdowne
1916 MacKinlay, Robert, M.B. .... Sarnia
1909 MacKinnon, A. J., M.B. .... Zurich
1872 MacKinnon, Angus, M.B. ...... Guelph
1919 MacKinnon, K. L., M.B. .... Renfrew
1896 Macklin, A. H., M.B. .... Goderich
1895 Macklin, Daisy M., M.D., C.M. . Stratford
1874 MacLaren, A., M.D. .... London, 424 Queen's Ave.
1896 MacLaren, P. S., M.D., C.M. .... Ottawa, 91 O'Connor St.
1906 MacLaren, R. T., M.D., C.M. .. Whitby
1903 MacLaurin, N. T., M.B. .... Toronto, 717 Spadina Ave.
1868 MacLean, Archibald, M.D., C.M. Sarnia
1899 MacLean, J. N., M.D., C.M. .... Magpie Mine
1911 Maclean, K. T., M.D. .... London, 442 Clarence St.
1916 MacLennan, D. S., M.B. ...... Toronto, 194 Albany Ave.
1901 MacLennan, D. N., M.D., C.M. . Toronto, 126 Bloor St. W.
1919 MacLeod, D. A., M.D., C.M. ... Hamilton, 185 Britannia Ave.
1908 MacLeod, J. A., M.B. .... Orangeville
1920 MacLeod, J. G., M.D., C.M. .... Dunvegan
1908 MacLeod, Neil, M.B. .... Ottawa, 121 Cartier St.
1901 MacLoghlin, Fforde E., M.B. ... Hamilton. 452 Main St. E.
1887 MacMahon, J. A., M.B. .... St. Catharines
1916 MacMahon, V. Paul, M.B. ...... St. Catharines
1908 MacMillan, A. D., M.D., C.M. ... Finch
1907 MacMillan, R. J., M.B. .... Toronto, 74 Gerrard St. E.
1900 MacMurchy, Helen, M.D. ...... Ottawa, Dept. Pub. Health
1916 MacMurchy, John A., M.B. .... Dresden
1897 Macnamara, A. T., M.B. ...... Toronto, 2052 Davenport Rd.
1888 MacNaughton, P., M.D., C.M. ... Cobourg
1917 MacNeil, G. W., M.B. .... Owen Sound
1918 Macpherson, A. W., M.B. ..... South River
1920 Macpherson, D. G., M.B., Ch.B. . Toronto
1908 Macpherson, G. A., M.B. ...... Toronto, 2343 Queen St. E.
1915 Macpherson, J. R., M.D. ...... Duart
1919 MacTavish, C. R., M.B. .... Grant

```
1919  Madden, O. M., M.B.  ........ Buffalo, N. Y.
1904  Magee, C. F.  ............... Carp
1921  Magner, William, M.B., B.Ch. .. Toronto, St. Michael's  Hosp.
1907  Magwood, S. N. J., M.B.  ...... Toronto, 414 Dovercourt Rd.
1913  Mahoney, J. L., M.B.  ........ Niagara Falls
1906  Mahood, A. E., B.A., M.D., C.M. Ottawa, 160 Metcalfe St.
1892  Mair, A. W.  ............... Chesley
1907  Mair, W. L.  ............... Holstein
1916  Maitland, H. B., M.B.  ........ Toronto, 54 Simpson Ave.
1921  Maitland, K. R., M.D., C.M.  .... Brighton
1921  Malcolmson, A. S., M.B.  ....... St. Catharines
1897  Malloch, Neil, M.D., C.M.  ...... Winchester
1899  Malone, H. V., B.A., M.D., C.M. Frankford
1898  Maloney, M. J., M.D., C.M.  .... Eganville
1918  Malyon, Roy H., M.B.  ........ Sundridge
1906  Manion, R. J., M.D., C.M.  ...... Fort William
1869  Mann, James, M.D.  .......... Renfrew
1911  Mann, J. B., M.B.  ........... Peterboro
1907  Mann, R. W., M.D., C.M.  ...... Toronto, 184 Bloor St. E.
1913  Manning, H. K., M.B.  ........ Toronto, 2 St. Clair Ave. W.
1908  Manson, J. Sproule, M.B.  ...... Toronto, 250 Huron St.
1917  Marcellus, T. N., M.D., C.M.  ... Georgetown
1910  Marcy, W. J. M., M.B.  ........ Oakville
1920  Markson, Moses, M.D., C.M .... Toronto, General Hospital
1872  Marlatt, C. W., M.B.  ........ St. Thomas
1877  Marlatt, George A., M.B.  ...... Toronto, 38 Symington Ave.
1915  Marlow, Fred C., M.B.  ........ Toronto, 647 Broadview Ave.
1901  Marlow, F. W., M.D., C.M.  ... Toronto, 417 Bloor St. W.
1896  Marquis, J. A., M.B.  ........ Brantford
1893  Marr, Delaski, M.B.  .......... Ridgetown
1895  Marselis, E. H., M.D., C.M.  ... Iroquois
1921  Martin, A. D., M.B.  .......... St. Mary's
1912  Martin, A. C., M.B.  .......... Hamilton, 173 West Ave. N.
1893  Martin, Frank, M.B.  ......... Dundalk
1905  Martin, H. P., M.B.  ......... Toronto, 36 Carlton St.
1914  Martin, H. S., M.B.  ......... Hamilton, 564 King St. E.
1915  Martin, H. C., M.B.  ......... Toronto, 53 College St.
1919  Martin, H. W., M.B.  ......... Hamilton, 173 West Ave. N.
1921  Martin, R. C., M.B.  ......... Newburgh
1919  Martin, W. E., M.B.  ......... Toronto, 1432 Queen St. E.
1885  Marty, John  ............... New Hamburg
1917  Martyn, W. M., M.B.  ........ Toronto, 538 St. Clair Ave. W.
1900  Mason, Homer, M.D., C.M.  .... Toronto, 119 Annette St.
1890  Mason, R. H., M.B.  ......... Kingston, The Ontario Hosp.
1905  Mason, W. E., M.D., C.M.  ..... Toronto, 585 Church St.
1903  Mason, W. R., M.D., C.M.  ...... Parry Sound
1917  Masse, L. V., M.D.  ........... Verner
1920  Masson, Duncan M., B.A., M.B.. Toronto, 112 St. Vincent St.
1886  Mather, W. M., M.D., C.M.  ..... Tweed
1916  Mathers, J. A., M.B.  ......... Hamilton, 220 Ottawa St. N.
1916  Matheson, D. C., M.B.  ........ Kingston, Queen's Univ.
1905  Matheson, J. J., M.B.  ........ Toronto, 2377 Dundas St. W.
1912  Mathieson, Lily B., M.B.  ...... Toronto, 341 Danforth Ave.
1914  Matthews, R. A., M.D.  ........ Toronto, 673 Broadview Ave.
1920  Matthews, W. R., B.A., M.D.  ... London, 611 Colborne St.
1912  Mavety, A. F., M.B.  ......... Toronto, 1 Baby Point Rd.
```

1890 Mavety, A. C., M.D., C.M. ...... Toronto, 173 Mavety Ave.,
1898 Maw, Herbert, .M.D., C.M. ..... Caledonia,
1892 Mayburry, A. W., M.D., C.M. ...... Toronto, 329 Bloor St. W.,
1897 Maybury, W. F., B.A., M.B. ... Ottawa, 40 Nepean St.,
1914 Maynard, J. C., M.B. .... Toronto, 151 Bloor St. W.,
1921 Mayne, Cecil H., M.B. .... Drayton,
1881 Mearns, W. A., M.B. .... Hanover,
1889 Meek, E., M.B. .... Port Rowan,
1878 Meek, Harry, M.B. .... London, 330 Queen's Ave.,
1903 Meighen, W. A., M.D., C.M. .... Perth,
1883 Meikle, T. D., M.B. .... Mount Forest,
1883 Meldrum, J. A., M.B. .... Weston,
1904 Meldrum, W. N., M.B. .... Norwich,
1903 Mellow, F. E., M.D., C.M. ..... Uxbridge,
1884 Mellow, S. J., M.D., C.M. ...... Port Perry,
1917 Membery, G. G., M.D., C.M. .... Adolphustown,
1905 Menard, A. J., M.D. .... Windsor,
1894 Mencke, J. R., M.D., C.M. ...... Bridgeburg,
1910 Menzies, P. K., B.A., M.B. .... Toronto, 155 Bloor St. E.
1899 Menzies, R. D., M.A., M.D., C. M. Iroquois Falls,
1878 Merrison, J. E., M.B. .... Sarnia,
1888 Merritt, W. H., M.D., C.M. .... St. Catharines.
1899 Messecar, J. W., M.B. .... Milles Roches,
1896 Metcalfe, A. A., M.D., C.M. .... Almonte,
1866 Metherill, G. W., M.D. .... Burlington,
1888 Meyers, D. Campbell, M.D., C.M. Toronto, 72 Heath St. W.
1890 Michell, A. V., M.B. .... Toronto, 835 Bathurst St.,
1903 Michell, W. A. R., M.B. .... Perth,
1919 Mick, E. C., M.B. .... Cobden,
1892 Middlebro, T. H., M.B. .... Owen Sound,
1913 Middleton, J. J., M.B. .... Toronto, Prov. Brd. Health,
1921 Middleton, R. H., M.B. .... Caledonia,
1887 Midgley, J. E., M.D., C.M. .... Detroit, Mich.,
1919 Millan, K. E., M.D., C.M. ...... Toronto, 5 Lowther Ave.,
1909 Millar, Adam H., M.B. .... Toronto, 70 Gerrard St., E.
1906 Millen, S. F., M.B. .... South Woodslee,
1877 Miller, A. H., M.D. .... St. Thomas,
1907 Miller, A. P., M.D., C.M .... Windsor,
1919 Miller, C O., M.B. .... Toronto, 266 Roncesvalles Av.,
1913 Miller, G. R., M.B. .... Stayner,
1920 Miller, James, M.B., Ch.B. ..... Kingston, Queen's Univ.,
1919 Miller, John R., M.B. .... Iroquois,
1895 Milligan, A. A., M.D., C.M. .... Toronto, 803 College St.,
1878 Millman, Thomas, M.D. .... Toronto, 490 Huron St.,
1916 Mills, C. V., M.B. .... Sandwich,
1919 Mills, J. D., M.D., C.M. .... Toronto, 1218 Davenport Rd.,
1921 Mills, Oscar G., M.B. .... Tottenham,
1920 Mills, S. G., B.A., M.B. .... Toronto, 756 Broadview Ave.,
1910 Millyard, W. S., M.B. .... Coboconk,
1889 Milne, W. J., M.D., C.M. ...... Blyth,
1889 Milner, B. Z., M.D., C.M. ..... Toronto, 100 St. George St.,
1893 Minnes, S., M.A., M.R., C.M. ...... Ottawa, 183 Metcalfe St.,
1908 Minns, F. S., M.D. .... Toronto, 120 St. Clair Ave. W.,
1909 Minthorn, H. L., M.B. .... Timmins,
1912 Mitchell, E. W., M.B. .... Cobalt,

```
1874  Mitchell, F. H. .............|.. Komoka,
1915  Mitchell, H. K., M.B. .......... Sioux Lookout,
1916  Mitchell, I. N., M.B. .......... Welland Junction,
1893  Mitchell, J. A., M.D., C.M. .... Drumbo
1899  Mitchell, J. P., M.B. .......... Toronto, 320 Bloor St. W.,
1921  Mitchell, N. H., M.B. .......... Hamilton, 42 Florence St.,
1917  Mitchell, W. T. B., M.B. ....... London, Westminster Hosp.,
1916  Mitton, O. W., M.D. ........... Granton,
1915  Moffat, A. B., B.A., M.B. ...... Toronto,1028 Logan Ave.;
1911  Moffat, H. B.,.M.B. ........... Ottawa, 278 O'Connor St.,
1921  Moffat, W. W., B.A., M.B. ..... Teeswater,
1906  Mohr, F. W. C., M.D., C.M. .... Ottawa, 377 Friel St.,
1903  Moir, Archibald, Phm.B., M.B. . Peterboro,
1896  Moles, E. B., M.D., C.M. ....... Brockville,
1893  Moloney, P. J., M.D., C.M. .... Toronto, Prov, Brd. Health,
1915  Monfette, Georges ............ Alexandria,
1895  Monteith, J. D., M.D., C.M. .... Stratford,
1916  Montgomery, Albert, M.B. ..... Toronto, 306 Ryrie Bldg.,
1921  Montgomery, R. C., M.B. .....; Harriston,
1890  Montgomery, Wilson, M.D., C.M. Embro,.
1919  Moody, A. J., M.B. .......... Windsor,
1915  Moon, A. A., M.B. ........... Windsor,
1921  Moon, Harold R., M.B. ....... Toronto, Wellsboro Apts.
1909  Mooney, C. N., M.B. ......... Toronto, 1893 Davenport Rd.,
1887  Moore, C. F., M.D., C.M. ...... Toronto, 17 Isabella St.,
1874  Moore, C. S. .............. London, 376 Wellington St.,
1899  Moore, Francis, M.B. ........ Clarksburg,
1909  Moore, H.H., M.D. ........... Timmins,
1901  Moore, James M.D., C.M. ..... Listowel,
1900  Moore, James, M.D., C.M. .... Brooklin,
1891  Moore, J. J., M.D., C.M. ...... Brooklin,
1904  Moore, M. Hilton, M.D., C.M. ... Athens,
1896  Moore, R., M.D., C.M. ........ Fort Frances,
1898  Moore, Samuel, M.D. ......... Toronto, 1041 Bloor St. W.,
1907  Moorhead, A. S., M.B. ......... Toronto, 146 Bloor St. W.,
1919  Moorhouse, V. H. K., B.A., M.B. Toronto, 40 Pleasant Blvd.,
1875  Moorhouse, W. H., M.B. ...... London, 249 Queen's Ave.,
1872  Moran, J. B., M.B. .......... Toronto, 1010 Gerrard St. E.,
1913  Morand, Raymond D., M.D. .... Windsor,
1901  Morgan, A. E., M.B. .......... Toronto, 817 Lansdowne Ave.,
1914  Morgan, C. R. L., M.D., C.M. ... Hamilton, The Mt. San.,
1910  Morgan, E A. W., M.B. ....... Toronto, 310 Bloor St. W.
1908  Morgan, A. H. E., M.B. ...... Chesley,
1898  Morgan, J. A., M.B. ......... Peterboro,
1915  Morgan, W. C., M.D. ......... Roslin,
1919  Moriarty, James, M.D. ....... Chatham,
1892  Morris, C. E. ............. London, R.R. 4.,
1906  Morris, J. I., M.B. ........... Hamilton, 524 King St. E.,
1921  Morris, Nelson D., B.A., M.B. ... Orillia,
1900  Morris, S. J., M.D. ........... Mount Elgin,
1899  Morrison, C. A. A., M.D., C.M. .. Kingston, 208 Bagot St.,
1914  Morrison, D. A., M.D., C.M. .... Brantford,
1921  Morrison, G. Wendell, M.D., C.M. New York City, 10 W. 131st St.
1918  Morrison, M. C., M.D., C.M. .... Thorndale,
1911  Morrison, N. A., M.B. ....... New Dundee,
1911  Morrison, Lindsay, M.B. ...... Toronto, 1845 Dufferin St.,
```

Morrison, T., M.B. .... Hamilton, 2 Grant Ave.,
Morrison, W., B.A., M.D., C.M. . Toronto, 248 Danf.rth Ave.,
Morrison, W. C., M.B. .... Sudbury,
Morrow, Calvin, M.D., C.M. ... Metcalfe,
Morrow, F. G., M.D. .... Hamilton, 44 Hughson St. S,.
Morrow, James J., M.D., C.M. . Toronto, 2881 Dundas St. W.,
Morrow, R., M.D. .... Guelph,
Morton, J. P., M.B. .... Hamilton, 148 James St. S.,
Mothersill, G. S., M.D., C M .... Ottawa, 254 O'Connor St.
Mothersill, L. J., M.D., C.M. ... Port Stanley,
Mowbray, F. B., M.B. .... Hamilton, 44 Hughson St. S,.
Moxley, J. H., M.D., C.M. ..... Hamilton, 930 King St. E.,
Moyle, H. B., M.A., M.B. ...... Mimico,
Moyle, R. D. .... London, R.R. 7.,
Muir, David, M.B. .... Toronto, 244 Sherbourne St.,
Mulligan, C. V., M.B. .... Toronto, St. Michael's Hosp.,
Mulligan, F. W., M.D., C.M. ... Petrolia,
Mulligan, J. W., M.D., C.M. .... Fort Coulonge, P. Q.,
Mulligan, W. H. .... Sudbury,
Mullin, J. H., M.B. .... Hamilton, 201 James St. S.,
Mulloy, P. G., M.D., C.M. ...... Morrisburg,
Mulock, M. J., M.D., C.M. ..... St. Catharines.
Mundell, D. E., B.A., M.D., C.M. Kingston, 228 Brock St.,
Munn, F. J., B.A., M.B .... Toronto, 1086 Bloor St. W.,
Munns, A C., M.B. .... Toronto, 1299 Lansdowne Ave.,
Munro, B. D., Phm.B., M.D., C.M. Toronto, 616 Spadina Ave.
Munro, D., M.D., C:M. .... Warsaw,
Munro, G C., M.D., C M .... Smithville,
Munro, J. H. .... Maxville,
Munro, W. A., M.B. .... Cornwall,
Munroe, A. T., M.D., C.M. .... Dalkeith,
Munroe, Finlay, M.D., C.M. .... Paris,
Murdoch, A., M.B. .... Rainy River,
Murphy, A. E., M.D., C.M. .... Stayner,
Murphy, A. L., M.D., C.M. .... Toronto, 713 Dovercourt Rd.,
Murphy, J. E., M.D., C.M. ..... Arnprior,
Murphy, S. H., B.A., M.D., C.M. Renfrew,
Murphy, W. S., B.A., M.D., C.M. Smith's Falls,
Murray, A. J., M.D., C.M. ...... London, 866 Wellington St..
Murray, A. McD., M.B. .... Toronto, 276 Danforth Ave.,
Murray, D. C., M.B. .... Toronto, 989 Gerrard St. E.
Murray, D. W. G., M.B. .... St. Paul's Station
Murray, H. H., B.A., M.B. .... Toronto, 1447 Queen St. W.
Murray, H. G., M.D., C.M. ..... Owen Sound.
Murray, Kenneth, M.B. .... Toronto, 312 St. Clair Ave., W.
Murray, L. M., M.D., C.M. ..... Toronto, 48 Bloor St., E.
Murray, R. S., M.D.. .... Mitchell
Murray, Thomas F., M.D. ..... Wallaceburg
Musgrave, J., M.A., M.D., C.M. .... Toronto, 511 Bloor St. W.
Musson, George, M.B. .... Toronto, 96 Avenue Rd.
Muterer, A. S., M.D. .... Schumacher
Mylks, G. W., M.D., C.M. ...... Kingston, 79 Williams St.
McAllister, Arthur, M.B. ...... Georgetown
McAlpine, John, M.D. .... Lindsay
McAlpine, Margaret, M.B. .... Toronto, 619 Bathurst St.
McAlpine, R. D., M.D. .... Dresden

```
1906  McAndrew, Joseph, M.B. ..... Georgetown
1908  McArthur, A. D., M.B. ........ Toronto, 594 Sherbourne St.
1919  McArthur, E. C., M.B. ........ Toronto, 594 Sherbourne St.
1918  McArthur, J. A., M.D. ........ Blackstock
1892  McAsh, John, M.B. .......... Tara
1921  McAvoy, J. R., M.D., C.M. ..... Napanee
1915  McBain, E. W., M.D. .......... St. Thomas
1919  McBane, J. K., M.D. .......... Rainy River
1895  McBroom, J. A., M.D., C.M. .... Brockville
1908  McBroom, W. T., M.D. ........ Toronto, 1144 Bloor St. W.
1912  McCabe, C. J., M.B. ......... Hamilton, 36 Gore St.
1889  McCabe, J. R., M.D., C.M. .... Strathroy
1909  McCabe, L. G., M.B. ......... Windsor
1896  McCaig, A. S., M.B. ......... Sault Ste. Marie
1918  McCallum, Duncan, M.B. ...... Churchill
1906  McCallum, S., M.A., M.D., C.M. . Niagara Falls
1900  McCallum, S., M.B. .......... Thornbury
1879  McCammon, J. A., M.D., C.M. ... Gananoque
1911  McCammon, J. G., B.A., M.D., C.M... Gananoque
1910  McCann, J. J. F., M.D., C.M. ... Renfrew
1916  McCarroll, F. L., M.D., C.M. ... Espanola
1921  McCart, H. W. D., M.B. ......... Toronto, 364 Spadina Rd.
1898  McCarthy, W. A., M.D., C.M. ... Kingston, 163 Brock St.
1906  McCarthy, Mary Callaghan, M.B. Sault Ste. Marie
1904  McCartney, G. E., M.B. ....... Fort William
1915  McCaul, H. C., M.D. ......... Princeton
1903  McCauley, W. A., M.D., C.M. ... Copper Cliff
1913  McCausland, Archibald, M.B. ... London, The Ontario Hospital
1916  McClelland, J. C., B.A., M.B. ... Toronto, 151 Bloor St. W.
1918  McClelland, J. Harold C., M.B. . Mimico
1891  McClelland, Mars, M.D., C.M. .. Peterboro
1909  McClelland, W. A., M.B. ...... Toronto, 2275 Dundas St. W.
1913  McClenahan, C. A., B.A., M.B. .. Mimico
1894  McClenahan, D. A., M.D., C.M. . Hamilton, 204 Herkimer St.'
1912  McClenahan, R. R., B.A., M.B. . Toronto, 54 Summerhill Gardens
1905  McClennan, A. W., M.B. ...... Toronto, 436 Palmerston Blvd.
1902  McClintock, J. A., M.D., C.M. .. Uxbridge
1920  McClintock, J. J., M.B. ....... Lethbridge, Alta
1888  McClinton, James B. H., M.D., C.M.. Midland
1919  McClinton, W. S., M.B. ....... Midland
1907  McClure, William A., M.B. ..... Woodbridge
1890  McColl, H. A., M.B. .......... Milton
1904  McColl, T. H., M.B. .......... Tilbury
1902  McCollum, J. A., M.B. ........ Toronto, 12 Avenue Rd.
1894  McCollum, W. J., M.B. ........ Toronto, 94 Shuter St.
1905  McComb, R. J. A., M.B. ....... Toronto, 53 College St.
1907  McCombe, J., M.D., C M ...... St. Catharines
1898  McConnell, J. H., M.D., C.M. ... Toronto, 1653 Dundas St., W.
1920  McConney, Florence S., B.A., M.B... Toronto, 81 Collier St.
1889  McConville, Isobel, M.D., C.M. . Kingston, 13 Montreal St.
1902  McCormack, J. M., M.D., C.M. ...... Toronto, 113 Spadina Ave.
1885  McCormack, Norman, M.D., C.M. Renfrew
1910  McCormack, Victor, M.B. ...... Toronto, 2668 Yonge St.
```

1920 McCormack, W. G,. M.B. .... Toronto, 176 Wright Ave.
1909 McCormack, W. G. M., M.B. ... Toronto, 110 Boon 'Ave. .
1909 McCormick, A. M., M.D., C.M. .. Ottawa, 165 Laurier Ave., W..
1898 McCormick, T. A., M.D., C.M. .. Walkerville
1919 McCormick, W. N., M.D. ...... Toronto, 380 King St., W.
1906 McCormick, W. J., B.A., M.D. . Toronto, 32 Gothic' Ave.
1921 McCorvie, C. Ray, M.B. .... Chatham
1918 McCosh, J. T., M.B. .... Toronto, 1978 Dufferin St.
1920 McCoy, E. M., B.A., M.D., C.M. . Belleville
1892 McCoy, S. H., B.A., M.B .... Ottawa, Dept. Mil. and Defence
1912 McCracken, J F., M.B. .... Hagersville
1911 McCracken, W. A., M.D., C.M. .. Martintown
1921 McCuaig, C. H., M.D., C.M. .... Bainsville
1905 McCue, P. F., M.B. .... Walkerton
1913 McCulloch, A. Ernest, B.A., M.B.Toronto, 165 St. Clair Ave., W.
1913 McCulloch, Charles D., M.B. .. Wellington
1904 McCulloch, E. A., B.A., M.B. .. Toronto, 165 St. Clair Ave.. W.
1902 McCulloch, John, M.D., C.M. ... Lindsay
1904 McCulloch, J. M., M.D., C.M. .. Peterboro
1905 McCulloch, R. J. P., M.B. ...... Toronto, 102 College St.
1909 McCulloch, W. G., M.B. .... Orono
1905 McCullough, C. C., M.D., C.M. .... Fort William
1892 McCullough, E. F., M.D., C.M. . Rockwood
1892 McCullough, H. A., B.A., M.B. . Torento. 16 Bloor St-, W.
1866 McCullough, James, M.D. ...... Toronto, 394 Bloor St., W.
1912 McCullough, J. S., M.A., M.B. .. New Liskeard
1916 McCullough, J. C., M.B. .... New Liskeard
1884 McCullough, J. S., M.D., C.M. ... Walter's Falls
1891 McCullough, J. S., M.B. .... Toronto, 394 Bloor St., W.
1890 McCullough, J. W. S., M.D., C.M.Toronto. Prev- Lrd. Health
1891 McCullough, O., B.A., M.D., C.M. .. Levack
1884 McCullough, Thomas, M.D., C.M.Chatsworth
1889 McCullough, T. P., M.D., C.M. .. Peterboro
1876 McCurdy, Archibald, M.B. .... Norwich
1898 McDermid, Archibald, M.D., C.M.Severn Bridge
1912 McDermott, J. P., M.D., C.M. .. Killaloe
1918 McDermott, J. F., M.D., C.M. ... Tavistock
1911 McDermott, J. J., M. D., C.M. ... Massey
1915 McDiarmid, J. S., B.Sc., M.D., C.M.. Dover Centre
1901 McDiarmid, W. B., M.D., C.M. .. Maxville
1890 McDonald, Alexander, M.D. ... Vankleek Hill
1908 McDonald, A., M.D., C.M. ..... Ottawa
1889 McDonald, D. D., M.D., C.M. .... Ottawa, 90 O'Connor St.
1912 McDonald, E. A., M.B. .... Toronto, 688 Broadview Ave.
1920 McDonald, George O., M.B. .... Collingwood
1895 McDonald, H. S., B.A., M.D., C.M.Dresden
1888 McDonald, James A., M.D., C.M.. Kincardine
1918 McDonald, John, M.D., C.M. ... Sault Ste. Marie
1921 McDonald, J. G. L., M.B. ...... Little Current
1916 McDonald, J. L., M.B. .... Toronto, 6 Edgewood Crescent
1919 McDonald, John M., M.B. ...... Highgate
1901 McDonald, Minnie A., M.D., C.M.Hagersville
1892 McDonald, P. A., M.D., C.M. .... Penetanguishene
1899 McDonald, R. G., M.B. .... Sarnia

1895 McDonald, William, B.A., M.B. .... Owen Sound
1890 McDonell, Mary H., M.D., C.M. . Hensall
1914 McDonough, V. A., M.B. ...... Toronto, 714 Dovercourt Rd.
1920 McDougall, B. W. A., M.D. .... London, 515 Princess Ave.
1903 McDougall, C. H., M.D., C.M. ... Strathroy
1866 McDougall, P. A., M.D., C.M. ... Ottawa, 40 Park Ave.
1892 McEachern, Donald, M.D., C.M. .... Linwood ,
1886 McEdwards, D., M.D., C.M. .... Hamilton, 4 Bay St.
1898 McElroy, A. S., M.D., C.M. .... Ottawa, 722 Bank St.
1921 McEwen, Annabel, M.B. .... London, 20 Ardaven Place
1896 McEwen, Duncan, M.D., C.M. .. Maxville
1905 McEwen, F. F., M.B. .... Aylmer
1890 McEwen, J. A., M.D. .... Kazubazua, P. Q.
1910 McEwen, J. A., M.B. .... Carleton Place
1905 McFadden, A. H., M.B. .... Cooksville
1920 McFadden, G. Fern, B.A., M.D., C.M. Hamilton, City Hospital
1908 McFadden, H. M., M.B. .... Thorndale
1900 McFall, W. A., M.B. ......:.... Toronto, 919 College St.
1916 McFarlane, D. C., M.D. .... London, 331 Queen's Ave.
1916 McFarlane, E. C., M.D. ....Priceville
1889 McFarlane, Murray, M.D., C.M. . Toronto, 190 Bloor St., E.
1888 McFarlane, M. A., M.D., C.M. .. Carleton Place
1887 McFaul, A. M., M.D., C.M. ..... Collingwood
1890 McFaul, J. H. .... Toronto, 474 Dovercourt Rd.
1915 McGanity, A. J., M.B. .... Kitchener
1893 McGarry, J. H., M.D, C.M. ..... Niagara Falls
1921 McGarry, John M., M.B. ...... Niagara Falls
1912 McGavin, E. H., M.B. .... Windsor
1921 McGeoch, James R., M.D. .... London, 485 Dufferin Ave.
1918 McGhie, A. G., M.D., C.M. ..... Cayuga
1918 McGhie, B. T., M.B. ....:.. London, Westminster Hosp.
1900 McGibbon, George C., M.D., C.M. Honeywood
1905 McGibbon, Peter, M.B. .... Bracebridge
1882 McGill, H. R., M.B. .... Midland
1888 McGillawee, J., B.A., M.D., C.M. .. Kitchener
1908 McGillicuddy, J. E., M.D.. ..... London, 127 Wortley Rd.
1890 McGillivray, C. F., M.A., M.B. . Whitby
1898 McGillivray, Donald, M.D., C.M. Toronto, 2 Elgin Ave.
1920 McGillivray, James E., M.B. ... Toronto, 20 Breadalbane St.
1889 McGillivray, T. S., M.D., C.M. . Hamilton, 154 James St., S.
1912 McGillvery, F. E. B., M.B. ..... Simcoe
1911 McGlennon, A. C., B.A., M.D., C.M... Colborne
1900 McGrady, J. M., M.D., C.M. ..... Port Arthur
1905 McGregor, J. K., M.B. .... Hamilton, 132 Main St.
1875 McGregor, J. O., M.B. .... Waterdown
1918 McGuffin, G. L., M.D. .... London, 461 Dufferin St.
1921 McHugh, M. J., M.B. .... Weston
1902 McIlwraith, D. G., M.B. .... Hamilton, 230 James St. S.
1894 McIlwraith, Kennedy C., M.B. .. Toronto, 30 Prince Arthur Ave.
1913 McIlwraith, L., M.D. ....Thamesville
1921 McInnis, E. L., M.D. ....St. Thomas
1910 McInnis, J. A., M.B. .... Timmins
1915 McIntosh, A. J., B.A., M.B. ... Toronto, 137 Pape Ave.

1875 McIntosh, D. J., M.D., C.M. ..... Vankleek Hill
1889 McIntosh, D. H., M.D., C.M. .... Carleton Place
1904 McIntosh, J. A. .... Chippawa
1910 McIntosh, J. H., M.B. .... Riceville
1894 McIntosh, L. Y., M.D., C.M. ... Fort William
1905 McIntosh, P. A., B.A., M.D., C.M. Spencerville
1920 McIntosh, P. D., M.B. .... Toronto, 16 Walker Ave.
1896 McIntosh, W. A., M.D., C.M. ... Simcoe
1906 McIntyre, A. A., M.D. .... Glencoe
1915 McIntyre, George, C., M.B. .... Toronto, 469 Parliament St.
1920 McKay, A. L., B.A., M.B. ...... Toronto, 25 Patricia Drive
1917 McKay, A. J., M.D. .... Hamilton, 398 Barton St. E.
1907 McKay, D. J., M.D. .... London, 616 Wellington St.
1889 McKay, Donald, M.D., C.M. .... Collingwood
1912 McKay, D. G. S., M.B. .... Fairbank
1914 McKay, H. A., M.B. .... Hamilton, The Ontario Hosp.
1895 McKay, T. W. G., M.D. .... Oshawa
1910 McKee, J. F., M.D.,-C.M. ...... Heathcote
1918 McKee, J. G., M.D., C.M. ...... Eik Lake
1907 McKee, W. F., M.D., C.M. ..... Cache Bay
1909 McKelvey, Alexander D., M.B. .. Toronto, 160 Bloor St., W.
1915 McKendry, J. J., B.A., M.D., C.M.... Winchester
1870 McKenna, Charles, M.B. .... Toronto, 236 College St.
1906 McKenna, J. A., M.B. .... Toronto, 236 College St.
1886 McKenzie, A. F., M.D. .... Alliston
1896 McKenzie, D. C., M.B. .... Fort Frances
1887 McKenzie, Dugald, M.B. .... Toronto, 182 Symington Ave.
1914 McKenzie, K. G., M.B. .... Toronto, 241 Jarvis St.
1893 McKenzie, W. J., M.B. .... Kingsville
1877 McKeough, G. T., M.D. .... Blenheim
1917 McKeown, Justin, M.B. .... North Bay
1889 McKeown, W., B.A., M.D., C.M. .... Toronto, 140 Wellesley Cres.
1914 McKibbin, A. E., M.B. .... Oshawa
1901 McKichan, M.D., B.A., M.B. ..... Toronto, 686 Broadview Ave.
1920 McKie, J. G. .... Oakville
1913 McKillip, T. H., M.B. .... Toronto, 149 College St.
1885 McKillop, Alexander, M.D., C.M. Dutton
1917 McKillop, C. J. A., M.D. .... St. Thomas
1898 McKillop, D. A., M.D. .... St. Thomas
1905 McKinley, D. F., M.B. .... Toronto, 863 College St.
1910 McKinley, N. J., M.D., C.M. .... Toronto, 82 College St.
1914 McKinley, W. E., M.B. .... Toronto, 1087 Gerrard St. E.
1904 McKinley, W. W., M.D., C.M. .. Port Hope
1898 McKinnon, F. W., M.D., C.M. ... Ottawa, 171 Metcalfe St.
1905 McKinnon, J. P., M.B. .... Guelph
1885 McKinnon, N. C., M.D., C.M. ... Brougham
1921 McKinnon, N. E., M.B. .... Toronto, 178 Cottingham St.
1906 McLachlan, D. F., M.B. .... Windsor
1889 McLachlan, J. Y., M.D. .... Glencoe
1901 McLaren, A. F., M.D., C.M. .... Ottawa, 212 Metcalfe St.
1885 McLaren, D. C., B.A., M.D., C.M. Ottawa, 141 Laurier Ave., W.
1900 McLaren, G. H., M.D., C.M. .... Toronto, 176 Bloor St., E.
1911 McLaren, K. A., M.B. .... Toronto, 504 Dovercourt Rd.
1912 McLaren, Laura M. .... Guelph

1909 McLaren, T. C., M.D., C.M. ...... Cobden
1903 McLaren, T. O., M.D., C.M. .... Lancaster
1915 McLaren, W. R., M.B. .... Sarnia
1915 McLarty, G. A., M.B. .... Toronto, 546 Palmerston Blvd.
1886 McLaughlin, Edward, M.D., C.M. Morrisburg
1888 McLaughlin, Peter, M.D., C.M. . Winchester
1904 McLaughlin, R. P., M.B. .... Ottawa, 113 Hawthorne Ave.
1872 McLay, Archibald, M.D. ...... Woodstock
1904 McLay, H. G., M.D. .... Aylmer
1913 McLay, J. F., B.A., M.B. ...... Grimsby
1911 McLay, S. M., B.A., M.B. ...... Woodstock
1908 McLean, A. A., M.B. .... London, 485 Dundas St.
1913 McLean, C. E., M.D., C.M. ...... Collin's Inlet
1906 McLean, G. D., M.B. .... Woodbridge
1904 McLean, H., M.B. .... Inwood
1899 McLean, J. R., B.A., M.D., C.M. Sault Ste. Marie
1876 McLean, John .... Orillia
1879 McLean, Peter D., M.B. .... Woodbridge
1914 McLean, William J., M.B. ..... London, Westminster Hosp.
1916 McLean, W. J., M.B. .... Shelbourne
1910 McLean, W. T., M.B. .... Toronto, 830 Bloor St., W.
1901 McLeay, Lollard, M.B. .... Gravenhurst
1872 McLellan, Charles, M.B. ...... Trenton
1878 McLellan, J. H., M.D. .... London, 56 Beaconsfield Ave.
1904 McLellan, J. C., M.D. .... Komoka
1888 McLennan, Donald, M.D., C.M. . Plattsville
1895 McLennan, Farquhar, M.D., C.M. Windsor
1914 McLeod, Alexander, M.D., C.M. . Wroxeter
1890 McLeod, Donald, M.D., C.M. ... Toronto, 62 College St.
1905 McLeod, J. G., M.B. .... Toronto, 18 Barton Ave.
1921 McLeod, J. H., M.B. .... Toronto, 384 Spadina Ave.
1919 McLeod, N. D., M.B. .... Brownsville
1887 McLurg, James, M.D., C.M. .... Sault Ste. Marie
1882 McMahon, T. F., M.B. .... Toronto, St. George Apts.
1906 McMane, Charles, M.B. .... Toronto, 665 St. Clair Ave. W.
1913 McManus, J. P. C., M.D., C.M. . Toronto, 156 Danforth Ave.
1909 McMillan, A. R., M.D. .... Sarnia
1919 McMillan, W. H., B.A., M.D., C.M. Thorold
1915 McMullen, D., M.B. .... Creighton Mine
1883 McMurchy, Arch., B.A., M.D., C.M... North Bay
1912 McMurchy, A. H., M.B. .... North Bay
1896 McMurrich, J. Bryce, M.D., C.M. Ste. Anne de Bellevue, P. Q.
1918 McNally, H. J., M.B. .... Waterloo
1889 McNally, T. J., M.D., C.M. .... London, Inst. Pub. Health
1883 McNaughton, J. A., M.D., C.M. . Brussels
1906 McNaughton, W. B., M.D., C.M. Arnprior
1891 McNeil, D. G., M.B. .... Arva
1903 McNeil, George, M.D. .... London, 245 Queen's Ave.
1918 McNevin, F. P., M.B. .... Toronto, 1909 Queen St., E.
1908 McNichol, O. A., M.D., C.M. .... Toronto, 134 Carlton St.
1898 McNichol, W. J., M.B. .... Hamilton, 254 Bay St., S.
1918 McNiece, E. W., M.D. .... Springfield
1895 McNiven, J. A., M.B. .... Acton
1898 McNulty, F. P., M.B. .... Peterboro
1882 McPhaden, Murdoch, M.D., C.M. Mount Forest

1887 McPhail, D. P., M.D., C.M. .... Highgate
1875 McPhedran, Alexander, M.B. ... Toronto, 151 Bloor St., W.
1905 McPhedran, A. G., M.B. .... Toronto, 923 College St.
1912 McPhedran, F. M., M.B. ..... Toronto, 151 Bloor St., W.
1905 McPhedran, J. H., M.B. .... Toronto, 155 Bloor St., E.
1907 McPhedran, Fletcher, B.A., M.B. Toronto, 151 Bloor St., W.
1911 McPhee, J. D., M.B. .... Port McNichol
1907 McPherson, A. W., M.B. .... Peterboro
1896 McPherson, C. F. S., M.D., C.M. Prescott
1911 McPherson, C. J., M.D., C.M. ... Ottawa, 3 Ossington Ave.
1895 McPherson, D W., M.D., C.M. .. Toronto, 556 Bathurst St.
1892 McPherson, D. A., M.D., C.M. .. Toronto, 187 St. Clair Ave., W.
1919 McPherson, E. E., M.B. .... Blenheim
1921 McPherson, R. J., M.B. .... Galt
1914 McQuade, E. A., M.B. .... Trenton
1915 McQuay, J. F., M.B. .... Toronto, 105 Howard St.
1891 McQueen, James, M.D., C.M. ... Galt
1912 McQuibban, G. A., M.B. .... Alma
1912 McQuibban, J. W., M.B. ...... Alma
1896 McRae, J. R., M.D., C.M. ...... Sault Ste. Marie
1906 McRae, T. T., M.B. .... Brussels
1889 McRitchie, T. L., M.D. .... Chatham
1916 McTaggart, G. D., M.D. ...:... Hamilton, 21 Sherman Ave., N.
1910 McTavish, Robert, M.B. .... Fort William
1911 McVean, Sara G., M.B. .... Hamilton, 401 King St., E.
1908 McVicar, C. S., M.B. .... Toronto, 300 Roncesvalles Av.
1880 McWilliam, John, M.B. .... London, 419 Dundas St.
1901 McWilliams, V. H., M.B. ...... Toronto, 288 Russell Hill Rd.
1905 Nagle, S. M., M.D., C.M. ...... Ottawa, 221 Laurier Ave., E.
1887 Nairn, Jas. M., M.D., C.M. ..... West Montrose
1885 Naismith, A. D., M.B. .... Staffordville
1911 Nancekivell, T. W., B.A., M.B. . Hamilton, 576 Concession St.
1917 Nash, H. C., M.B. .... St. George
1920 Nathanson, Joseph N., M.D., C.M. Ottawa, 450 McLaren St.
1916 Naylor, A. H., M.B. .... Creighton Mine
1915 Naylor, R. W., M.B. .... Toronto, 527 Palmerston Blvd.
1904 Neal, F. C., M.B. .... Peterboro
1919 Neelands, Lucy G., M.B. ...... Forest
1900 Neeley, David B., M.B. .... Whitby
1909 Neely, F. L., M.D. .... Hamilton, The Ontario Hosp.
1920 Nelson, E. J., M.B. .... Acton
1919 Nelson, F. H., M.D. .... Sebringville
1905 Nelson, J. S., M.D., C.M. ...... Westboro
1911 Nelson, S. W. H. .... Toronto, 415 Bloor St., W.
1918 Nesbitt, J. H., M.B. .... Mount Dennis ;
1918 Nettleton, E. W., M.B. .... Toronto, 15 Ross St.
1911 Nettleton, J. M., M.B. .... Toronto, 530 St. Clair Ave., W.
1878 Nevitt, Richard B., M.D. ...... Toronto, 46 Bloor St., W.
1915 Newell, Charles, M.B. .... Toronto, 467 Woodbine Ave.
1877 Newell, James, M.D., C.M. ..... Watford
1908 Newell, O. J., M.B. .... Hamilton, 323 Wentworth St. E.
1921 Newhouse, J. A., M.B. .... Snelgrove
1905 Newman, C. R., M.B. .... Toronto, 1713 Dufferin St.
1915 Newman, W. R., M.B. .... Toronto, 160 Oakwood Ave.
1893 Nichol, A. H., B.A., M.B. ...... Listowel

```
1873  Nichol, Angus, M.D. .......... Sebringville
1919  Nichol, D. H., M.D., C.M. ...... London, Westminster Hosp.
1897  Nichol, Roy, B.A., M.D. .......... Cornwall
1896  Nichol, W. H., M.B. .......... Brantford
1913  Nicholson, Harry M., M.B. .... Hamilton, 134 James St., S.
1911  Nicholson, William F., M.B. .... Hamilton, 69 Sherman Ave., S.
1919  Nicklin, H. R., M.B. .......... Milverton
1890  Niddrie, R. J., M.D., C.M. ...... Toronto, 484 Dovercourt Rd.
1887  Niemeier, O. G., M.D., C.M. ........ Toronto, 797 Indian Rd.
1911  Niemeier, O. W., M.B. ......... Hamilton, 82 Sherman Ave., S.
1917  Nixon, L. W., M.D., C.M. ...... Richmond
1890  Noble, C. T., M.D., C.M. ....... Sutton West
1890  Noble, John, M.D., C.M. ...... Toronto, 219 Carlton St.
1895  Noble, R. T., M.B. ........... Toronto, 216 St. Clair Ave. W.
1886  Noecker, C. T., M.B. ......... Waterloo
1919  Nolan, E. W., M.B. .......... Toronto, 1611 Danforth Ave.
1921  Noonan, W. T., M.B. .......... Mount Forest
1914  Norman, James, M.D., C.M. .... Toronto, 745 Ossington Ave.
1907  Norman, T. H., B.A., M.B. .... Toronto, 35 St. John's Rd.
1889  Northmore, H. S., M.D., C.M. ... Bath
1895  Northwood, A. E., M.B. ....... Chatham
1916  Norwich, Arthur C., M.B. ...... Toronto, 74 Sorauren Ave.
1869  Noxon, Allan ............... Toronto, 833 Bathurst St.
1887  Oaks, Anthony, M.B. .......... Preston
1907  Oaks, W. H. ................ Barrie
1900  O'Brien, J. R. ............. Ottawa, 78 Laurier Ave., E.
1901  O'Brien, P. W., M.B. .......... Toronto, 126 McCaul St.
1918  O'Brien, S. H., M.D., C.M. ...... New York City, Harlem Hosp.
1899  O'Connor, C. E., M.D., C.M. .... Kingston, 279 King St., E.
1915  O'Connor, F. DeS., M.B. ....... Tamworth
1915  O'Connor, F. X., M.D.C.M. ..... Kingston, 11 West St.
1907  O'Connor, F. J., M.D.C.M. ..... Kingston, 193 Earle St.
1915  O'Donnell, J. E., M.D., C.M. ... Fort Frances
1919  O'Dwyer, P. J., M.D. ......... Zurich
1909  Ogden, W. E., M.B. .......... Toronto, 9 Spadina Rd.
1915  O'Gorman, V. K., B.A., M.B. ... Sudbury
1906  O'Hara, W. J., M.B. ......... Toronto, 1057 Gerrard St., E.
1904  Oille, J. A., M.D. ........... Toronto, 112 College St.
1892  Oldham, J. H., M.D., C.M. ..... Yarker
1912  O'Leary, G. A., M.B. ......... Toronto, 145 Margueretta Ave.
1890  Oliver, C. B., M.D., C.M. ..... Chatham
1899  Oliver, Edward B., M.D., C.M. .. Fort William
1896  Oliver, J. H., M.D., C.M. ...... Sunderland
1919  Oliver, Robert, M.D., C.M. .... Hamilton, 191 Britannia Ave.
1886  Olmsted, Ingersoll, M.B. ....... Hamilton, 215 James St., S.
1893  Olmsted, W. E., M.B. ......... Niagara Falls
1920  Ord, J. W. E., M.D., C.M. ...... Burton-onTrent, Eng.
1904  O'Reilly, B. R., M.D., C.M. ..... Toronto, 183 St. Clair Ave., W.
1883  O'Reilly, E. B., M.B. ......... Hamilton, 5 West Ave., S.
1912  O'Reilly, Joseph, M.D., C.M. .... Calabogie
1899  Orme, J. W., M.D. .......... Crediton
1899  Orme, T. D., M.D. ........... Lucan
1900  Orr, Dorothea, M.D., C.M. ..... Toronto, 577 Dovercourt Rd.
1877  Orr, Rowland, B., M.B. ...... Toronto, 310 Roncesvalles Ave.
1909  Orr, T. S., M.B. ........... Hamilton, 690 Main St., E.
1886  Orton, T. H., M.D., C.M. ...... Guelph
```

1915 O'Sullivan, Paul M., M.A., M.B.Toronto, 313 Brunswick Ave.
1913 Otton, S. W., M.B. .... Newmarket
1908 Ovens, A. P., M.D. .... Newbury
1915 Overend, S. A., M.D., C.M. ..... Hamilton, 37 Alberta Ave.
1918 Owen, Trevor, M.B. .... St. Catharines
1918 Paddell, H. W., M.D. .... London, 377 Huron St.
1899 Page, C.A., M.D., C.M. .... Oakville
1918 Page, E. L., M.D., C.M. .... Hamilton, General Hospital
1891 Page, Thomas, M.B. .... Toronto, 941 Bathurst St.
1920 Page, W. C., B.A., M.D., C.M. ..Hamilton, 80 Herkimer St.
1866 Paget, A. H., M.D. .... Toronto, care of 173 Yonge
1921 Paiement, J. E. H., M.D. ...... Sturgeon Falls
1907 Pain, Albert, M.B. .... Hamilton, 910 King St. E.
1920 Palmer, H. I., M.B. .... Brantford
1914 Palmer, L. C., M.B. .... Toronto, 1081 St. Clair Av., W.
1889 Palmer, R. H., M.B. .... Brantford
1920 Palmer, R. E., M.B. .... Toronto, Wellesley Hosp.
1919 Pardy, W. V. V., M.D. .... Mount Brydges
1919 Parent, J. P., M.D. .... Chatham
1902 Parent, R. H., M.D. .... Ottawa, 105 Wurtemburg St.
1894 Parfitt, C. D., M.D., C.M. ..... Gravenhurst
1911 Park, F. S., M.B. .... Toronto, 461 Avenue Rd.
1875 Park, Hugh, M.B. .... Niagara Falls
1904 Park, J. M., M.B. .... Hamilton, 125 Gladstone Ave.
1890 Park, P. P., M.D., C.M. .... Hamilton, 853 Main St., E.
1888 Park, P. C., M.D., C.M. ...... Hamilton, 164 James St. S.
1919 Park, Roswell, M.D. .... Hamilton, 853 Main St. E.
1879 Park, Theodore J., M.D. .... Amherstburg
1893 Park, W. F., M.B. .... Amherstburg
1921 Parke, G. H., M.D., C.M. .... Pointe Claire, Que.
1877 Parke, W. T., M.D. .... Woodstock
1909 Parker, C. B., B.A., M.B. ..... Toronto, 52 College St.
1915 Parker, G. P., M.B. .... Toronto, 817 Bathurst St.
1890 Parker, S. G., M.B. .... Toronto, 210 Bloor St., W.
1919 Parkhill, D. A., M.D., C.M. ... Vars
1918 Parks, W. R., M.B. .... Toronto, 544 Dovercourt Rd.
1894 Parlow, A. B., M.D., C.M. ..... Ottawa, 411 McLaren St.
1919 Parney, F. S., M.B. .... Toronto, Isolation Hosp.
1912 Parr, R. L., M.B. .... Toronto, 702 Bathurst St.
1903 Parry, J. R., B.A., M.B. .... Hamilton, 282 Bay St., S.
1900 Parry, R. Y., B.A., M.B. ...... Hamilton, 183 James St., S.
1885 Parry, W T., M.D., C.M. ...... Toronto, 578 Spadina Ave.
1887 Parsons, C. J. .... Ardoch
1892 Parsons, H. C., B.A., M.D., C.M. Toronto, 6 Clarendon Ave.
1896 Partridge, A. W., M.B. .... Burk's Falls
1895 Paterson, H. McL., M.B. ...... Rodney
1921 Paterson, Peter W., M.D. ...... Kerrwood
1908 Paterson, R. K., M.D., C.M. .... Ottawa, 443 Somerset St.
1909 Paterson, R. H., B.A., M.B. .... Hamilton, 122 James St., S.
1911 Paton, J. P., M.B. .... Kenora
1921 Patrick, W. S., M.D., C.M. .... Toronto, 5 Evelyn Crescent
1903 Pattee, F. J. .... Hawkesbury
1886 Pattee, R. P. .... Hawkesbury
1911 Patterson, C. A., M.D., C.M. ... Smith's Falls
1919 Paterson, J. R., M.D., C.M. .... Glen Allan
1906 Patterson, W. R., B.A., M.D., C.M. Toronto, 8 Oakmount Rd.
1888 Patton, J. C., M.D., C.M. ..... Toronto, 189 Gerrard St., E.

1901 Paul, H. E., B.A., M.D., C.M. ... Toronto, 82 College St.
1885 Paul, J. J., M.D., C.M. .... Sunderland
1915 Paul, Reginald, M.B. .... Pefferlaw
1920 Paul, R. R., M.D., C.M. .... Athens
1921 Paul, W. S., M.D., C.M. .... Kingston, 106 Clergy St., W.
1914 Pearse, Robin .... Toronto, 206 Bloor St., W.
1893 Pearson, F. G. E., M.D., C.M. .. Brantford
1915 Pearson, Gerald H. J., B.A., M.D. Ottawa, 436 Jackson Bldg.
1895 Pearson, H C., M.D., C.M. .... Toronto, 88 Dunn Ave.
1910 Peart, T. W., M.B. .... Burlington
1914 Peck, J. W., M.D., C.M. .... Hensall
1910 Pedlar, W. C., M.B. .... Sturgeon Falls
1921 Pedley, W. H., M.B. .... Woodstock
1921 Peever, M. G., M.D. .... London, 512 Wellington St.
1919 Pelton, H. A., M.D., C.M. ..... Thamesville
1918 Pennecott, C. W., M.D. .... London, 430 Hamilton Rd.
1911 Penney, W. G., M.B. .... Toronto, 1469 Danforth Ave.
1910 Pentecost, R. S., B.A., M.B. .... Toronto, 90 College St.
1908 Pepin, W. C., M.D. .... Windsor
1888 Pepler, W. H., M.D., C.M. ..... Toronto, 600 Spadina Ave.
1919 Pequegnat, L. A., M.B. .... Toronto, 741 Dovercourt Rd.
1887 Perfect, A. H., M.D., C.M. .... Toronto, 201 Annette St.
1919 Perkins, S. H., M.D., C.M. ..... Hamilton, 641 Barton St., E.
1918 Perlman, David, M.B. .... Toronto, 353 Bathurst St.
1901 Perry, A. R., M.D., C.M. ...... Mount Forest
1919 Peterson, E. H., M.D., C.M. ... Hornepayne
1911 Phair, J. T., M.D. .... Toronto, 130 Balmoral Ave.
1877 Phelan, Daniel, M.D., C.M. ..... Kingston, 191 Johnson St.
1917 Phelps, Albert, M.D. .... Walkerville
1887 Phillips, J. A., M.D., C.M. ..... Brantford
1914 Phillips, J. G., M.D., C.M. .... Toronto, 2339 Queen St., E.
1910 Philp, George R., M.B. .... Toronto, 607 Sherbourne St.
1887 Philp, T. S., M.D., C.M. .... Picton
1866 Philp, William, M.D. .... Hamilton, 92 Hess St., N.
1890 Philp, W. H., M.B. .... Toronto, 1087 Bloor St., W.
1910. Phipps, T. R., M.B. .... Toronto, 242 Broadview Ave.
1916 Phoenix, E. E., M.D. .... Toronto, 873-875 Kingston Rd.
1914 Pickard, O. W. A. .... Detroit, Mich.
1911 Pickard, T. R., M.B. .... Guelph
1883 Pickering, Latimer .... Toronto, 277 Dundas Crescent
1921 Pickett, P. E., M.B. .... Toronto, 79 Victor Ave.
1876 Pingel, A. R., M.B. .... London, 316 Queen's Ave.
1921 Pippy, Olive .... Ottawa, 5 Howick Place
1902 Pirie, G. R., M.B. .... Toronto, 182 Bloor St., W.
1910 Pirie, H. H., M.D., C.M. ...... Dundas
1893 Pirritte, F. W., M.B. .... Sarnia
1907 Platt, E. O., B.A., M.B. .... Belleville
1912 Platt, G. A., M.A., M.D., C.M. .. Picton
1920 Platt, M. A., M.B. .... London, 110 Wellington St.
1907 Playfair, L. L., M.D., C.M. .... Hamilton, 225 James St. W.
1913 Plewes, W. F., M.B. .... Toronto, 543 Broadview Ave.
1916 Plews, T. V., M.B. .... Cainsville
1920 Plouffe, A. Francis, M.D. ...... Montreal, P. Q.
1919 Pocock, W. T., M.D., C.M. ..... Kearney
1920 Podnos, Arthur, M.B. .... Toronto, 119 Grange Ave.
1911 Poirier, J. Leo, M.B. .... St. Catharines

```
1915 Poisson, A. L., M.D. .......... Windsor
1910 Poisson, Paul, M.D. .......... Tecumseh
1914 Pollock, J. M., M.D., C.M. ...... Moose Creek
1911 Pollock, M. A., B.A., M.B. ..... Toronto, 149 Beverley St.
1912 Poole, A G., Phm.B., M.B. ..... Toronto, 166 Simcoe St.
1901 Porter, A. S., M.D., C.M. ...... Timmins
1899 Porter, Frank, M.D., C.M. ..... Waubaushene
1894 Porter, G. D., M.B. ........... Toronto, 162 Crescent Rd.
1921 Porter, J. G., McM., M.D., C.M. . St. Thomas
1917 Porter, Hugh J., M.D. ........ Hamilton, 248 Locke St., S.
1868 Porter, R. J., M.D. ........... Walkerton
1901 Potts, J. *M., M.D., C.M. ....... Stirling
1906 Powell, Charles, M.B. ........ Port Arthur
1887 Powell, F. H., M.D., C.M. ...... Ottawa, 240 Bronson Ave.
1875 Powell, N. A., M.D., C.M. ..... Toronto, 167 College St.
1876 Powell, R. W., M.D., C.M. .... Ottawa, 180 Cooper St.
1920 Powell, W. G., B.A., M.B. ..... Stratford
1868 Powers, L. B., M.D., C.M. ...... Port Hope
1899 Powers, Martin, B.A., M.D., C.M. Rockland
1918 Pratt, C. V., M.B. ............ Toronto, 183 Annette St.
1895 Pratt, J. I., M.B. ............ Port Arthur
1907 Pratt, W. C., M.D., C.M. ...... Listowel
1900 Pratt, Wilton, M.D., C.M. ...... Smith's Falls
1914 Pratten, F. H., M.B. ......... London, Queen Alexandra San.
1908 Prentice, A. J., M.B. ......... Toronto, 208 Oakwood Ave.
1905 Presault, J. W., B.A., M.D., C.M. Capreol
1906 Preston, C E., M.D., C.M. ...... Ottawa, 215 Metcalfe St.
1920 Preston, H. E., M.B. ......... London, Westminster Hospital
1920 Preston, H. F., M.B. ......... Napanee
1875 Preston, R. F., M.D., C.M. ..... Carleton Place
1866 Preston, R. H.. M.D. .......... Newboro
1919 Price, F. E., M.D., C.M. ...... Alton
1921 Price, Joseph, M.D., C.M. ..... Niagara-on-the-Lake
1921 Price, Revecca, M.B. ......... Toronto, 78 Grosvenor St.
1888 Primrose, A., M.D. .......... Toronto, 100 College St.
1884 Pringle, A. F., M.D., C.M. ..... Dunnville
1911 Pringle, G. W., B.A., M.D., C.M. Toronto, 1957 Yonge St.
1894 Proctor, E. L., M.D., C.M. ..... Kitchener
1919 Proud, W. A., M.B. .......... Guelph
1888 Proudfoot, John, M.D. ........ Monkton
1908 Publow, C.A., M.D., C.M. ...... Picton
1912 Publow, G. A., M.D., C.M. ..... Thorold
1920 Puffer, D. S., M.B. ........... Toronto, 49 Grenadier Ave.
1916 Pugh, E. C., M.B. ............ Toronto, 246 Danforth Ave.
1896 Purvis, J. W. F., M.D., C.M. ... Brockville
1918 Purvis, L. C., M.D., C.M. ...... Stittsville
1878 Pyne, R. A., M.D. ........... Toronto, 287 Indian Rd.
1892 Quackenbush, A., M.D., C.M. ... Northpines
1887 Quance, S. H., B.A., M.D., C.M. Hagersville
1907 Quigley, J P., M.A., M.D., C.M. . Kingston, 197 Johnston St.
1904 Quinlan, P. F., M.B. .......... Stratford
1910 Quinn, F. P. ................ Ottawa, 196 Lisgar St.
1920 Quinn, H. J., M.B. ........... Brantford
1910 Quinn, J. S., M.D., C.M. ....... Preston
1920 Quint, Walter S., M.B. ........ Toronto, 147 Bloor St. W.
```

```
1913 Quirk, E. L., M.D., C.M. ...... Aylmer, P. Q.
1908 Racey, G. W., M.B. .......... Parkhill
1880 Radford, J. H., M.D., C.M. .... Gait
1919 Rae, Cecil A., M.B. ........ Toronto, Isolation Hospital
1909 Rae, Edgar, B.A., M.B. ....... Toronto, 254 Greenwood Ave.
1882 Raikes, Richard, M.B. ........ Midland
1911 Ramsay, G. A., M.D. ......... London, 385 Waterloo St.
1919 Rankin, Arthur B., B.A., M.B. .. London, 20 Hayman Court
1878 Rankin, J. P., M.B. ......... Stratford
1918 Rankin, Roy W., M.B. ........ Toronto, 484 Clendenan Ave.
1902 Ranney, A. E., M.D., C.M. ..... North Bay
1896 Rannie, J. A., M.B. .......... Chesley
1911 Ravary, J. M., M.D., C.M. ..,.. Ottawa, 433 Rideau St.
1915 Raw, William E. ............ Hamilton, 34 Hess St. S.
1917 Rawlings, H. A., M.B. ........ Ottawa, 6 Regina Apts.
1920 Read, W. W., M.D., C.M. ...... Wingham
1902 Reason, C. H., M.D. .......... London, 538 Dundas St.
1886 Reaume, J. O., M.D., C.M. ..... Windsor
1906 Reazin, H. L., M.B. .......... Toronto, 1662 Queen St. W.
1917 Reddick, J. W., M.B. ........ Toronto, 18 Keewatin Ave.
1878 Reddick, Robert ............. Ottawa, 176 Second Ave.
1898 Redmond, R. C., B.A., M.D., C.M. Wingham
1877 Reeve, J. E. ................ Toronto, 18 Carlton St.
1894 Reeves, James, M.D., C.M. .... Eganville
1904 Reid, E. Victoria ........... Toronto, 385 Broadview Ave.
1907 Reid, F. I. ................. Merlin
1920 Reid, F. L., M.D., C.M. ....... Kingston, 204 Bagot St.
1907 Reid, G. R. ................ Toronto, 20 College St.
1906 Reid, Hanna E., M.B. ........ Toronto, 534 Dovercourt Rd.
1907 Reid, J., M.D., C.M. .......... Leamington
1887 Reid, J. B., M.D., C.M. ....... Tillsonburg
1906 Reid, J. D., M.D., C.M. ....... Prescott
1920 Reid, J. Spence, B.A., M.B. .... Tillsonburg
1906 Reid, Minerva E., M.B. ....... Toronto, 125 Annette St.
1905 Reid, William, M.B. .......... Wyoming
1907 Reid, W. H., M.B. ........... St. George
1919 Reist, C. O., M.D., C.M. ...... Preston
1905 Reive, W. G., M.B. ........... Welland
1889 Rennie, G. S., M.D., C.M. ..... Hamilton, 32 Walnut St.
1916 Renton, G. W., M.D. ......... London, 443 Ridout St.
1917 Renwick, J. A., M.D. ......... Thamesford
1896 Reynar, A. F., M.D.; C.M. ..... Palgrave
1889 Reynolds, A. J., M.D., C.M. ... Mount Forest
1911 Reynolds, B. C., M.D., C.M. ..... Ottawa, 132 O'Connor St.
1906 Reynolds, E. C. A., M.D., C.M. .. Erin
1905 Reynolds, M. H., B.A., M.D., C.M. Ottawa, 132 O'Connor St.
1920 Reynolds, R. P., M.D. ........ London, 28 Askin St.
1918 Rheaume, J. R., M.D. ......... Windsor
1921 Rice, Oscar, M.D. ............ Stratton
1907 Rich, W. T., M.B. ............ Lindsay
1917 Richards, G. E., M.B. ......... Toronto, 325 St. George St.
1910 Richards, J. N., M.B. ......... Warkworth
1901 Richardson, A. W., B.A., M.D., C.M.. Kingston, 247 Johnson St.
```

1892 Richardson, C. C., M.B. .... Windsor
1895 Richardson, E. K., M.B. ...... Toronto, 232 High Park Ave.
1911 Richardson, E. F., M.B. .... Campbellford
1916 Richardson, E. A., M.B. .... Toronto, 1214 Dufferin St.
1904 Richardson, G. F., M.D., C.M. ... Sprucedale
1909 Richardson, R. S., M.B. ...... Toronto, 647 Broadview Ave.
1913 Richardson, S. A., M.B. .... Wallaceburg
1902 Riches, J. F. S., M.B. .... Toronto, 453 Dovercourt Rd.
1914 Richmond, L. A., M.B. .... Hamilton, 336 Main St. E.
1908 Ricker, A. C., B.A., M.B. .... Toronto, 120 Roncesvalles Ave.
1886 Riddell, A. B., M.D., C.M. .... Bayham
1915 Riddell, A. R., B.A., M.D. ...... Toronto, 86 Spadina Rd.
1915 Rigg, Dearden, M.B. .... Dunnville
1912 Rigg, J. F., M.B. ...:....... Niagara-on-the-Lake
1911 Riley, C. F., M.D. .... Toronto, 216 Carlton St.
1907 Ripley, A. T., M.B. .... West Lorne
1914 Risdon, E. F., M.B. .... Toronto. 30 Avenue Rd.
1918 Riseborough, E. C., M.B. ...... Chatham
1921 Ritchie, A. B., M.B. .... Hamilton, 897½ King Street East.
1920 Rittinger, Fred, M.B. .... Kitchener
1904 Robb, John M., M.B. .... Blind River
1907 Robb, W. M., M.D,. C.M. ..... Toronto, 740 Dovercourt Rd.
1920 Robbins, F. C., M.B. .... Toronto, 56 Tranby Ave.
1885 Roberts, H. G., M.D., C.M. .... Toronto, 32 Bloor St. W.
1907 Robert, J. X., M.B. .... Simcoe
1896 Roberts, E. L., M.B. .... Guelph
1903 Roberts, James, M.D., C.M. .... Hamilton, 105 Eastbourne Ave.
1899 Roberts, J. A., M.B. .... Toronto, 38 Charles St. E.
1907 Robertson, D. E., M.D. ...... Toronto, 112 College St.
1902 Robertson, D. M. .... Ottawa, 96 Wurtemburg St.
1914 Robertson, Edna C., M.B. ...... Birch Cliff
1916 Robertson, H. C., M.B. .... Birch Cliff
1871 Robertson, J. A., M.B. .... Stratford
1918 Robertson, J. Murray, M.B. .... Toronto, 379 Spadina Ave.
1903 Robertson, J. J., M.D., C.M. ... Belleville
1909 Robertson, L. B., B.A., M.B. ... Toronto, 143 College St.
1901 Robertson, L. F., B.A., M.D., C.M. Stratford
1891 Robertson, T. F., M.D., C.M. ... Brockville
1890 Robertson, William, M.D., C.M. Elora
1917 Robertson, W. A., M.D., C.M. ... Toronto, 107 Cowan Ave.
1919 Robertson, W. G., M.B. .... Douglas.
1884 Robertson, W. N., M.D., C.M. ... Toronto, 119 Morley Ava
1909 Robertson, W. H., M.B. .... Toronto, 913 Bloor St. W.
1921 Robillard, J. O., B.A., M.D., C.M. Ottawa, 195 Nicholas St.
1913 Robinson, C.K., M.D., C.M. .... Battersea
1905 Robinson, E. J., M.D., C.M. ... Williamstown
1913 Robinson, H. P., B.A., M.B. .... Smithville
1900 Robinson, J. W., M.D. .... Brantford
1919 Robinson, J. L., M.D., C.M. ... Toronto, 127 Westmount Ave.
1874 Robinson, Robert H. .... Toronto, 532 Palmerston Blvd.
1915 Robinson, T. A., M.D., C.M. ... Toronto, 147 Howard Pk. Ave.
1883 Robinson, T. H., M.B. .... Kleinburg
1886 Robinson, T. M. .... St. Jacob's
1883 Robinson, W. J., M.B. .... London, The Ontario Hospital
1915 Robinson, W. L., B.A., M.B. ... Toronto, 15 Glen Grove Ave. W.
1919 Robson, C.H., M.D., C.M. .... Toronto, 26 Foxbar Rd.
1916 Robson, R. B., M.B. .... Walkerville

1878 Robson, W. T., M.D. .... Ilderton
1919 Rochon, O. J., M.D. .... Tilbury
1913 Rochon, P. E., B.A., M.D. .... Clarence Creek
1888 Roger, J. P., M.D., C.M. ...... Whitby
1877 Rogers, A. Frankford, M.D., C.M. Ottawa, 251 Cooper St.
1881 Rogers, D. H., M.D., C.M. ..... Gananoque
1909 Rogers, G. W., M.B. .... Essex
1913 Rogers, H. P., M.B. .....:.... Toronto, 22 Earlscourt Ave.
1902 Rogers, James, M.D. .... Forest
1889 Rogers, J. T., M.D., C.M. ...... Hamilton, 114 Main St. W.
1891 Rogers, J. F. B., M.D., C.M. .... Port Burwell
1893 Rogers, J M., M.B. .... Ingersoll
1920 Rogers, Keith F., M.D., C.M. ... Toronto, 282 Avenue Rd.
1911 Rogers, N. W., M.B. ....:. Stroud
1921 Rogers, S. Oliver, M.B. .... Toronto, 151 Monarch Pk. Ave.
1869 Rollins, J. A. .... London, 8 Bellevue Ave.
1907 Rolls, A. M., M.B. .... Toronto, 32 Biggar Ave.
1907 Rolph, A. H., B.A., M.B. ...... Toronto, 78 Crescent Rd.
1905 Rolph, F. W., M.A., M.D., C.M. . Toronto, 13 Madison Ave.
1890 Rooney, R. W., M.D., C.M. .... Orangeville
1892 Rosebrugh, F. A., M.D., C.M. ...... Hamilton, 98 James St. S.
1897 Ross, A. E., B.A., M.D., C.M. .. Kingston, Supt., General Hosp.
1902 Ross, Cecil C., M.D. .... Hyde Park
1921 Ross, C. B., B.A., M.D., C.M. ... Lucan
1910 Ross, C. F. W., M.B. .... Georgetown
1904 Ross, Fred A., M.B. .... Barrie
1902 Ross, G. W., M.A., M.B. .... Toronto, 627 Jarvis St.
1872 Ross, Hugh, M.B. .... Clifford
1896 Ross, H. H., M.B. .... Seaforth
1892 Ross, J. F., M.D., C.M. .... Kirkfield
1904 Ross, Victor, M.B. .... Hamilton, 537 King St. E.
1883 Ross, W. K. .... Brockville
1912 Roszell, A. E., M.B. .... Caledonia
1895 Rounthwaite, F. S., B.A., M.D., C.M.. Toronto, 2158 Queen St. E.
1907 Routledge, A. Roy, M.D., C.M. .. London, 372 Maitland St.
1877 Routledge, G. A. .... Lambeth
1908 Routley, F. W., M.B. .... Maple
1915 Routley, T. C., M.B. .... Toronto, 127 Oakwood Ave·
1891 Rowan, Richard, M.D., C.M. .... Toronto, 562 Dovercourt Rd.
1879 Rowe, G. G., M.D. .... Toronto, 1329 Queen St. W.
1908 Rowland, C. E., B.A., M.B. ..... Walkerville
1912 Rowntree, H. L., M.B. .... Toronto, 1203 Bloor St. W.
1913 Rowswell, A. C., M.B. .... Toronto, 11 Runnymede Rd.
1921 Roy, Armand, M.D. .... St. Isidore de Prescott ·
1897 Royce, Gilbert, B.A., M.B. ..... Toronto, 100 College St.
1907 Ruby, R. H., M.B. .... Kemptville
1919 Rudd, E. J. K., M.D., C.M. .....· Foleyet
1896 Rudolf, R. D., M.B., C.M. ...;.. Toronto, 100 College St.
1905 Rundle, F. J., M.D., C.M. ...... Oshawa
1902 Rundle, H. C. P., M.D., C.M. ... Brighton
1920 Rush, J W., M.B. .... Toronto, 335 Jarvis St.
1921 Ruskin, I. W., M.B. :......... Toronto, 405 Dundas St. W.
1905 Russell, A. L., M.B. .... Bailieboro

1912 Russell, C.S., B.A., M.D., C.M. · Hamilton, 1088 Barton St. E.
1899 Russell, G. A., M.D. .... Canfield
1894 Russell, J. P., M.D., C.M. ..... Toronto, 1972 Queen St. E.
1903 Russell, J. W., M.D. .... Toronto, 1084 College St.
1920 Russell, N. H., M.B. .... Toronto, 26 Kendall Ave.
1908 Russell, W. G. F., M.D. .... Toronto, 85 Sorauren Ave.
1902 Rutherford, Allan B., M.B. ..... Owen Sound
1900 Rutherford, James W., M.B. .... Chatham
1903 Rutherford, R. W., M.B. ...... Chatham
1901 Rutherford, R. M., M.D., C.M. .· Hawkesbury
1921 Rutherford, S. E., M.D., C.M. ..Tillsonburg
1889 Rutherford, S. T., M.D., C.M. ...Stratford
1906 Rutherford, T. D., M.D., C.M. .. Burford
1921 Rutherford, W. B., M.B. ....· Blenheim
1919 Rutledge, E. J., M.D., C.M. .... Ottawa, 495 Somerset St.
1893 Ruttan, F. S., M.D., ... Hamilton, 146 Park St. N.
1866 Ruttan, J. B., M.D. .... Wellington
1889 Ryan, Edward, B.A., M.D., C.M. Kingston, The Ontario Hosp.
1908 Ryckman, Warren C., M.B. .:.. Hamilton, 576 Main St. E.
1901 Ryerson, E. S., M.D., C.M. .... Toronto, 14 DeLisle Ave.
1878 Ryerson, G. A. S., M.D. ...... Toronto, 2 College St.
1893 Rykert, A. F., B.A., M.D., C.M. . Dundas
1919 Rymal, L. C., M.B. .... Hamilton, 303 York St.
1901 Sadlar, G. S., M.D., C.M. ...... Combermere
1919 Sadleir, J. F., M.D. .... Sarnia
1895 Sagar, D. S., M.D. .... Brantford
1921 Sanders, J. L., B.A., M.D., C.M. Ottawa, 435 MacLaren St.
1896 Sands, W. W., M.D., C.M. ..... Kingston, City Clerk's Office
1889 Sangster, W. A., M.B. .... Stouffville
1908 Sargent, F. R., B.A., M.D., C.M. Sydenham
1916 Sargent, W V., M.D., C.M. ...... Kingston, 28 Frontenac St.
1916 Sarjeant, P. A., M.B. .... Toronto, Sick Children's Hosp.
1892 Saulter, W. W., M.D., C.M. ....Ottawa, 564 Somerset St.
1913 Saunders, J. B., M.D., C.M. ..... Brockville
1920 Sauriol, L. E., M.D., C.M. ..... Wolfe Island
1913 Savage, T. M., M.B. .... Guelph
1866 Savage, W. F., M.D. .... Guelph
1909 Sawers, C. W., M.D. .... Watford
1886 Scadding, H. C., M.D., C.M. ... Toronto, 182 Bloor St. W.
1905 Scarlett, E., M.B. .... Hamilton, 94 Bay St. S.
1906 Schaef, H. E., M.D. .... London, 1225 Dundas St.
1908 Scheck, W. S., M.D., C.M. ..... Toronto, 220 Roncesvalles Ave.
1890 Scherk, F. H., M.B. .... Toronto, 67 Balsam Ave.
1899 Schmidt, G. A., M.D., C.M. .....Cobalt
1900 Schnarr, R. W., M.B. .... Kitchener
1912 Schram, John S., M.D. .... London, 544 Talbot St.
1915 Schram, N. F., M.D. .... London, 40 Wharncliffe Rd.
1915 Scobie, T. J., M.D., C.M. ..... Ottawa, 969 Wellington St.
1921 Scott, C. I., M.B. .... Toronto, General Hosp.
1917 Scott, C. V., B.A., M.B. .... Toronto, General Hosp.
1915 Scott, D. E., M.D. .... Lion's Head
1914 Scott, F. R., M.B. .... Toronto, 122 Roncesvalles Ave.
1911 Scott, G. O., M.D., C.M. ...... Ottawa, 436 Jackson Bldg.
1916 Scott, G. R., M.B. .... Peterboro
1871 Scott, J. G. .... Seaforth
1919 Scott, J. H., M.D., C.M. ...... Poplar

1880 Scott, J. G., M.D., C.M. .... Ottawa, 265 Elgin St.
1888 Scott, P. J., M.D., C.M. .... Southampton
1901 Scott, P. L., M.B. .... Toronto, 19 Avenue Rd.
1885 Scott, Stuart, M.D., C.M. ...... Newmarket
1898 Scott, W. A., B.A., M.B. ...... Toronto, 627 Sherbourne St.
1913 Scott, W. A., B.A., M.B. .... Toronto, 75 Bloor St. E.
1919 Scott, W. C. M., M.D., C.M. ..... Ottawa, 265 Elgin St.
1887 Scott, W. D., M.D., C.M. .... Peterboro
1891 Scott, W. J., M.D., C.M .... Lanark
1918 Scott, William, M.B. .... Cookstown
1877 Scovil, S. S., M.D., C.M. .... Kenora
1916 Scullard, Garner, M.B. .... Chatham
1895 Seaborn, E., M.D., C.M. ...... London, 469 Park Ave.
1874 Seager, F. R., M.D. .... Brigden
1894 Seager, James, M.D., C.M. ..... Ottawa, 561 Somerset St.
1921 Sears, Harley A., M.D., C.M. ... Brandon, Man., Mental Hosp.
1918 Seaton, J. G., M.D. ....Sheffield
1913 Seaton, W. B., M.B. .... Toronto, 74 Hilton Ave.
1912 Sebert, Louis J., M.B. .... Toronto, 73 Bloor St. E.
1901 Secord, E. R., M.D., C.M. ...... Brantford
1905 Serson, J. R., M.D., C.M. ...... Mimico
1903 Service, H. E., M.D., C.M. ..... Tillsonburg .
1915 Sexton, T. J., M.B. .... Merriton
1920 Shannon, E. H., M.B. .... Toronto, 649 Bathurst St.
1891 Shannon, G. W. A., M.B. ..... St. Thomas
1918 Sharp, F. B., M.D., C.M. ...... Napanee
1891 Sharp, Morris, M.D. .... Tilbury
1916 Sharpe, J. H., M.B. .... Toronto, 87 Gertrude St.
1895 Sharpe, W. D., B.A., M.D. ..... Brampton
1877 Shaver, A. W. .... West Hamilton
1920 Shaver, Roy C., M.B. .... Stayner
1891 Shaw, J. W., M.D., C.M. ...... Clinton
1892 Shaw, R. W., M.D. .... London, 287 King St.
1895 Shaw, R. W., M.D., C.M. ..... Manitowaning
1882 Shaw, W. F., M.D., C.M. .... Callander
1905 Sheahan, F. J., M.B. .... St. Catharines
1895 Sheahan, John, M.B. .... St. Catharines
1907 Sheahan, J. J. .... Chapleau
1878 Sheard, Charles, M.B. .... Toronto, 314 Jarvis St.
1911 Sheard, Charles, Jr., M.B. ..... Toronto, 52 College St.
1911 Sheard, Robert H., M.B. .... Toronto, 72 Isabella St.
1909 Shenstone, N. S., B.A., M.D. ... Toronto, 196 Bloor St. W.
1898 Shepard, A. A., B.A., M.B. ..... Sault Ste. Marie
1887 Shepherd, H. E., M.D. .... Toronto, 18 Gloucester St.
1880 Shepherd, L. E., M.D. .... Apsley
1921 Sheppard, Richard J., M.B. .... Queenston
1871 Sherk, George, M.D., C.M. ..... Nanticoke
1911 Shields, H. J., B.A., M.B. ...... Toronto, 102 College St.
1914 Shields, J. D., M.B. .... Ottawa, B. P. C., Canada
1913 Shields, R. L., M.B. .... Kitchener
1918 Shiell, A. G., M.D. .... Listowel
1890 Shiell, R. T., B.A., M.B. ...... Toronto, 317 Sherbourne St.
1895 Shier, D. Webster, M.D., C.M. .. Toronto, 619 Markham St.
1910 Shier, R. V. B., M.B. .... Toronto, General Hospital
1907 Shier, W. C., B.A., M.B. ...... Uxbridge
1894 Shillington, A. T., M.D., C.M. .. Ottawa, 281 Gilmour St.

1887 Shillington, J. W., M.D., C.M. .. Ottawa, 157 Gloucester St.
1907 Shirreff, W. T., M.D., C.M. ..... Ottawa, 74 Third Ave.
1919 Shirton, G. K., M.D. .... Waterford
1907 Shoebotham, W. M., M.D. ...... London, 620 Richmond St.
1917 Shore, O. J., M.D. .... Glanworth
1919 Shorey, K. M., M.B. .... Kingston, Mowat Sanitorium
1916 Shouldice, E. E., M.B. .... Toronto, 461 Dovercourt Rd.
1898 Shultis, John, M.D., C.M. ..... Port Colborne
1921 Shunk, Everton, S. M., M.B. ... Toronto, 398 Runnymede Rd.
1914 Shute, R. J., M.D. .... Windsor
1894 Shuttleworth, C. B., M.D., C.M. Toronto, 478 Huron St.
1921 Sicard, L. J. S., M.D., C.M. .... Buckingham, Que.
1915 Siddall, W. G., M.D. .... Watford
1918 Siegel Morris, M.B. .... Hamilton, 639 Main St. E.
1896 Silcox, W. L., M.B. .... Hamilton, 181 Herkimer St.
1889 Silverthorn, Gideon, M.D., C.M. . Toronto, 266 College St.
1919 Simmons, J. R., M.D., C.M. .... Springbrook
1885 Simmons, J. U., M.D., C.M. .... Frankford
1916 Simpkins, H. A., M.D. .... Lawrence Station
1904 Simpson, A. A. J., M.D., C.M. .. Kintail
1921 Simpson, G. Victor, M.D. ...... Niagara Falls
1910 Simpson, J. A., M.B. .... Hamilton, 908 King St. E.
1910 Simpson, J. S. .... Toronto, 137 Avenue Rd.
1881 Simpson, John, M.D., C.M. .... Lindsay
1908 Simpson, L. J., M.B. .... Barrie
1920 Simpson, Roy W., M.B. ...... Grand Valley
1915 Simpson, T. J., M.B. .... Collingwood
1884 Simpson, T. W., B.A., M.D., C.M. Napanee
1900 Simpson, W. O., M.D., C.M. .... Toronto, 314 Queen St. E.
1912 Sims, H. L. .... Ottawa, 200 Metcalfe St.
1906 Sinclair, Alexander, M.B. ..... Sault Ste. Marie
1912 Sinclair, C. W., M.B. .... Aylmer
1874 Sinclair, Coll. .... Aylmer
1888 Sinclair, D. J. .... Woodstock
1894 Sinclair, H. H., M.D., C.M. ..... Walkerton
1918 Sinclair, J. W., M.B. .... Toronto, 423 Wellesley St.
1869 Sinclair, J. M. .... Toronto, 1807 Dufferin St.
1894 Sinclair, J. P., M.B. .... Gananoque
1916 Sinclair, T. A., M.A., M.B. ..... Walkerton
1914 Sinclair, W. E., M.B. .... Toronto, 124 Bloor St. W.
1911 Singer, Bessie, T., M.B. ...... Toronto, 433 Palmerston Blvd.
1891 Sirrs, Letitia K., M.D., C.M. ... Campbellville
1889 Sisley, Opie, M.D. .... Toronto, 2 Main St. E.
1911 Skeeles, L. O. C., M.B. .... Toronto, 2133 Gerrard St. E.
1921 Slack, Albert J., M.D. .... London, Inst. Public Health
1914 Slater, R. F., M.B. .... Hespeler
1910 Slater, W. Dean, M.B. .... Toronto, 159 College St.
1907 Slemon, C. W., M.D., C.M. ..... Bowmanville
1866 Sloan, William, M.D. .... Ottawa, 191 Dunn Ave.
1880 Small, H. B. .... Ottawa, 150 Laurier Ave. W.
1877 Smellie, T. S. T., M.A., M.D., C.M. Port Arthur
1906 Smillie, A. B., M.B. .... Niagara Falls
1910 Smillie, Jennie, M.B. .... Toronto, 1075 Dovercourt Rd.
1920 Smith, A. H. C., M.D. .... South Porcupine
1882 Smith, A. D., M.B. .... Mitchell
1919 Smith, A. W., M.D. .... Dorchester
1891 Smith, C. F., M.D., C.M. ...... St. Mary's

1896 Smith, C. H., M.D., C.M. ...... Petrolea
1866 Smith, D. Day, M.D. .... Hamilton, 310 Main St. E.
1903 Smith, D. T., M.D., C.M. ...... Ottawa, 497 Somerset St.
1903 Smith, David, M.B. .... Stratford
1897 Smith, D. King, M.B. .... Toronto, 22 Wellesley St.
1890 Smith, Duncan, M.D. .... Fingal
1913 Smith, Earl, M.B. .... Brantford
1909 Smith, Estella O., M.B. .... Toronto, 1109 College St.
1917 Smith, Frank K., M.B. .... Welland
1894 Smith, F. W., M.D., C.M. ....St. Thomas
1880 Smith, G. B., M.D., C.M. ...... Toronto, 80 College St.
1904 Smith, George E., B.A., M.B. ... Toronto, 244 Bloor St. W.
1902 Smith, G. W. T., M.B. .... North Bay
1887 Smith, G. G., M.D. .... L'Original
1911 Smith, H. G., B.A., M.B. ...... Orillia
1896 Smith, I. G., M.B. .... Ottawa, 1164 Wellington St.
1915 Smith, I. K., M.B. .... Toronto, 60 College St.
1902 Smith, J. A., M.B. .... Sudbury
1916 Smith, J. C., M.B. .... Lakefield
1890 Smith, J. L., M.B. .... Durham.
1909 Smith, J. M., M.B. .... Beaverton
1914 Smith, J. N., M.D. .... Hamilton, 7 Proctor Blvd.
.1918 Smith, J. R., M.B. .... Orillia
1892 Smith, Joseph R., M.D., C.M.... Grimsby
1919 Smith, Mary M., M.D., C.M. ...Gravenhurst.
1914 Smith, M. T., M.B. .... Carleton Place
1919 Smith, R. J., M.B. .... Dundas
1918 Smith, R. P., M.B. .... Hamilton, 158 James St. S.
1914 Smith, R. S., M.B. .... Hamilton, 1008 Barton St. E.
1907 Smith, S. H., M.D., C.M. ...... Streetsville
1902 Smith, T. W., M.D., C.M. ...... Hawkesbury
1912 Smith, W. D., M.B. .... Creemore
1888 Smith, W. Harley, B.A., M.B. .. Toronto, 143 College St.
1907 Smith, W. J., M.B. .... Brampton
1912 Smith, W. W., M.B. .... Port Arthur
1893 Smuck, J. W., M.D., C.M. ..... Toronto, 74 Beaconsfield Ave.
1921 Smylie, R. T., M.B. .... Toronto, 243 Dovercourt Rd.
1897 Sneath, C. R., M.D., C.M. ..... Toronto, 385 Broadview Ave.
1895 Sneath, T. H., M.D., C.M. ..... Dromore
1905 Snelgrove, F. J., B.A., M.B..... Toronto, 901 Bathurst St.
1902 Snell, A E., B.A., M.B. .... Ottawa, c/o D.G.M.S., Mil. H.Q.
1913 Snetsinger, H. A., M.B. ...... Toronto, 661 Pape Ave.
1889 Snider, E. T., M.D., C.M. ...... Cayuga
1901 Snyder, George B., M.B........ Niagara Falls
1921 Snyder, Maurice, M.D., C.M. ... Toronto, 403 Dundas St. W.
1905 Soady, J. H., B.A., M.B........ Toronto, 935 St. Clair Ave. W.
1909 Solway, L. J., B.A., M.B. ..... Toronto, 425 Bloor St. W.
1880 Soper, Augustus .... Galt
1918 Soules, M H., M.B. .... Toronto, 1103 Gerrard St. E.
1885 Spankie, Wm., B.A., M.D., C.M. .... Wolfe Island.
1907 Sparks, G. L., M.B. .... Fort William
1905 Sparks, J. F., B.A., M.D., C.M. ... Kingston, 100 Wellington St.
1916 Sparks, W E. L., M.B. .... Toronto, 178 Sherbourne St.
1892 Sparling, A J., M.D., C.M. ..... Pembroke
1916 Spearing, Frederick, B.A., M.B. : Beeton

1890 Speers, A. H., M.D., C.M. ..... Burlington
1916 Speers, A. L., M.B. .... Mount Hope
1908 Speers, J. H., M.B. .... Toronto, 849 Bloor St. W.
1906 Speirs, J. A., M.B. .... Toronto, 263 Victoria St.
1890 Spence, A. M., M.D., C.M. ...... Lucknow
1906 Spence, C. Ellwood. M.B. ...... Fort William
1905 Spence, Edward, M.D. .... London, 545 King St.
1918 Spence, Roy J., M.B. .... Toronto, 1209 Danforth Ave.
1919 Spicer, S. L., M.D. .... Toronto, 1244 King St. W.
1911 Spohn, P. D., M.B. .... Toronto, 20 High Park Ave.
1920 Spratt, Wray L., M.B. .... Ottawa, 75 Fairmont Ave.
1915 Sproul, M. J., M.D., C.M. ..... Apple Hill
1912 Sproule, H. F., M.B. .... Mount Dennis
1907 Sproule, W. B., M.B. .... Thessalon
1885 Stacey, C. E., M.D., C.M. ..... Toronto, 161 College St.
1919 Stackhouse, W. R., M.B. ...... Ridgeway
1904 Staley, A. A., M.D., C.M. ...... Toronto, 473 Broadview Ave.
1911 Stalker, G. B., B.A., M.B. ...... Hanover
1878 Stalker, Malcolm, M.B. .... Walkerton
1905 Stallwood, J. B., M.B. .... Beamsville
1895 Stammers. C. L. B., M.D., C.M. .. Smith's Falls
1900 Stanley, J. R., M.B. .... St. Mary's
1919 Staples. S. J., M.D., C.M. ..... Woodville
1915 Stark, W. Berkeley, M.B. ..... Toronto, 85 Lynwood Ave·
1890 Starr, Clarence L., M.B. .... Toronto, 224 Bloor St. W.
1889 Starr, F. N. G., M.D., C.M. .... Toronto, 112 College St.
1914 St. Aubin. H., M.D. .... Stony Point
1903 Stauffer, B. L., M.B. .... Manilla
1920 Stauffer, Margarv M., M.D. ..... Toronto, 1492 King St. W.
1898 St. Charles. W. P., M.D., C.M. .. Toronto, 422 Sherbourne St.
1909 Stead, J. H., M.A., M.D., C.M. .. Oakville
1919 Steele, E. L., M.D. .... London, 536 Colbourne St.
1888 Steele, Michael, M.D., C.M. ..... Tavistock
1915 Steinberg, Archibald. M.B. ... Hamilton, 714 King St. E.
1894 Stenhouse. J. T., M.A., M.B. ... Toronto, 175 Bloor St. E.
1890 Stenton, D. K., M.D. .... St. Thomas
1918 Stephenson. B. G., M.D. .... Toronto, 549 West Marion St.
1903 Stevens, Joaquin M., B.A., M.D. Woodstock
1912 Stevens. R. S., B.A., M.D., C.M. Ottawa, 127 Gloucester St.
1879 Stevenson. F. C., M.B. .... Bradford
1918 Stevenson, G. H., M.B. .... London
1920 Stevenson, Harold G., B.A., M.B. Toronto, 57 Dixon Ave.
1895 Stevenson, H. A., M.D., C.M. ... London, 391 Dundas St.
1918 Stevenson, L. D., B.A., M.D., C.M. Kingston, Queen's University
1887 Stevenson, W. J., M.D., C.M. ... Aurora
1896 Stevenson. W. J., M.D., C.M. .. London. 391 Dundas St.
1899 Stewart, A D., M.B. .... Fort William
1905 Stewart, A. E., M.B. .... McGregor
1920 Stewart, Alvie E., M.B. .... Merlin
1902 Stewart, C. A., M.D., C.M. ...... Dunvegan
1919 Stewart, D. L., M.D. .... Thamesville
1912 Stewart. Elizabeth L., M.B. .... Toronto, 206 Bloor St. W.
1918 Stewart, George R., M.D., C.M. .. Ridgeway
1907 Stewart, George S., M.B. ...... Hamilton, 321 Locke St. S.
1919 Stewart, J. Stokes, M.D., C.M. .. Hamilton, 394 Main St. E.
1906 Stewart, J. R., B.A., M.D., C.M. . Cobden

1918 Stewart, L. A. S., M.D., C.M... Ottawa, 196 Elgin St.
1908 Stewart, Robert, M.B. ...... Wingham
1919 Stewart, R. B., M.A., M.D. ..... Toronto, 415 Bloor St. W.
1884 Stewart, R. L., M.B. .... Toronto, 626 Church St.
1884 Stewart, Samuel, B.A., M.D., C.M. Thamesville
1887 Stewart, W. O., M.B. .... Guelph
1908 Stinson, S. B., M.B. .... Brantford
1915 Stock, V. F., B.A., M.B. ...... Toronto, 166 George St.
1919 Stoll, E. L., M.B. .... Toronto, 419 Church St.
1920 Stone, E. L., M:B. .... Kingston, 233 Brock St.
1910 Stone, J. G. R., M.B. .... Windsor
1889 Stone, J. R., M.B. .... Parry Sound
1919 Stonehouse, G. G., M.D., C.M. .. Wallaceburg
1920 Stoness, J. F., B.A., M.D., C.M. ... Ottawa, St. Luke's Hosp.
1915 Storey, V. H., M.B. .... Bowmanville
1901 Storey, W. E., M.B. .... Kemptville
1886 Storms, O. G., M.D., C.M. ..... Hamilton, 53 Bay St. S.
1915 Storms, T. H. D., B.A., M.B. ... Hamilton, 53 Bay St. S.
1919 Stover, C B., M.B. .... Windsor
1921 Stover, Irwin, M.B. .... Chatham
1914 St. Pierre, Damien .... Ford City
1906 Strathy, G. S., M.D., C.M. ..... Toronto, 143 College St.
1903 Stratton, C. M., B.A., M.D., C.M. Napanee
1911 Streight, S. J., M.B. .... Toronto, 155 Bloor St. E.
1912 Struthers, J. D., M.B. .... Toronto, 667 Pape Ave.
1899 Struthers, W. E., M.D., C.M. ... Toronto, 558 Bathurst St.
1918 Stuart, L. M., M.B. .... Guelph
1883 Stuart, Peter, M.D. .... Guelph
1881 Stutt, Edward, M.D., C.M. ..... Toronto, 195 Beverley St.
1920 Sullivan, B. C., M.B. .... Toronto, 493 Sherbourne St.
1919 Sullivan, Herbert, M.B. ...... Toronto, General Hospital
1908 Sullivan, H. J., M.D., C.M. .... Hamilton, 58 S. Wellington St.
1907 Sutherland, Bruce C., M.D., C.M. Hamilton, 146 James St. S.
1904 Sutherland, D. M., M.B. .... Woodstock
1906 Sutherland, E. M., B.A., M.D., C.M. North Augusta
1910 Sutherland, J. W., B.A., M.B. .. Ottawa, 100 Pretoria Ave.
1921 Sutherland, J. L., M.B. ...... St. Catharines
1885 Sutherland, J. G., M.D., C.M. .... St. Catharines
1910 Sutton, A. E., M.B. .... Toronto, 798 Danforth Ave.
1905 Sutton, A. B., M.B. .... Port Credit
1914 Sutton, H. C., M.B. .... Port Credit
1904 Sutton, N. F., M.B. .... Norwood
1904 Sutton, N. H., M.B. .... Peterboro
1919 Sweeney, Denis, M.B. .... Arthur
1912 Sweeney, P. J., M.B. .... London, 720 Dundas St.
1920 Swinden, J. B. .... Toronto, 68 Orchardview Blvd.
1916 Switzer, B. C., M.B. .... Creemore
1921 Switzer, J. W., M.B. .... St. Mary's
1914 Syer, E. C., M.B. .... Hamilton, 1306 King St. E.
1919 Sykes, G. F., M.B. .... Woodstock
1875 Sylvester, G. P., M.B. .... Toronto, 79 Isabella St.
1904 Taggart, E. A. .... Ottawa, 98 Metcalfe St.
1896 Tait, N. J., M.D., C.M. .... Toronto, 147 Bloor St. W.
1920 Tallon, J. A., B.A., M.D., C.M. . Montreal, P.Q., 775 Wellington

1904 Tandy, J. H., B.A., M.D., C.M. . Toronto, 628 St. Clair Ave. W.
1921 Tanguay, Rodolphe, M.D. ...... Chelmsford
1916 Tanner, G. E., M.B. .... Midland
1918 Tate, E. C., M.B. .... Toronto, 425 Broadview Ave.
1914 Taugher, W. J., M.D., C.M. .... Prescott
1914 Taylor, Addison, M.B. .... Toronto, 841 Bloor St. W.
1871 Taylor, Alexander, M.D. ...... Goderich
1910 Taylor, A. H., M.B. .... Goderich
1876 Taylor, A. B., M.D. .... Hanover
1893 Taylor, C. J., M.D., C.M. ...... Toronto, 643 Christie St.
1901 Taylor, C. L., M.D., C.M. .... Forest
1920 Taylor, Clifford E., M.D., C.M. . Cobalt
1911 Taylor, H. A., M.B. .... Wallaceburg
1920 Taylor, H.D., B.A.. M.D., C.M. . Toronto, 51 Redwood Ave.
1912 Taylor, N. B., M.B. .... Toronto, 184 Spadina Rd.
1916 Taylor, R. H., M.D. .... Dashwood
1919 Taylor, R. B., M.D., C.M. ..... Timmins
1896 Taylor, W. H., M.D., C.M ..... Toronto, 64 Wellesley St.
1888 Taylor, W. O., M.D., C.M. ..... Cobalt
1892 Teeter, Oscar, M.B. .... Amherstburg
1899 Teeter, R. J., M.D., C.M. ..... Waterford
1891 Temple, C. A., M.D., C.M. ..... Toronto, 398 Palmerston Blvd.
1868 Temple, J. Algernon, M.D., C.M. Toronto, 186 Warren Rd.
1899 TenEyck, John F., M.D., C.M. .. Toronto, 53 Wellesley St.
1919 Tennant, C. S., M.B. .... Hamilton, The Ontario Hosp.
1909 Tennent, R. W., M.D., C.M. .... Belleville
1916 Tew, W. P., M.B. .... London, 402 Dundas St.
1920 Thackeray, J. B., M.B., B.S. ... Ottawa, 285 McLeod St.
1915 Theoret, Felix, M.D. .... Rockland
1891 Third, James, M.D., C.M. ..... Kingston, 67 West St.
1921 Third, J. R., B.A., M.D., C.M. .. Kingston, 12 Wellington St.
1890 Thistle, W. B., M.D., C.M. .... Toronto, 171 College St.
1896 Thomas, C. H., M.D., C.M. .... Toronto, 710 Dovercourt Rd.
1910 Thomas, J. T., M.B. .... Caledon
1892 Thomas, Julia, M.D., C.M. ..... Toronto, 436 Jarvis St.
1916 Thomas, N. O., M.B. .... Fort William
1906 Thomas, Robert A., M.D., C.M. .. Toronto, 976 College St.
1910 Thomas, R. H., M.B. .... Toronto, 167 College St.
1884 Thompson, A. S., M.B. .... Strathroy
1911 Thompson, A. A., M.B. .... Port Colborne
1903 Thompson, A. S., M.D., C.M. ... Havelock
1891 Thompson, B. E., M.B. .... Stoney Creek
1893 Thompson, C. W., M.B. .... Clinton
1912 Thompson, F. L., M.B. .... Toronto, 40 St. Clair Ave. W.
1907 Thompson, G. J. A., M.A., M.D. London, 156 Elmwood Ave.
1906 Thompson, H. D., M.D., C.M. ... Toronto, 1084 St. Clair Ave. W.
1901 Thompson, Septimus, M.D. ..... London, 443 Clarence Ave.
1911 Thompson, S. E., M.D., C.M. .. Kingston, 162 King St.
1889 Thompson, W. W., M.D., C.M. ..Niagara Falls South.
1887 Thomson, Adam, M.D., C.M. ... Galt
1921 Thomson, A. F., M.D., C.M. ... Galt
1918 Thomson, Arthur, M.A., M.B. ..Toronto, 258 Wellesley St.
1894 Thomson, David, M.D., C.M. ...Marmora
1888 Thomson, H. B., M.D., C.M. ... Toronto, 120 Rainsford Rd.
1915 Thomson, Murray G., M.B. .... Brantford
1891 Thomson, W. A., M.D., C.M. ...London, 753 Richmond St.

1907 Thornton, F. B., M.B. .... Toronto, 96 Northcliffe Blvd.
1920 Throop, W. E., B.A., M.D., C.M. ... Frankville
1907 Thrush, C. A. M., M.B. .... Dunnville
1919 Tichborne, S. F., M.D., C.M. ... Inwood
1892 Tilley, A. S., M.D., C.M. ...... Bowmanville
1899 Tillman, W. J., M.D. .... London, 222 Central Ave.
1909 Tindale, W. E., M.B. ...... Toronto, 711 Dovercourt Rd.
1904 Tindle, T. J. C., M.D., C.M. .... Flinton
1921 Tipping, C. E., M.B. .... Toronto, 218 Wright Ave.
1906 Tisdale, R. W., M.B. .... Delhi
1877 Tisdale, Walter, M.B. .... Simcoe
1879 Todd, J. A., M.B. .... Toronto, 165 College St.
1908 Todd, Rachel, M.D., C.M. ...... Toronto, 56 Brock Ave.
1911 Toll, W. C., M.B. .... Simcoe
1918 Tomlinson, N. F., M.B. .... Claremont
1886 Toole, C. A., M.D., C.M. ...... Port Dover
1907 Torrington, H. M., M.B. ...... Sudbury
1914 Tovell, H. M., M.D. .... Toronto, 206 Bloor St. W.
1887 Tovell, Matthew, M.D., C.M. .... Sydenham
1919 Tower, J. L., B.A., M.D., C.M. .. Belleville
1909 Towers, T. L., M.B. .... London, 23 Alma St.
1888 Towle, R. E., M.D., C.M. ...... Toronto, 229½ Jones Ave.
1921 Trackman, J. A., M.B. .... Toronto, 256 Simcoe St.
1901 Trebilcock, F. C., M.D., C.M. ... Toronto, 722 Spadina Ave.
1875 Trimble, R. J., M.D. .... Queenston
1907 Trottier, A. C. H., M.D. .... Belle River
1920 Trottier, V. A., M.D. .... Windsor
1913 Trow, C. E. A., M.B. .... Shakespeare
1911 Trow, E. J., M.B. .... Toronto, 40 Avenue Rd.
1885 Trudel, Aime, M.D. .... Orleans
1906 Truman, L. A., M.B. .... Hamilton, 780 Main St. E.
1886 Tuck, J. A., M.D., C.M. .... Toronto, 604 Bathurst St.
1871 Tucker, M. M., M.D. .... Orono
1918 Tucker, R. M., M.B. .... Allanburg
1919 Tucker, R. J., M.B. .... Paisley
1888 Tufford, A. F., M.D., C.M. .... St. Thomas
1921 Turnbull, Alexander, B.A., M.B. . Canfield
1908 Turnbull, E. G. .... Barrie
1914 Turnbull, J. G., M.B. .... Leamington
1902 Turner, Alexander, M.D. ...... St. Thomas
1905 Turner, A., M.D. .... Dutton
1889 Turner, H. A., M.D., C.M. ... Millbrook
1907 Turner, R. McP., M.B. .... Toronto, 391 Gerrard St. E.
1911 Turofsky, H. A., B.A., M.B. ... Toronto, 347 Bathurst St.
1912 Tutt, W. R., M.B. .... Sarnia
1920 Tweedie, W. C., M.D., C.M. .... Rockland
1908 Tye, P. L., M.B. .... Milverton
1912 Tyrer, E. R., M.B. .... Hillsdale
1915 Tyrer, W. L., M.B. .... Hamilton, 1048 Barton St. E.
1887 Tyrrell, J. D., M.D. .... Toronto, 546 Sherbourne St.
1876 Tyrrell, R. S., M.B. .... Toronto, 1 Rusholme Rd.
1905 Unsworth, A. D., M.B. .... Hamilton, 14 Duke St.
1890 Uren, J. F., M.D., C.M. .... Toronto, 520 Church St.
1913 Urie, G. N., B.A., M.D., C.M. ... Guelph
1919 Urie, P. R., M.D., C.M. .... Guelph

1920 Urquhart, G. T., M.B. .... Owen Sound
1882 Urquhart, John. M.B. .... Oakville
1906 Valin, R. E., M.D., C.M. ...... Ottawa, 82 Daly Ave.
1911. Valiquet, M. U., B.A., M.D. ... Ottawa, 320 St. Patrick St.
1878 Vanderburg, J. F., M.B. ...... Merritton
1921 Vanderburg, L. C.. M.D.,.C.M. .. Kingston, Queen's University
1915 Vanderburg, W. A., B.A., M.D., C.M. Hamilton, 518 King St. E.
1907 Vanderlip, Frank, M.B. .... Brampton
1882 Vandervoort, E. D., M.B. ..,.. Deseronto
1920 Van Luven, Otto, M.B. .... Hamilton, 154 James St. S.
1915 Van Wyck, H.B. .... Toronto, 154 Danforth Ave.
1912 Vaughan, M. Carlton, M.B. .... Buffalo, N.Y.
1912 Veitch, A. H., M.B. .... Toronto, Dufferin & St. Clair
1919 Veitch, H. D., M.B. .... Toronto, 2070 Gerrard St. E.
1920 Verity, Lloyd E., M.B. .... Brantford
1911 Vernon, E. G., M.B. .... Clarkson
1911 Verrall, W. S., M.B. .... Toronto, 12 Bloor St. E.
1917 Volume, D. A.. M.D. .... Kingston, 4 Chestnut St.
1871 Vrooman, A. E., M.B. .... Lindsay
1905 Vrooman, F. S., M.B. .... Toronto, 999 Queen St. W.
1888 Vrooman. J. P., M.D., C.M. .... Napanee
1892 Waddy, J. P. .... York Mills
1895 Wade, A. S., M.D., C.M. .... Renfrew
1907 Wade, J. J., M.D.. C.M. .... Roseneath
1889 Wade, R. J., M.D., C.M. ...... Brighton
1919 Wagner, A. L., M.B. .... Elmira
1900 Wagner, C. J.. ,...... .... Toronto, 400 Jarvis St.
1902 Wainwright, C. S., M.B. .... Orillia
1921 Walden, A. P., M.B. ....:::... Guelph
1915 Waldron, C. W., M.B. .... Toronto, 691 Spadina Ave.
1901 Wales, Harry C., M.B. .... Toronto, 663 Manning Ave.
1916 Walker, Agnes M., M.B. .... Alliston
1867 Walker, A., Holford, M.D. .... Toronto, Athelma Apts.
1899 Walker, C. W., M.B. .... Brigden
1913 Walker, F. M., M.B. .... Alliston
1918 Walker, F. N., M.B. .... Toronto, 1854 Gerrard St. E.
1907 Walker, F. J., M.B. .... Wheatly
1908 Walker, Herbert, M.B. .... Dunnville
1910 Walker, M. J. O., M.D., C.M. ,.. Merrickville
1911 Walker, R. R., M.B., C.M. .... Hamilton, 177 Hunter St. W.
1913 Wallace, C. K., B.A., M.D., C.M. .. Ottawa, 498 Gladstone Ave.
1881 Wallace, David, M.D., C.M. ... Kemptville
1909 Wallace, F. W., M.B. .... Toronto, 207 Carlton St.
1920 Wallace, James, M.A., M.D., C.M. Merlin
1921 Wallace, John H., M.D. .... London, St. Joseph's Hosp.
1894 Wallace, Norman C., M.B. .... Guelph
1882 Wallace, Robert R., M.B. ..... Hamilton, 60 Bay St. S.
1909 Wallace, W. G., B.A., M.D., C.M. .. Ottawa, 181 Lisgar St.
1903 Wallace, W. T., M.B. ,....... Guelph
1919 Wallbridge, C. T., M.B. .... Deseronto
1895 Wallbridge, F. G., M.D., C.M. .. Belleville
1906 Wallis, A. G., M.B. .... Thessalon
1889 Wallwin, Henry, M.D., C.M. ... Barrie

1920 Wallwin, W. E., M.D., C.M. ... Barons, Alberta
1915 Walmsley, J. H., B.A., M.D., C.M. Picton
1890 Walsh, F. D. .... Guelph
1915 Walsh, S. Y., M.B. ....:.... Keene
1921 Walters, A. G., M.B. .... Niagara Falls
1899 Walters, John J., M.B. .... Kitchener
1887 Walters, W. R., M.B. .... Toronto, 1502 Danforth Ave.
1921 Walwyn, W. McL., M.B. ...... Weston
1919 Ward, Everett, F. G., M.B. ... Foxboro
1893 Wardell, H. A., M.B. .... Hamilton, 84 Cannon St. E.
1888 Wardlaw, J. S., M.D., C.M. ... Galt
1887 Warner, A. F., M.D., C.M. ..... Toronto, 205 Yonge St.
1920 Warner, W. P., M.B. .... St. Thomas
1903 Warren, C. A., M.B. .... Toronto, 536 St. Clair Ave. W.
1913 Warren, D. A., B.A., M.B. ..... Hamilton, 771 Main St E.
1916 Warriner, C. H., B.A., M.B. ... Toronto, 37 Carlton St.
1884 Watson, A. D., M.D., C.M. .... Toronto, 10 Euclid Ave.
1912 Watson, B. P. .... Toronto, 100 College St.
1921 Watson, C. H., M.B. .... Orillia.
1921 Watson, George F., M.B. ..... Elmira
1891 Watson, John, M.B. .... Toronto, 829 College St.
1874 Watson, J. H., M.D. .... Toronto, 167 Avenue Rd.
1887 Watson, W. R., M.D., C.M. ... Elmira
1914 Watson, W. V., M.B. .... Toronto, 120 Quebec Ave.
1915 Watt, G. M., M.B. .... Brantford
1910 Watt, J. C., M.B. .... Toronto, 20 Hawthorne Ave.
1905 Watterson, T. A., M.B. .... Ottawa, 403 Albert St.
1886 Watts, E. J., M.D., C.M. ..... Toronto, 187 Dunn Ave.
1905 Watts, F. E., M.B. .... Toronto, 155 Bloor St. E.
1921 Waud, R. A., M.D. .... London, Victoria Hospital
1872 Waugh, W. E. .... London, 537 Talbot St.
1918 Weaver, Walter J., M.B. ...... Niagara Falls
1896 Webb, Alfred, M.B. .... Newmarket
1913 Webb, F. E., M.B. ..:.:...... Toronto, 1010 Gerrard St. E.
1891 Webster, David F., M.B. ..... West Lorne
1889 Webster, John, M.B. :........ Whitby
1899 Webster, J. D., B.A., M.B. ..... Toronto, 907 College St.
1891 Webster, R. E., M.D., C.M. .... Ottawa, 196 Metcalfe St.
1869 Webster, Samuel .... Norval
1889 Webster, T. S., M.D., C.M. .... Toronto, 581 Spadina Ave.
1920 Weekes, W. E., M.D. .... Wardsville.
1886 Weekes, W. J., M.D., C.M. ..... London. 436 Waterloo St.
1905 Weidenhammer, F. J., M.B. ... Waterloo
1904 Weir, B. C., M.B. .... Auburn
1911 Weir, G. S., M.D. .... London, 139 Oxford St. W.
1918 Weir, James F., B.A., M.D. .... London.
1921 Weissgerber, L. A., M.B. ...... Toronto, 80 College St.
1882 Welford, A. Beverley, M.B. .... Woodstock
1913 Wellman, A. Lorne, M.B. ...... Waterloo
1917 Wells, C. A., M.B. .... Toronto, 38 Runnymede Rd.
1910 Wells, E. Roger, M.B. .... Toronto, 82 College St.
1891 Wells, F. H., M.B. .... Port Elgin
1921 Welwood, T. R., B.A., M.B. .... Toronto, 2016 Davenport Rd.
1919 Werden, W. A., M.B. .... Mimico
1891 Wesley, J. H., M.B. .... Newmarket

1910 Wesley, R. W., M.B. .... Toronto, 2 Spadina Rd.
1886 West, Robert, M.D., C.M. ...... Woodstock
1886 West, Stephen, M.D., C.M. .... Angus
1918 West, S. E. T., M.B. .... Angus
1911 Weston, F. W., B.A., M.B. ..... Toronto, 45 Avenue Rd.
1909 Weston, R. E. A., M.B. ...... Tillsonburg
1920 Wheler, E. G., M.B. .... Toronto, Sick Children's Hosp.
1907 Whillans, J. A., B.A., M.B. .... Swansea
1895 White, E. A., M.B. .... Fenelon Falls
1913 White, G. E., M.B. .... Windsor
1912 White, J. G., M.D., C.M. ...... Mt. Clemens, Mich.
1892 White, J. W., M.D., C.M. ..... Toronto, 25 Toronto St.
1894 White, J. A., M.B. .... Lindsay
1913 White, J. H., B.A., M.B. ...... Brussels
1894 White, Prosper D., M.D., C.M. ... Detroit, Mich.
1908 White, S. T., M.D., C.M. ...... Shelburne
1916 White, T. E., M.B. .... Hamilton, 14 Cannon St. W.
1883 Whiteley, J. B., M.D., C.M. ..... Goderich
1902 Whiteley, L. N., M.B. .... Gorrie
1920 Whitelock, C. K., M.B. .... Harrowsmith
1889 Whiteman, G. A., M.D., C.M. ... Picton
1874 Whiteman, Robert, M.B. ...... Kitchener
1909 Whittaker, C. C., M.D. .... London, The Ontario Hosp.
1903 Whitton, D. A., M.D., C.M. .... Ottawa, 133 First Avenue
1905 Whyte, B. C. M., M.D., C.M. ... Port Hope
1910 Whyte, M. B., B.A., M.B. ...... Toronto, 75 Langley Ave.
1919 Whytock, A. B., B.A., M.D., C.M. Madoc
1915 Whytock, H. W., B.A., M.D., C.M. ... Madoc
1894 Wickett, Thomas, M.D., C.M. ... Hamilton, 25 Nightingale St.
1893 Wickson, David D., M.D., C.M. . Toronto, 263 Christie St.
1912 Widdis, J. B., M.D., C.M. ..... Fisherville
1906 Wigham, J. W., M.B. .... Toronto, 1299 Bloor St. W.
1906 Wigle, C. A. .... Wiarton
1877 Wigle, Hiram .... Wiarton
1916 Wildfang, Harvey J., M.D. .... Langton
1919 Wiley, H. I., M.D. .... Windsor
1895 Wiley, W. D. .... Brantford
1921 Wilkes, A. B., B.A., M.D., C.M. ... Lenham, Eng.
1912 Wilkins, W. E., M.D., C.M. ..... Cobourg
1877 Wilkinson, F. B., M.B. .... Sarnia
1919 Wilkinson, S. A., M.B. .... Chapleau
1912 Wilkinson, W. M., M.B. .... Oakville
1906 Wilkinson, W. M. .... Magpie Mine
1914 Williams, Charles F., M.D., C.M. Cardinal
1904 Williams, E. J. F., B.A., M.D., C.M.. Brockville
1902 Williams, Ernest, M.D. .... London, 363 Queen's Ave.
1909 Williams, G. W., M.B. .... Aurora
1889 Williams, Hadley, M.D. .... London, 439 Park Ave.
1887 Williams, J. Francis, M.D., C.M. Bracebridge
1901 Williams, J. P. F., M.B. ...... Toronto, 550 Palmerston Blvd.
1893 Williams. J. J., M.B. .... Woodstock
1920 Williams, J. V., M.B. .... Kingston, Sydenham Hospital.
1910 Williams, L. B., M.B. .... Toronto, 1725 Dufferin St.
1908 Williams, R. A., M.B. .... Ingersoll
1904 Williams, W. T., M.D., C.M. ... Toronto, 544 Palmerston Ave.

1921 Williamson, Agnes B., M.B. .... Beaverton
1899 Williamson, A. R.,B., M.A., M.D.,
C.M. .... Kingston, 240 King St. E.
1908 Willinsky, A. I., B.A., M.B. ..... Toronto, 316 Bloor St. W.
1919 Willoughby, J. B., M.D., C.M. .. Napanee
1889 Willson, A. I., M.B.. .... Plattsville
1907 Willson, Herbert G., B.A., M.D. . Toronto, 186 Spadina Rd.
1878 Wilson, Archibald, M.B. .... Toronto, 1032 Bathurst St.
1915 Wilson, C. E., M.B. .... Toronto, Grace Hospital
1908 Wilson, C. E., M.B. .... Napanee
1900 Wilson, D. C., M.D., C.M. .... Parkhill
1921 Wilson, D. G., M.B. .... Gananoque
1905 Wilson, F. Cameron, M.D., C.M. Napanee
1898 Wilson, F. W. Ernest, M.D., C.M. Niagara Falls
1916 Wilson, F. B. G., Phm.B., M.B. . Toronto, 42 Orchardview Blvd.
1921 Wilson, F. H.. M.B. .... Stouffville
1904 Wilson, G. E., M.B. .... Toronto, 205 Bloor St. E.
1915 Wilson, Ivan D., M.D. .... London, 365 Dundas St.
1875 Wilson, J. D., M.B. .... London, 134 Carling St.
1872 Wilson, J. A., M.D. .... Guelph
1912 Wilson, J. P., M.B. .... Richmond Hill
1916 Wilson, M. J., B.A., M.B. ..... Toronto, 191 Spadina Rd.
1908 Wilson, N. King, M.B. .... Toronto, 380 Bloor St. W.
1906 Wilson, O. M. .... Ottawa, 185 Metcalfe St.
1894 Wilson, Thomas, M.D., C.M. .... Ottawa, 90 Lyon St.
1914 Wilson, T. G., M.D., C.M. ...... Moorefield
1875 Wilson, W. J., M.D. .... Toronto, 380 Bloor St. W
1892 Wilson, W. T., M.D., C.M. ...... Penetanguishene
1913 Windsor, A., M.D. .... Detroit, Mich.
1915 Winkler, W. N., M.B. .... Toronto, 393 Dundas St. W.
1886 Winnett, Frederick, M.D., C.M. Toronto, 2 Maple Ave.
1901 Winter, D. E. .... Ottawa, 732 Albert St.
1903 Winters, G. A., B.A., M.B. ..... Westmount, P. Q.
1915 Wishart, D. E., B.A., M.B. ..... Toronto, 45 Grosvenor St.
1885 Wishart, D. J. G., B.A., M.D., C.M... Toronto, 47 Grosvenor St.
1875 Wishart, John, M.D., C.M. ..... London, 195 Dufferin Ave.
1903 Withrow, O. C. J., M.B. ...... Toronto, 38 Albany Ave.
1919 Wismer, H. S., M.D. .... Toronto, 260 Queen's Ave.
1919 Wittick, M. A., M.D. .... Toronto, 1244 King St. W.
1907 Wodehouse, R. E., M.B. .... Toronto, 287 Kennedy Ave.
1921 Wood, E. T., M.D., C.M. ...... Brockville
1918 Wood, Edward H,, M.B. .... Peterboro
1902 Wood, Isabella S., M.D., C.M. .. Toronto, 321 Bathurst St.
1909 Wood, J. H., M.B. .... Toronto, 1062 Dovercourt Rd.
1876 Wood, J. W., M.D. .... Lindsay
1893 Wood, P. B., M.D. .... Windsor
1907 Woodhall, Frank, M.B. .... Hamilton, 433 King St. E.
1910 Woodhouse, Catherine F., B.A., M.B. Toronto, 58 Duke St.
1916 Woodruff, G. A., M.D., C.M. ... Elmvale
1920 Woods, J. R., B.A. .... Chatham
1911 Woods, J. C., B.A., M.D., C.M. .. Ottawa, 283 Sussex St.
1893 Woods, N. W. .... Bayfield
1920 Woods, W. E., M.B. .... Fergus
1899 Woods, W. H., M.D., C.M. .... Mount Brydges

1904 Woolner, W. A. W., M.B. ..... Ayr
1881 Woolverton, F. E., M.B. .... Toronto, 82 Westmount Ave.
1909 Workman, H. C., B.A., M.D., C.M. Port Colborne
1910 Worley, E. G. .... Ashton
1919 Wortman, C. M., M.D. .... London, 600 Dufferin Ave.
1873 Wright, A. H., B.A., M.D. .... Toronto, 30 Gerrard St. E.
1903 Wright, A. B., M.B. .... Toronto, 206 Bloor St. W.
1911 Wright, C. S., M.B. .... Toronto, 12 Madison Ave.
1914 Wright, C. F., M.D. .... Smooth Rock Falls
1885 Wright, W. H., M.D. .... Tottenham
1905 Wright, Walter W., M.B. ...... Toronto, 143 College St.
1914 Wynne, C. S., M.B. .:........ Toronto, 2532 Yonge St.
1920 Wythe, P. T. H., M.D., C.M. .... Hamilton, 468 King St. W.
1919 Yeates, A. M., M.D. .... Hamilton, 143 James St. S.
1912 Yelland, H. M., M.B. .... Peterboro
1900 Yeo, W. T., M.D., C.M. .... Toronto, 1455 Queen St. W.
1889 Yeomans, H. A., M.D., C.M. .... Belleville
1892 Youell, J. H. G., B.A., M.B. ... Aylmer
1919 Young, C. O., B.A., M.B. ...... Sarnia
1906 Young, C. A., M.D., C.M. ...... Ottawa, 283 MacLaren St.
1912 Young, C. R., M.B. .... Little Current
1916 Young, D. R., M.D. .... Emo
1908 Young, F. S., M.D., C.M. ..... Seeley's Bay
1895 Young, George S., B.A., M.B. .. Toronto, 143 College St.
1916 Young, H. Gordon, M.B. ...... St. Mary's
1904 Young, J. M., B.A., M.D., C.M. . Walkerville
1889 Young, S. N., M.D., C.M. ...... Ridgetown
1897 Young, Thos. A., M.D., C.M. ... Scarboro
1896 Young, T. W. H., M.D., C.M. ... Peterboro
1887 Young, W. A., M.D. .... Toronto, 145 College St.
1912 Zumstein, E. W., M.B. .... Delhi
1920 Zumstein, G. T., M.B. .... St. Catharines
1895 Zumstein, J. M., M.B. .... Smithville
1890 Zwick, Frank, M.B. .... Stirling
1921 Zwick, Frank F., M.B. .... Toronto, St. Michael's Hosp.

INDEX